# Savage Portrayals

# SAVAGE PORTRAYALS

*Race, Media, and the*
*Central Park Jogger Story*

**NATALIE P. BYFIELD**

TEMPLE UNIVERSITY PRESS
Philadelphia

*For*
*Clarence, Kenya, Camara,*
*and Judi*

TEMPLE UNIVERSITY PRESS
Philadelphia, Pennsylvania 19122
*www.temple.edu/tempress*

Library of Congress Cataloging-in-Publication Data

Byfield, Natalie P., 1960–
    Savage portrayals : race, media, and the Central Park jogger story / Natalie P. Byfield.
      pages   cm
    Includes bibliographical references and index.
    ISBN 978-1-4399-0633-0 (cloth : alk. paper)
    ISBN 978-1-4399-0634-7 (pbk. : alk. paper)
    ISBN 978-1-4399-0635-4 (e-book)
    1. Central Park Jogger Rape Trial, New York, N.Y., 1990—Press coverage.   2. Rape—
New York (State)—New York—Press coverage—Case studies.   3. Violent crimes—New York
(State)—New York—Press coverage—Case studies.   4. Discrimination in criminal justice
administration—New York (State)—New York—Case studies.   5. African Americans in
mass media.   6. Hispanic Americans in mass media.   7. Racism—United States.   I. Title.

HV6568.N5B94 2014
364.15'32097471—dc23                                                          2013016594

Printed in the United States of America

031214P

# Contents

# Acknowledgments

**I AM ETERNALLY GRATEFUL** for the generosity of spirit of the members of the Central Park Five—Antron McCray, Kevin Richardson, Yusef Salaam, Raymond Santana, and Korey Wise—whose lives provided the inspiration for this project and who have embraced me as I worked to tell a part of their stories. The idea to write about the media coverage of the attack on the Central Park jogger began for me while I covered the story as a journalist. At that time, what the account should look like and the message it should deliver were just a blurry image. My journey to completing this book included many difficult roads that I could not have traveled had it not been for the support of numerous people, whose belief in my project—which sought to forge an alternative path, away from traditional metanarratives in sociological research—kept me going through many dark days when the task seemed impossible.

Early support came from members of my dissertation committee at Fordham University, particularly Robin Andersen and E. Doyle McCarthy from the university's Communication and Media Studies and Sociology and Anthropology departments, respectively. Since our days in the sociology doctoral program, the intellectual generosity of Joyce Weil has been a continuous source of help to me.

My current home institution, St. John's University in Queens, New York, has provided institutional and financial support that has helped bring this project to fruition. The university's Institute for Writing Studies has been vital. My writing partnership with Anne Geller, director of the institute's Writing Across the Curriculum, sustained me, particularly during the school year. She heard and read many versions of significant parts of the manuscript. Her insightful questions prompted the self-reflection needed as I worked to create my narrative path. I must also thank the director of the institute's Writing Center, Harry

Denny, who helped me wrestle a chapter of the manuscript into shape. A grant from the St. John's Center for Teaching and Learning supported my work with Herstory, the memoir writing group whose structured memoir writing pedagogy provided a foundation for some of my work. I am indebted to Herstory and its founder Erika Duncan, who read and critiqued my early forays into memoir writing. A grant from the St. John's Summer Support of Research Program was invaluable for helping me complete the project. My department at St. John's provided institutional support via several graduate research assistants, particularly Donna Truong and Frances Adomako, who provided important help. I am very thankful for the encouragement I have received from colleagues in my department, particularly Roderick Bush, Judith Ryder, and Roberta Villalón.

I am also indebted to colleagues outside my institution who read drafts of the proposal and the manuscript and provided guidance, mentorship, and detailed and thoughtful feedback. In particular, the intellectual support and generosity of Carolyn Brown, Judith Byfield, Karen Fields, Venus Green, Wanda Hendricks, Donna Murch, and Deborah Gray White propelled me forward. In addition, I thank Deirdre Royster, whose insightful comments early in the process were instrumental.

I must express my deep feelings of gratitude to my colleagues, friends, and family outside of academia, whose various forms of support helped make this book possible. Ken Burns, Sarah Burns, and David McMahon supported my project in their own work. In particular, Sarah Burns provided research support. My editors at Temple University Press have been invaluable. In particular, I thank Janet Francendese and Mick Gusinde-Duffy, as well as copy editor Lynne Frost, who have been central. I am also deeply grateful to my extended family, whose support for me is always palpable. I thank my parents, Hugh and Ruby Byfield; their lifelong support has been inspirational. I also thank my siblings, Judith, Brian, and Byron. The Browne, Dock, Sheppard, Whitehead, and Wright families also have been the core of my world for decades and have kept me going. In particular, my mother-in-law, Sarah Dock, and lifelong friend Ruth Browne have championed me unflaggingly. My final words of thanks go to my husband, Clarence, and my children, Kenya and Camara, to whom this project is, in part, dedicated. Their support throughout this long process has been breathtaking.

# 1

## Reconnecting New Forms of Inequality to their Roots

### Measuring the Distance between the Eras of Color-Blind Racism and Jim Crow Racism

**THE PERSONAL** and professional agendas I pursue in this book grew from a desire to right a wrong. In 1989, members of the media, as well as portions of the political establishment and elements of the criminal justice system in New York City, wrongfully accused a group of black and Latino male teens of sexually assaulting a white female who had been jogging in Central Park. She would become known simply as "the jogger." Six teenage boys were charged with the crime. Five of them would eventually be convicted in two trials; the sixth would settle the charges against him in a plea bargain. About thirteen years after the prosecutions, the Manhattan District Attorney's office petitioned the court to vacate the convictions because the actual rapist had stepped forward admitting his guilt. This person, a known and convicted serial rapist and murderer already serving a life sentence, confessed to the attack and said that he had acted alone. Only *his* DNA could be connected to the jogger. Despite these developments in the case in 2002, some members of the political establishment and the criminal justice system continue to support the wrongful convictions of the young men.

The rape of Trisha Meili, a twenty-eight-year-old investment banker working in Manhattan's financial district, drew international media attention through a narrative focused on an allegedly new type of street crime called "wilding." Simply put, the term meant intentionally behaving in a crazy manner, causing harm to others, and damaging property. According to police, the rape of Meili was the culmination of an evening of wilding in Central Park that began with other incidents of physical assault and harassment. With that police declaration, rape and wilding would become joined in the public consciousness. Although the other incidents mentioned in the police description of the evening's events included assaults that caused various degrees of injury, one thing can be said for certain: It is unlikely the public at large would ever have heard about the other incidents in the park that night had the jogger not been raped. Meili's sexual assault became the central issue in any discussion of wilding in Central Park on the night of April 19, 1989.

I heard about the rape the same way most New Yorkers did—early the following morning from the news media. But this story affected me differently than it did most people because I worked as a journalist. I wrote for the *Daily News,* and I covered the city for a living. When I arrived in the newsroom the day after the attack, it was clear this would be a big story. I had already suspected as much, but I never imagined on that first day that I would end up spending almost two months working on the story, let alone that I would still be involved with the case nearly a quarter century later. This rape was different. Despite my young age and relative inexperience, the jogger incident stood out to me as an important moment because of the reaction that unfolded in my newsroom and in the city.

The incident seemed to galvanize the media and the public because the teens charged with raping Meili—a white woman—were black and Latino. Even in 1989, when the civil rights gains since 1965 were supposed to have erased racial hierarchies and overt discrimination, the incident revived fears of black men preying on white women and engaging in random acts of violence. Such fears and assumptions were rarely expressed or acknowledged in mainstream discourse as the unapologetic racism of slavery and the Jim Crow era, which ended in 1965, gave way to a more subtle expression of many of the same attitudes, dubbed "color-blind racism" by Bonilla-Silva (2006: 28–29). The sexual assault of Trisha Meili tapped into intractable racist ideas that linked people of color and the underclass with social pathology and sexual transgression.

New York City and other metropolitan areas were in the grip of rising crime rates, some of which were attributed to the spread of crack cocaine (Grogger and Willis 2000). This drug, which is a cheaper form of cocaine, spread in the inner cities, and with the media's help, became associated with blacks and Latinos. Although the use of both powder and crack cocaine grew across the nation in the 1980s, it was low-income black and Latino male youths in the inner cities who primarily became associated with the broken lives, crime, and violence that often accompany drug abuse. For many in the mainstream, the Meili rape appeared to be an extension of the pathologies associated with people of color, which the tougher, post-1970s law enforcement tactics and harsher sentencing had failed to deter.

In the context of numerous reports of increasing rates of crime for young black and Latino males, suspicion and skepticism toward these individuals have been treated as commonsensical in the logic of the mainstream. But this logic also normalizes the privilege assigned to some groups—such as affluent white males—which likely prevents the negative life outcomes experienced by others. The problem with mainstream logic and the practices it engenders is that their underlying assumptions are not regularly challenged. This is especially true of the interworkings of race, class, and gender. People routinely behave in ways that support the mainstream conception of hierarchical social structure, even if they do not realize it and derive no benefit from such behavior. For example, women routinely defer to men, people generally defer to those with more wealth or higher social status, and so forth.

Although claims that we live in a meritocratic society rationalize the existence of these hierarchies, their persistence undermines the fundamental ideas of equality and fairness on which this nation was founded. How do we account for persons or groups who consistently remain at the bottom of such hierarchies, particularly those related to race, class, and gender? For much of the nation's history, these outcomes were explained "scientifically" in terms of natural deficits of the female sex or of those not born into the upper classes, or the innate inferiority of southern Europeans and non-white races. From the early 1900s, science began to show that attributes associated with one's racial classification are not rooted in biology. Since the post–civil rights era, we have largely discredited narratives that use genetics to ascribe certain traits—such as laziness, high intelligence, promiscuity, or leadership—to particular individuals and groups. Also, we have mostly eliminated such genetic arguments as legitimate rationalizations for excluding individuals and groups from fully participating in society.[1]

Many people reference this progress to suggest that race, class, and gender no longer serve as obstacles to full participation in U.S. society and to claim that we are approaching a fully meritocratic society. New ideologies and narratives have been developed to reflect the more inclusive social order. These narratives attribute racially disparate outcomes to individual choice, culture, or market forces; they form the basis of the color-blind racism described by Bonilla-Silva (2006: 28–29), who argues that race-neutral discourse obscures discrimination and the harm it causes. The notion of race neutrality that frames laws, policies, and practices often, in fact, produces or exacerbates racially disparate outcomes. Some examples of supposedly race-neutral laws and practices are the New York Police Department's stop-and-frisk program and the War on Drugs. Consequences of the new refusal to address ongoing issues of racism include racial profiling policies and the persistently small number of people of color in high-level jobs.

The coverage of the Meili rape case demonstrates how the biological explanations of earlier eras could be transformed for a race-neutral frame. Although news stories about the jogger case emphasized the suspects' ages and suggested that their youth might explain the outsized public reaction to the rape, the most memorable headlines did not refer to age at all. Instead, inflammatory words such as "wilding" and "savage"—words appropriate to an era when ideas about biological inferiority supported traditional racism and its segregationist practices—characterized the coverage. This case became an extreme example of how new narratives about racial groups based on the notion of color-blind racism make it possible for the use of racist tropes from the past and the existence of unequal racial outcomes to be dismissed by mainstream institutions as having little or no relationship to the country's historical and material foundations of racial inequality. Those whites who espouse color blindness could argue that expressions which in the past had been designed to demean a racial group no longer denigrate and subordinate; and racially disparate outcomes which in the past had represented anti-black or anti-brown practices no longer occur due to racism.

As a young African American female journalist watching and participating in the unfolding of the jogger coverage, I felt the sting and the heat of racism as I plotted my own course through the newsroom and the city. I became aware of how the structures of race, class, and gender defined how I operated as I reported the story. The evidence suggests that the case had a long-term impact that reached well beyond the lives of the wrongfully convicted youngsters. It reshaped the margins of race, class, and gender for black and brown low-income males for years to come. The coverage likely contributed to changes in the way we address juvenile justice, with profound consequences for the life outcomes of juveniles of color. Thus, the case stands as a uniquely important element in the evolution of our race-based social structure.

## Researching Intersecting Forms of Oppression, Mainstream Media, and Marginality

*Savage Portrayals* is an autoethnographic study of my experiences covering the rape of the Central Park jogger. The autoethnography, which is based on intensely personal descriptive narratives, is built atop a content analysis of the words and terms used in the newspaper coverage of the rape, the trials, and beyond. I use these two approaches to show the role of the press in constructing racial meaning. I also connect the media coverage of the attack on the jogger to the creation of unequal life outcomes for young, low-income black and Latino males. In addition, I show the relationship between the media's contemporary use of race, class, and gender tropes and the pre–civil rights history of these notions. To do this, I draw from the work of an interdisciplinary group of scholars in the fields of sociology, history, media studies, and cultural studies.

I contextualize my personal narratives and the representations used in the press coverage within America's raced, class-based, and gendered social structure through the incorporation of sociological studies of systemic racism and the formation of racial categories (Bell 1992; Bonilla-Silva 2006; Du Bois 2003; Feagin 2001; Ferber 1998; K. E. Fields 2002; Omi and Winant 1994) as well as some scholarship on African American history (Allen 1997; Bardaglio 1994; B. J. Fields 1990; Fredrickson 1971a; J. D. Hall 1983; Roediger 1999, 2005; Saxton 1984, 2003; White 1999). I use theories and studies of intersectionality[2] to demonstrate how structures of race, class, and gender came together to delimit my interactions during this period. Intersectional analysis interprets how structures of race, class, and gender intersect in myriad ways to create unique social locations that both oppress and privilege their members. My content analysis of newspaper coverage of the jogger story aims to draw connections between media representations and the real world. Therefore, I also incorporate the work of media studies and cultural studies researchers to provide an analytical foundation for examining the role of the media in shaping our contemporary social order (Gans 1979; S. Hall 2007; S. Hall et al. 1978; Tuchman 1978; van Dijk 1993a, 1993b). I use these wide-ranging areas of scholarship to investigate American social structure, as well as to examine what is central to our society, what we marginalize, and what holds us together—in other words, the main currents of our world. Thus, this investigation of the media coverage of the jogger case looks at the mainstream: what shapes it and how it operates to maintain affluent white males in a position of dominance.

I see the mainstream as a site for corralling support for dominant groups. As an instrumental entity, it includes and excludes categories of people, cultural symbols, forms of meaning making, forms of expression, and forms of interaction in the society based on the needs of the dominant groups.[3] The degree of one's possession of the attributes of the mainstream determines how easily one can gain right of entry to navigate its institutions. Historically, in U.S. society, people who are white, middle class or affluent, citizens, and male typically access and plot a course through the mainstream with relative ease. People possess the requisite traits for entrée into the mainstream in varying degrees; and they are shut out in varying degrees depending on the features they hold. *Savage Portrayals* looks at how in the era of color blindness the mainstream media coverage of the rape of the Central Park jogger maintained white male group dominance and further marginalized low-income black and Latino males through vilification of the purported attackers and defining them as hyperdeviant.

## Our History of Racial Formation

To connect the contemporary forms of racial groupings and racial representations in the U.S. social structure to the particular race, class, and gender history of the country, I use the racial formation theory developed by Omi and Winant (1994). This theory contends that given the ways in which the notion of race has been used in the history of the development of capitalism, the European conquest of the New World, colonialism, and slavery and the slave trade, racial classifications are both structural and representational concepts. During the aforementioned periods of history, societies organized themselves around their notions of race, and in the process, categories of race were "created, inhabited, transformed, and destroyed" (Omi and Winant 1994: 55). This process is what Omi and Winant called "racial formation." In this context, race is defined as "a concept which signifies and symbolizes social conflicts and interests by referring to different types of human bodies" (Omi and Winant 1994: 55).[4] And the race-based social movements, policies, state actions, collective activities, and individual interactions that were employed in the process of racial formation are referred to by Omi and Winant (1994) as "historically situated racial projects."

I argue in this study that the development of the contemporary mass media was a type of historically situated racial project because it helped to consolidate the category of people we classify as "white" (see Byfield, forthcoming). The inauspicious beginnings of our modern media system provided the foundation for contemporary racial representations. The role of the press in the construction of what it means to be "white" and "black" is among the racial projects my study analyzes. From the nineteenth century, the white, black, and alternative presses have participated in a variety of racial projects to develop hegemonic and counterhegemonic constructions of the black male image. Such racial projects promote the transformation of the meanings of racial categories, which makes the construction of those groups an ongoing enterprise.

One of the most notable shifts in the conceptualization of racial categories is the transition from viewing them as a matter of biology to accepting race as a social construction. Interpreting race as a biological factor essentialized the concept. Regarding race as biology meant that the various racial categories in which people were grouped were assigned irreducible meanings, yet these meanings were contingent on the era in question. For example, whiteness would be equated with morality and blackness with hypersexuality, as if these traits had been encoded in the DNA of those who were members of these racial categories. Late-nineteenth-century mainstream constructions of the black male image depicted black males as the "black beast rapist" and imagined this character to be biologically controlled (Fredrickson 1971a).

Social scientists began discrediting biological notions of race from the early twentieth century (Omi and Winant 1994). Moving forward, it became more and more acceptable in the mainstream to view racial categories as socially constructed phenomena (Banton 2009; Omi and Winant 1994: 65). While thinking of race as a biological phenomenon fell out of favor, particularly after the modern civil rights movement, there developed the converse conceptualization of race as an illusion. Scholars argue that this view too is flawed (see Bell

1992; Bonilla-Silva 2006; Feagin 2001; Omi and Winant 1994). Societies and systems of signification have been constructed around the meanings assigned to the various categories of race. But whether or not race exists as a biological factor, it continues to be real for people as they interact and find their way in institutions and through other social structures in society. Deeply embedded structural inequalities reproduce racial disparities that continue to give meaning to racial representations created by dominant groups, even in the post–civil rights era.

In New York City at the time of the Central Park jogger incident, many of the events unfolding in the city and providing the backstory for this period revolved around race or were racialized (i.e., viewed through the prism of race). There had been several violent racial confrontations; a crack cocaine "epidemic" that had fueled street crime and drug-related violence; a vigorous tough-on-crime agenda in the local, state, and national political arenas (i.e., the War on Drugs); a rebounding financial sector recovering from a crippling recession; and a mayoral campaign infused with racial tension because it involved the first serious African American candidate for mayor of New York City. Viewing these events through the contemporary lens of racial color blindness prevents one from seeing their relationship to traditional systems of inequality based on race and gender. Dominant groups would interpret the violent racial confrontations as unique incidents, the crack problem would be seen as immoral behavior in poor black and Latino communities, the War on Drugs would represent race-neutral laws and policies, the dearth of employment opportunities for people of color in the public and private sectors would be interpreted as a result of the unpreparedness of those people, and the racial tension some perceived in the mayoral campaign would be viewed as race baiting.[5]

My impressions while covering the jogger story were that race more than any other categorical life factor, such as gender or class, was central to the case. Evidence for this seemed abundant, from the language in the media coverage to the commentary from average citizens as well as public and elected officials, some of whom I interviewed for the story. When some media reports and the assistant district attorney trying the case argued that the incident and the ensuing handling of the case by the media, politicians, and prosecutors had nothing to do with the race of the people involved, I initially interpreted these assertions to be platitudes being used to deflect complaints about racism. Reflecting on the case from a sociological perspective, I now construe such statements as reflecting two things: the ideology of color-blind racism and the new social locations being created by contemporary intersections of race, class, and gender. In the post–civil rights ideology of color blindness, mainstream whites use racial frames that minimize racial discrimination. When these whites tell themselves that they do not see color, actions or policies that lead to disparate racial outcomes can be ignored because discrimination based on biological factors is no longer perceived to be a major problem (Bonilla-Silva 2006: 29). Purveyors of such discourse are unconcerned about or unaware of the greater likelihood of a group such as low-income black and Latino males being denied their rights.

Unlike the period of "traditional" racism, post–civil rights society has to contend with inclusion. American institutions can no longer exclude people based on race and gender. In this new era, nonbiological attributes such as expressions, geography, and dress are used to construct identity and often to represent one's social location. Leaders of institutions can exclude people who possess what are perceived to be attributes from a particular social location without running the risk of being accused of racism. For example, low-income black males have a disproportionately high rate of criminal convictions. With nearly "one in three young black men . . . [expected to] spend some time in prison," this condition is used as a defining feature of their particular social location (Pager 2007: 3). Members of this group are frequently shut out of jobs because employers frown on criminal convictions, but employers who exclude such individuals cannot be accused of racism. Thus, racial analyses must now focus on the conditions that allow those in power to discriminate against a group of people from a particular social location who have features or attributes that exclude them from the mainstream.

## Gender in the Era of Color-Blind Racism

The 1970s not only ushered in a changing discourse on race but also saw a changing discourse on gender. Proponents of the ideology of color blindness argued for a diminished role for the state in managing racial interactions because legal segregation was over. But, in contrast, the changing discourse on gender called for an increasing role for the state (Bumiller 2008). The women's movement was largely concerned with prosecuting a "war" on sexual violence and would require the state to fulfill its duty to protect women equally. But, as Bumiller (2008: 5) points out, the concord between the women's movement and the neoliberal state for the purposes of protecting women from rape and intimate partner violence expanded the reaches of the state "beyond feminist organizations and their agendas." The state, in its agreement with this aspect of the feminist agenda, incorporated feminist as well as other organizations in its "regulatory role" (Bumiller 2008). It required these organizations, many of which were part of the health and social services bureaucracies, to use the state's agendas and priorities to manage the women who used the services intended to help and protect them from sexual violence. The state prioritized welfare reform and crime control. Bumiller (2008: 7) notes

> Mainstream feminist demands for more certain and severe punishment for crimes against women fed into these reactionary forces. This

resulted in a direct alliance between feminist activists and legislators, prosecutors, and other elected officials promoting the crime control business. Although the feminist's "gender war" did not have the same impact on incarceration as the "war on drugs," it still contributed to the symbolic message. . . . The prominence of sexual violence on the crime control agenda led to the creation of specialized sex crime units in large urban police and prosecutors' offices.

What mainstream feminists failed to recognize was the different impacts the state's policies and agendas had on women, depending on their race or class or some other attribute, such as citizenship status. Bumiller (2008) argues that one of the big failings of the gender war has been its failure to adequately address how racism has historically been at the foundation of people's conceptualizations of sexual violence. Black women *and* black men were victimized historically by American society's approach to sexual violence. Black women were subjected to sexual violence with no recourse when slavery denied them any rights over of their own bodies and white male property owners could rape at will and blame their actions on the black woman's sexual appetite. As late as the 1970s, black women who were raped were less likely to have their sexual assault viewed as an act worthy of legal consequence (Lizotte 1985). Conversely, black men were vulnerable to lynching, particularly in the period after the Civil War and into the twentieth century, often due to trumped-up charges based on their so-called biological propensity to rape white women. Scholars have blamed this post–Civil War development on fear of the economic competition black men posed as freedmen.

In the contemporary world, the war against sexual violence heightened fear of the stranger, and one particularly dangerous stranger was seen to be the black male (Bumiller 2008). Thus, embedded in the American imagination of sexual danger is the black male (Bumiller 2008; A. Davis 1981). With this history, treating the issue of sexual violence as "race neutral" would be problematic, according to Bumiller (2008: 21). However, in line with the ideology of color-blind racism, mainstream feminists advanced an agenda based on the idea that race could be a neutral concept in America. Regarding the gender wars of the 1970s, Bumiller (2008: 22) notes, "When the war against sexual violence emerged on the public agenda, it revived the specter of black men as sexual predators, while continuing to devalue the safety of black women." This had consequences for both black women and black men.

Many black feminists would argue that the inability of mainstream (i.e., predominantly white middle- and upper-class) feminists to recognize the disparate impact of the feminist agenda on women outside the mainstream came from the mainstream feminists' lack of awareness about the ways in which structures based on race, class, and gender can intersect to create distinct social locations that distinguish one woman from another, marginalizing black women's membership in the categorical grouping "women." In her essay "Individuality and the Intellectuals: An Imaginary Conversation between W.E.B. Du Bois and Emile Durkheim," social theorist Karen E. Fields (2002) investigates the relationship of the individual to the collective, particularly when the collective of which one is a part becomes complicit in one's own subordination. One of the issues Fields addresses is the naturalization of one's objectification within collectivities, in other words, the process of group membership.

Fields (2002: 438) builds her argument on Durkheim's ([1912] 1995) seminal study *Elementary Forms of Religious Life*, in which Fields states, "Durkheim studies the collective alchemy by which *reason* converts bald-faced inventions into external and constraining facts of nature, capable of resisting individual doubt." Thus, within collectivities we develop "abstract notions of common essence" (K. E. Fields 2002: 438). Durkheim ([1912] 1995) discovered this social fact in his study of aboriginal Australians' racial identification, in which clans used totems such as kangaroos to signify their identity and in which they claimed a shared identity with the actual kangaroo. "Through periodically repeated ritual, and through symbolic reminders between times, the name-essence is experienced as palpably real. In that way, it gains an objectivity that makes individual dreams of repudiating the shared identification not so much undreamable as irrelevant. Such shared identifications are not negotiable contracts" (K. E. Fields 2002: 438). Mainstream white feminists wanted to use the jogger as an iconic symbol for all women.

The shared identification used by members of categorical groups is made real to members, says Fields (2002: 439), through "frenzied rites" that Durkheim ([1912] 1995) called "effervescences collectives." I am arguing here that the frenzied rites that Durkheim saw in his assessment of racial identification among aboriginal Australians could serve as an analogy for racial projects throughout U.S. history, such as the very formation of the United States, the establishment of state and federal policies that separated Native Americans from their lands, lynchings, the modern civil rights movement, and possibly even the events surrounding the Central Park jogger incident. Durkheim ([1912] 1995) points out that the product of the effervescences collectives is the shared identification objectified in the form of a totem.

As the mainstream media represent primarily the dominant parties among race, class, and gender groupings, the outsized response to the jogger's rape became a frenzied rite or a racial/political project that strengthened categorical group loyalties along the lines of race, class, and gender. The challenge this rape presented in the city at the time spun around how the people who were subordinated in each of these groups would view the incident and how fairly those who were dominant within each of the groups would treat the young suspects and their supporters. The scene outside the courthouse during the trials of the accused would sometimes include supporters of the jogger (mostly white women) and supporters of the young suspects (mostly people of color, both male and female) in confrontational opposition. In another arena, the case pitted the black press and the mainstream press against each other.

The white women, representatives of the mainstream women's movement, were driven by their opposition to sexual violence in general; but underneath the reaction in this particular case also lay, as Bumiller (2008: 22) states, the "specter of black men as sexual predators," a powerful symbol uniting whites as a group. Some supporters of the suspects, drawn to the injustices being inflicted on the teens, no doubt had on their minds past racially unifying frenzied rites, such as the Scottsboro case, in which nine black boys in Scottsboro, Alabama, were falsely convicted of raping two white women as the groups traveled on a freight train in the south.[6] Crenshaw (1991) notes that an analysis that focuses on either race *or* gender without considering how these axes of oppression and privilege intersect may end up contributing to oppression in other areas:

> When feminists fail to acknowledge the role that race played in the public response to the rape of the Central Park jogger, feminism contributes to the forces that produce disproportionate punishment for Black men who rape white women, and when antiracists represent the case solely in terms of racial domination, they belittle the fact that women particularly, and all people generally, should be outraged by the gender violence the case represented. (p. 1282)

The black presses in the city were largely focused on evident racial disparities in the treatment of the young suspects. They also criticized the disparity in the treatment sexually assaulted black women receive.

People who are subordinate within the large group collectives do not have the same relationship to the symbols that unite the group as those who are dominant. The collective's icon (e.g., the jogger, in this case) becomes an object of oppression, something that reinforces the marginalization of those subordinate within the group. Because there is a disparity in outcomes between white and black rape victims, using the jogger as a symbol of sexual violence for all women makes the black woman's experience invisible within the category of women. When black women did not participate in the frenzied rites used to build group loyalty (i.e., did not vigorously support the jogger), they were perceived as being more concerned with race than with gender.[7]

Black feminist scholar Valerie Smith (1998: xx) contends that the jogger case had a particularly polarizing effect because the mainstream press's approach to the case was based in part on the "presumptive blackness of rapists and whiteness of rape victims." But the significance of this case does not hinge simply on the fact that it stands as further proof that race, class, and gender are inseparable. It also provides evidence of how, in the age of color-blind racism, issues of race, class, and gender can mask each other. I am particularly drawn to Smith's assessment of the case and her approach to intersectional analysis. She argues that the case should be viewed as a cultural event or moment that collapses categorical life experiences of race, class, and gender unto themselves. She contends that when one categorical life experience obscures the others, it "masks both the operation of others and the interconnections among them" (1998: xv).

In the case of the rape of the jogger in Central Park, people were so polarized that issues of race appeared to drown out concerns in other areas. However, in this particular instance, despite the horrific violence heaped on the jogger, another vulnerable group—young black and Latino male teens—was further marginalized and suffered injustices because of the way the press, prosecutors, and politicians handled the incident (Bumiller 2008; Crenshaw 1991). I argue here that the media, as an instrument of mainstream society, played a major role in the negative outcomes for the young suspects.

Everyone, regardless of their social location, must contend with the mainstream and its criteria for inclusion and exclusion. Mainstream discourses, narratives, and mores marginalize those who do not serve the interests of affluent white males. In the context of the events surrounding the rape of the Central Park jogger, the five teens accused did not stand a chance. Numerous scholars have already established that the media is one of the most important institutions in shaping mainstream opinion (e.g., Gans 1979; Herman and Chomsky 1988; van Dijk 1993a, 1993b). The focus of my study is on the role of the media in reconstructing a new mainstream from some of the contemporary narratives about race. In the more inclusive mainstream of the post–civil rights era, American society supposedly left behind biological notions of race. But groups that were subordinated under the biological conceptualization of race are again marginalized and oppressed in the new racial order. Young black and Latino males continue to be one of the most "otherized" groups in society, particularly if they articulate their identity using manner, speech, and forms of meaning not sanctioned by the mainstream.

Although the mainstream is often a central part of the discussion in social science research particularly, in the context of theories or notions about ethnic and racial assimilation, multiculturalism, or upward mobility (Alba and Nee 2005; Omi and Winant 1994: 14–23; Romero 2011; Young 2008), it is often discussed implicitly in the context of methodology. I take the position that the mainstream and the way it operates must be visible in our analyses, particularly because all groups must contend with mainstream filters. In the era of color-blind racism, it behooves us to examine how the mainstream continues to be a force for inclusion and marginalization in a society that legislates inclusion.

# Methodology

This is a mixed methods study using both qualitative and quantitative techniques to provide insight into the things that create meaning within the categorical groups one belongs to. These techniques are applied to the media coverage of the Central Park jogger incident to generate empirical data that will allow us to better understand how the mainstream—through contemporary discourses, narratives, and mores—impacts the construction of large categorical groups of race, class, and gender, among other things. To see what forms of expression, interaction, and meaning making are allowed in the mainstream and are significant to this case, I conducted a content analysis of fourteen years of newspaper coverage of the jogger incident and an autoethnography based primarily on my own experiences as a journalist covering the case. This study is not a measure of the accuracy of the rendition of reality produced by the media. Social theorist Niklas Luhmann (2000) argues in *The Reality of the Mass Media* that because the media form a knowledge-producing or cognitive system, it is impossible to make a distinction between the internal reality of the newsroom and the external reality of the world outside the newsroom. There is no way to know the actual genesis of the knowledge being generated in news products because one cannot determine which reality (internal or external) served as the primary source for that knowledge. Luhmann (2000: 5–8) solves the problem by suggesting that people researching cognitive systems should "observe observers as they construct reality" and discern *how* they construct reality. My content analysis and autoethnography aim to achieve this.

## Content Analysis: All the News That's Fit to Measure

Content analysis[8] is a technique often used for gathering and analyzing textual data. It has been and continues to be the foremost scientific methodology for research on newspaper journalism or communications (Krippendorff 2004; Slater 1998).[9] It serves as one of the main methodological approaches in my study because it is a research tool that probes the symbolic world of groups or individuals (Krippendorff 2004; Slater 1998). I used an ethnographic understanding of newsroom organization and newspaper production to design my content analysis. The environment that shaped the context of this analysis is a major metropolitan newsroom. I developed my theories about the newsroom from a number of sources, including my own work as a journalist in New York City from 1985 until 1993, both freelance and on staff, for a variety of publications. This first-hand knowledge of the field contributed significantly to my notions about the operation of the mainstream media world. In addition, the work of social theorists and media studies scholars (Fishman 1978; Gans 1979; S. Hall et al. 1978; Luhmann 2000; Tuchman 1972, 1973, 1978; van Dijk

1993a, 1993b) also shaped my organization and interpretation of the content analysis.

Print journalists produce stories about the world using words and images, which presumably construct or reflect the world outside their doors.[10] My content analysis does not examine images. It focuses instead on words and terms used by media producers to describe the jogger incident and the rest of the world outside the media. The words and terms provide measures for a variety of features of media content. They reflect how media producers conceptualize society and the things about society that they privilege. I quantify words and terms in the coverage that are indicators of important categorical experiences in society that are specifically relevant to the case under examination, such as race, class, gender, and age. It is my hope that measuring words and terms that are indicators for these concepts will reveal how media producers conceptualize society. Given that the Central Park jogger case is germane to new narratives about race and gender, the content analysis also measures words and terms related to the jogger's status as a victim, referred to here as "victimhood," and it measures words and terms related to violence. The jogger's status as a victim is tied to the new narratives created by the gender war. The significance of violence as part of the narratives of the gender war (Bumiller 2008) and the War on Drugs makes it important to assess how the concept of violence is used in mainstream narratives. Measurements of the use of words and terms that act as indicators for these six concepts—race, class, gender, age, victimhood, and violence—point to how media producers conceptualize categorical life experiences and the importance of victimhood and violence to those categories.

In addition to the texts that indicate the categorical life experiences mentioned above, there are other equally momentous textual elements in newspaper stories. I refer to these other crucial elements as "media language," which is composed of words, terms, and various structures of news stories that are so familiar to audiences that they serve as yet another vehicle for communicating media messages. Such forms of communication are similar to what van Dijk (1993b) labels "media discourse" in mainstream media. This discourse is based on a cognitive model shared by mainstream (predominantly white) journalists and their audiences (van Dijk 1993b). Media language can also be viewed as aspects of the conventions that journalists follow to convert into news the multitude of events unfolding in daily life (Tuchman 1972, 1973, 1978). Much of this media language is related to the components of the structure of news stories and the components of prominence of newspaper articles. Components of the structure of news stories include the headline, the lead (i.e., the first paragraph, which contains the most important information), the sources, and the smaller story topics used to construct larger facts[11] of the story. These features of media language tell the audience how media producers want them to interpret a story. Components of prominence represent another type of significant media language in news reporting. The components of prominence include the internal desk[12] that generated the news story (see Chapters 4 and 5), the type of story (e.g., hard news, feature, editorial, or news analysis),[13] the proximity of the story relative to page one (prominent placement),[14] the frequency with which an event is covered, and the use of a photo or other image in the story.[15] These features of media language communicate to the audience the level of importance media producers have assigned to a story.

I measured all of the aforementioned textual elements and components of media language in the coverage of the jogger incident for a fourteen-year period. The content analysis incorporates newspaper stories about the jogger incident from the time of the first reports on April 21, 1989,[16] and continues until December 2003, about a year after the original suspects were exonerated. This fourteen-year span is broken into four time periods that correspond with the ebb and flow of the coverage. The first phase runs from April 21, 1989, to June 9, 1989. This period covers the immediate aftermath of the incident, during which time the media constructed the overall narrative of the coverage. The bulk of my reportage about the incident occurred during this period. The second period of the content analysis covers June 10, 1989, to mid-March 1991. I refer to this period as the legal phase of the coverage. All the court cases involving the original prosecutions took place during this period. The third period covers the balance of 1991 through 2001. During this time, coverage of the incident as the subject of a story almost completely subsided. However, the Central Park jogger incident continued to be used as a reference in stories published on other subjects. The final period of the content analysis runs from the beginning of 2002 until the end of December 2003. In this period, the Manhattan's District Attorney's office reexamined the case and petitioned the court to vacate the convictions of the initial defendants. This period also incorporates the aftermath of the court ruling. In much of the content analysis, I merge the data from time periods 3 and 4 because of the small number of articles that appeared during period 3.

A data set consisting of a collection of approximately 502 newspaper articles published in the *New York Times* and the *New York Daily News* between April 21, 1989, and December 31, 2003, forms the base of the analysis. The *Times* articles were selected in two steps. Once a Lexis-Nexis search for the full time range of the study had produced a list of articles and publication dates, those dates were searched on microfilm, and the articles that met the selection criteria were copied along with the full pages on which they were published. The *Daily News* stories from 1996 to 2003 were collected in the same fashion. However, 1996 represents the first year that the *Daily News* began participating in the Lexis-Nexis database. Thus, for the years from 1989 to 1996, *Daily News* articles were retrieved by going through microfilm for the entire period and copying the articles in which the Central Park jogger incident and its aftermath was the subject of the story.

To ensure randomness of sampling, each article in the data set was given a unique number, and each time period formed a stratum from which my sample was randomly selected. Each assigned number for the articles was written on a piece of paper, which was folded and placed in a box. From that box, half of the numbers were randomly selected. This was repeated for each of the periods. I examined a sample of 251 stories with a codebook of approximately 161 variables.

The first part of the analysis addresses the frequencies of occurrence of the indicators of categorical life experiences, such as race, class, gender, age, and victimhood. This portion of the study was intended to reveal the words and terms mainstream media content producers relied on to discuss the various categorical groupings in the story. To my surprise, over the fourteen years of coverage and within each of the designated time periods, indicators of race are near the bottom of the list when measuring frequency of use of indicators for categorical life experiences. (See Figure 1.1.) This initially raised the possibility that the story was not primarily about race. The use of class indicators overall surpassed the use of indicators for race and gender. Until I saw these results, I had never imagined that the coverage contained more messages about class than about race. Up to that point, none of the literature I had read about the coverage had suggested this. These results raised a number of interesting questions. Were race and class still interchangeable given the growth of the black middle class in the post–civil rights era? Was race declining in significance, as some scholars had postulated (Wilson 1978)? Was ethnicity less of a barrier into the mainstream (Alba and Nee 2003)? Or, as an intersectional reading of the case suggested, was race being masked by other categorical life experiences? Was it color-blind racism at work (Bonilla-Silva 2006)?

Part of what must be kept in mind when considering the frequency of use of class indicators is that in the stories themselves, most of the class indicators refer to the jogger and her family. (See Table 3.2.) As these indicators are all elements of mainstream society, it would seem that within the categorical life experience referred to as "class," blacks and Latinos are marginalized by the producers of mainstream media content. This made me wonder if marginalization in other categorical life experiences could account for why one domain appears to eclipse the others.

Another part of the analysis addresses the frequency of occurrence of components of the structure or organization of news stories. Those components include specific words and terms as well as structures (such as the headline, the lead, sources, and smaller story topics) that represent journalistic conventions that allow media workers to construct news from events and to convey messages of objectivity about the process used to create the news (Tuchman 1972,

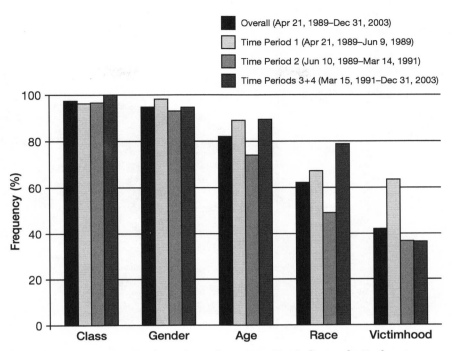

**FIGURE 1.1**   Percentages of Articles with at Least One Indicator for Each
Categorical Life Experience during Coverage of the Central Park Jogger Case,
April 21, 1989–December 31, 2003, by Time Period

1973, 1978). As noted earlier, these features of media language convey to the
readers how the media producers want them to interpret a story. Some people
read stories and accept all of the messages from media producers; others
develop different degrees of oppositional reading (S. Hall 2007). One notable
finding from the analysis of journalistic conventions is that the term "alleged"
was rarely used in the coverage of the Central Park jogger incident; in my
sample of 251 articles across fourteen years of stories, the word appeared only
twelve times.

Oftentimes media organizations address the issue of bias by trying to incorporate a multiplicity of perspectives. There is generally a great deal of reliance
within the media on external sources for information from other societal institutions. On initial inspection, there appears to be a symbiotic relationship
between—on the one hand—news reporters, photographers, and editors and—
on the other hand—sources. Media researchers (Gans 1979; Herman and Chomsky 1988; Luhmann 2000; Schudson 1978; Tuchman 1978; van Dijk 1993b)
often present sources as an important factor in the story selection process, interpreting the role of sources as one that holds a great deal of sway over the

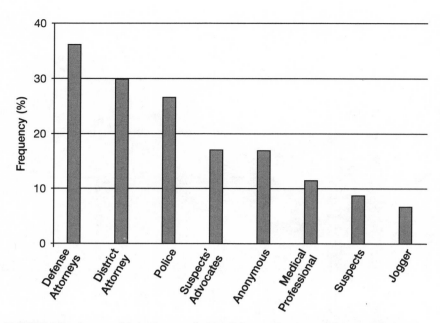

**FIGURE 1.2**  Sources Most Frequently Used during Coverage of the Central Park Jogger Case, April 21, 1989–December 31, 2003

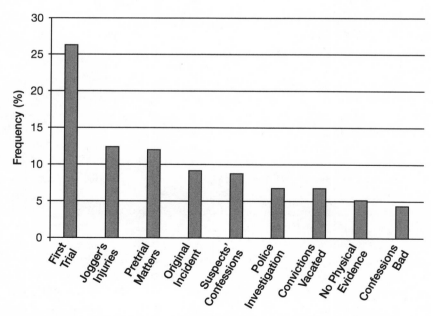

**FIGURE 1.3**  Topics Most Frequently Used in the Lead during Coverage of the Central Park Jogger Case, April 21, 1989–December 31, 2003

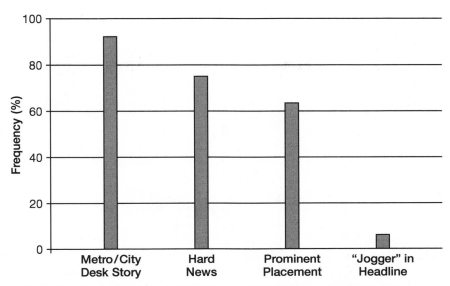

**FIGURE 1.4** Important Structural Elements of Media Language during Coverage of the Central Park Jogger Case, April 21, 1989–December 31, 2003

symbolic arena. One surprising finding from the articles I sampled is that the source most relied on throughout the coverage was the group of defense attorneys. They were featured in 36 percent of the articles. (See Figure 1.2.) However, the coverage clearly did not favor the young suspects. Measuring the frequency of use of particular story topics reveals which topics were relied on to create the facts of the coverage. Given the outcome of the case, it is no surprise that the "confessions bad" topic was used least frequently in leads. (See Figure 1.3.) The other significant area of media language involves the prominence of news articles (influenced by factors such as the desk that generated the story, the type of story, and prominence of placement). Findings for these factors are plotted in Figure 1.4.

## Autoethnography: The Researcher Bearing Witness

While content analysis can reveal much about the coverage of the Central Park jogger incident, such findings alone (even when statistical associations can be established with confidence) fail to fully elucidate one important component of the larger picture: the social milieu. How did the social world of the newsroom and the social processes that went into the reporting enable so much bias and marginalization to take place? Traditional ethnographic research is often applied to such situations. However, given my role in the coverage, I felt it necessary to go beyond traditional ethnography and take advantage of the dual roles I have played in the case.

Autoethnography seemed an ideal methodology for me to incorporate into this study because it is a technique that allows the researcher to also be a subject in a study. At the time of the jogger incident, I was a reporter on the city desk at the *New York Daily News*. I covered the story on a near-daily basis for about two and half months, reporting primarily any jogger-related event occurring at the hospital where the jogger was recovering. The period of my involvement at this level covers all of the first time period of the content analysis. I suddenly found myself in the middle of an international story in which I had to interact regularly with all of the major decision makers in the newsroom. The newness of the situation was striking for me. I was front and center in the news-gathering process at one of the largest papers in the nation. Because of my role in the coverage, I have served as a subject in other studies about the case (Benedict 1992; Burns 2011). Naturally I would want to include my experiences in my own study of the events, and this is the first time I have documented my personal account in this way. Because autoethnographies are a departure from traditional ethnographic studies, it is important to establish the distinction between the two and to discuss the benefits of the autoethnographic approach for this project.

Ethnography is a prominent qualitative research method in sociology that is typically used to study culture or people within the context of their culture. It is field research that emphasizes providing a very detailed description of a culture from the viewpoint of an insider in the culture to facilitate understanding of it (Neuman 2011: 423). Geertz (1973: 5) calls the analysis of culture "an interpretative science . . . in search of meaning." Ethnography incorporates specific requirements, functions, and processes. The requirements include entering and gaining access to a field site, "adopting an attitude of strangeness" or using new eyes to view the field site, noticing "social breakdowns," having the researcher become the "primary instrument or medium through which research is conducted," recording data in a variety of types of field notes, and mapping or diagraming social relationships (Neuman 2011: 420–463). An ethnographer functions in the following ways: "connects what the researcher studies to the context in which it appears [and] . . . get[s] inside the 'heads' or meaning systems of diverse members [of a social setting] and then switch[es] back to outsider" (Neuman 2011: 425–426). Because it is a science, ethnography must incorporate reliability and validity. Ethnographic reports provide two voices: the voice of the researcher, "the authority," and the voice of the subject, "the native." Ethnography has been used with the underlying assumption that the social scientist must be in a position of dominance or authority because only the scientist is equipped to interpret the "native voice" (Stoddart 1991).

Autoethnography is similar to traditional ethnography in that it focuses on the individual in a cultural context and seeks to present or report individual experience in such a way that it "makes the characteristics of a culture familiar for insiders and outsiders" (Ellis, Adams, and Bochner 2011). As in ethnography, in autoethnography the researcher can identify "social breakdowns," can become the "primary instrument or medium through which research is conducted," can reveal underlying systems of meaning, and can map or diagram social relationships.[17] However, the autoethnographer will not necessarily have the "new eyes" of a stranger who gained access to a field site. Nor will the autoethnographer necessarily have a variety of types of field notes. Nor does he or she abide by the "notion of researcher as controller" (Boyle and Parry 2007: 188). The most significant difference between autoethnography and traditional ethnography is that in autoethnography one individual receives the bulk of the focus of the analysis, and that individual is the researcher.

The autoethnographic methodology, which merges the researcher and the subject, delves into the self through a type of memoir[18] or autobiographical process. The synthesis of the roles of the researcher and subject into one enables the use of memory, emotions, witnessing, and dialogue. In its approach to the inner self, Boyle and Parry (2007: 186) note

> Autoethnography is characterized by personal experience narratives . . . , auto-observation . . . , personal ethnography . . . , lived experience . . . , self-ethnography . . . , reflexive ethnography . . . , emotionalism . . . , experiential texts . . . , and autobiographical ethnography. . . . Thus autoethnographic accounts are characterized by a move from a broad lens focus on individual situatedness within the cultural and social context, to a focus on the inner vulnerable and often resistant self.

Boyle and Parry (2007) make the case that this methodology stands to make a contribution because the researcher/subject is a witness to aspects of organizational culture that researchers typically do not have access to. Using this approach for the study of organizations is useful because personal stories in which the researcher/subject can bear witness to moments that are oftentimes hidden from examination unearth "tacit" aspects of organizational culture (Boyle and Parry 2007). This focus on the individual, Boyle and Parry (2007: 186) argue, allows the "organizational researcher to intimately connect the personal to the cultural through a 'peeling back' of multiple layers of consciousness, thoughts, feelings and beliefs."

Ellis, Adams, and Bochner (2011) contend that the autoethnographic process requires the following:

> An author retroactively and selectively writes about past experiences . . . write[s] about "epiphanies"—remembered moments perceived to have significantly impacted the trajectory of a person's life . . . , times of existential crises that forced a person to attend to and analyze lived

experience . . . [because] these epiphanies reveal ways a person could negotiate "intense situations" and "effects that linger—recollections, memories, images, feelings—long after a crucial incident is supposedly finished" [Bochner 1984: 595]. . . . Autoethnographers [must] . . . use their methodological tools and research literature to analyze experience.

Ellis, Adams, and Bochner (2011) identify eight different forms of autoethnographies. One in particular is familiar to many sociologists. It resembles some important texts that incorporate intersectional analyses (Ferguson 2000; Romero 2011; Wilkins 2008). These works are extremely self-reflexive. They represent what Ellis, Adams, and Bochner (2011) would term "narrative ethnographies," which are defined as texts that "incorporate the ethnographer's experiences into the ethnographic descriptions and analysis of others."

My autoethnographic work in this book is still another departure from the more familiar sociological approach. It is most similar to what Ellis, Adams, and Bochner (2011) refer to as "personal narratives." This form of autoethnography, which is described as one of the most "controversial," incorporates "stories about authors who view themselves as the phenomenon and write evocative narratives specifically focused on their academic, research, and personal lives" (Ellis, Adams, and Bochner 2011). This type of autoethnography poses a challenge to traditional science, either quantitative or interpretive. *Savage Portrayals* incorporates a series of my personal narratives,[19] many of which are based on memories, several reporter's notebooks compiled in the spring of 1989, and newspaper articles I wrote during this period. In my personal narratives, I am presented as a subject with multiple voices. There is me the subject who is the young reporter, personally experiencing the meaning and significance of the jogger coverage. With another voice, I am again a subject, but one who is no longer a working journalist and who is looking back on the case after some time elapsed. And, finally, there is me the subject who as a sociologist is analyzing (1) my past selves as well as the histories of race, class, and gender in the United States; (2) data gathered from a content analysis of the representations that appeared in two New York City newspapers at the heart of the story; and (3) data gathered from discussions and interviews with people associated with the case.

As always, new or infrequently used methodologies raise philosophical, epistemological, and practical questions about science. At its heart, the autoethnographic research technique is philosophically grounded in the realm of phenomenology. This field concerns itself with how people learn about the everyday world and make sense out of it or, more technically, how people assemble reality. Several aspects of this work make phenomenology an important place to base it philosophically. Gaye Tuchman (1978) has already grounded in phenomenology studies of media processes that seek to show how the construction of everyday life into news through professional rituals and conventions is related to the construction of reality. Intersectionality constitutes part of the theoretical frame used in the study to analyze my roles and the organizational and sociohistoric context on which my actions and those of other social actors were based. More and more, intersectionality is being coupled with phenomenology because intersectionality seeks to understand individual experiences based on the multiple subjectivities of the researcher and the subject as they interact with each other and with social structures (K. Davis 2008). "Recent trends in postmodern and feminist theory also contribute to the narrative and autobiographical exploration of field research" (L. Berger 2001: 506), and intersectionality has decidedly been a part of it.

Autoethnography holds epistemological assumptions that differ from those of quantitative and interpretative sciences. For example, the intense reliance on the researcher's multiple subjectivities raises epistemological concerns about the efficacy of this method as a type of science since there is no pretense of objectivity. Some researchers who use this method argue that "it makes no sense to impose traditional criteria in judging the value of a personal text" (Wall 2006: 9). And I should note that countless critiques about questionable objectivity in quantitative and interpretative sciences have been proffered (Berger and Berry 1988; Harding 1986). Wall (2006) argues that we should find alternative criteria for assessing autoethnography, such as literary criteria. Scholars (Boyle and Parry 2007; Wall 2006) have made the case that autoethnography is a very useful method for extracting "tacit" knowledge.

From the practical view of science, this study raises questions about writing conventions, the researcher's voice, legitimate data, ethics in research, and questions of validity/authenticity, reliability, and generalizability. I address the issue of writing conventions and ethics a little later and first try to dispel some of the other concerns in the context of my field. As a postmodern approach, autoethnography does eliminate the need for neutrality. Researchers using this approach (Ellis, Adams, and Bochner 2011; Wall 2006, 2008) argue that one can find a way of incorporating the self ("that was always there"; Wall 2006: 11) that allows one to balance "academic tradition with personal expression" (Wall 2006: 10). Autoethnography scholars (Ellis, Adams, and Bochner 2011; Wall 2008) contend that memory serves as legitimate data. Wall (2008) makes the case that memory is already a constitutive act in any type of ethnography, because we must contend with the memories of the researcher and of those being studied. In terms of validity, reliability, and generalizability, when they are "applied to autoethnography, the context, meaning and utility of these terms are altered" (Ellis, Adams, and Bochner 2011). In this context, reliability is based on the "narrator's credibility"; validity means that the study "evokes in readers a feeling that the experience described is lifelike, believable, and possible"; and generalizability, in this context, means that the readers can "determine if the story speaks to them . . . about their lives" (Ellis, Adams, and Bochner 2011).

The autoethnographic component of my study builds personal narratives from memories of my interactions with other social actors in two social contexts: the newsroom and my life growing up in New York City. These narratives are interwoven with scholarly literature about relevant themes such as (1) my categorical memberships as a black immigrant woman from a lower-income family; (2) how I perceive the boundaries of these groupings; (3) the strategies I use to navigate these social contexts given my particular social location; and (4) how institutionalized forms of domination based on race, class, and gender affect those strategies. These personal narratives allow readers to walk in my shoes, live those experiences with me, and come to moments of realization with me. They were strategically selected to supplement the content analysis and its findings that the news-making process in the construction of the Central Park jogger story was systematically biased against the young suspects and likely exacerbated the marginalization of young black and Latino low-income males.

A word about the ethics involved here: Ellis, Adams, and Bochner (2011) recommend that for ethical purposes autoethnographers submit their personal narratives to the people incorporated in the stories. Even if you change the names of other social actors described in your personal narrative, their identities, in some situations, can easily be determined. Therefore, Ellis, Adams, and Bochner (2011) argue that

> this obligates autoethnographers to show their work to others implicated in or by their texts, allowing these others to respond, and/or acknowledging how these others feel about what is being written about them and allowing them to talk back to how they have been represented in the text. Similar to traditional ethnographers, autoethnographers also may have to protect the privacy and safety of others by altering identifying characteristics such as circumstance, topics discussed, or characteristics like race, gender, name, place, or appearance.

In my particular case, the autoethnography of the newsroom involves analyzing the news-gathering process and including people germane to decision making in the newsroom. Some of my personal narratives include stories about individuals who alone held a particular position in the newsroom organizational structure. Therefore, there is no way to hide their identity without severely misrepresenting the social context that led to some of the outcomes. In my personal narrative, the editor-in-chief is identified by name. Some individuals are represented by pseudonyms, and names of others have been eliminated. At this time, both the former *Daily News* editor-in-chief and the Sunday editor, who are featured in my stories, are deceased. I have done my best to hide the descriptive details of other social actors, unless they have already implicated themselves by going public or by writing about these events. Some of the personal narratives include social actors who are friends and family members. I have discussed with them their inclusion in my stories.

Now, I want to say a few words about writing conventions. Since scientific research is a community affair, I am sure scholars will continue to debate the efficacy of using personal narratives as a research methodology. A case is already being made to make room for such an approach in our field and placing it under an umbrella called "lyrical sociology." The creation of such a genre in sociology would blur the divide between the humanities and the social sciences. Wall (2006: 154) hints at such an eventuality by suggesting that the alternative criteria used to assess autoethnography be literary in nature. Lyrical sociology, as described by Abbott (2007), is an alternative approach to the two dominant metanarratives in sociology, one being the "story" of variables and attempts at causal explanations found in quantitative methodologies and the other being the "story" of social actors and explanations of social processes found in qualitative methodologies.

Abbott (2007) describes lyrical sociology as having two distinctive components: its stance and its mechanics. The stance of a researcher using lyrical sociology to report his or her findings incorporates the intense engagement of the researcher with the topic, locating the work in the researcher's consciousness as an author and as someone emotionally involved in a social world, incorporating the researcher's state of being when writing about "in the moment" events from the social world, and using personification and figurative language (Abbott 2007: 73–76). The mechanics of employing lyrical sociology in the written presentation include use of the researcher/writer's emotional reactions to events, use of images, and use of the present tense to render those "in the moment" events to recreate an experience of social discovery for the reader. The aim is to help the reader experience a particular state of being and moment in time that led social actors to the particular choices and precipitated the outcomes we now know. As such, it represents a "congeries of images" (Abbott 2007: 76).

So as not to create confusion about the relationship of my work, described as personal narrative, to lyrical sociology, which Abbott (2007: 77) describes as "anti-narrative," I think it necessary to say that Abbott is referring to the metanarratives in our field surrounding qualitative and quantitative research and *not* the smaller narratives that might develop from the use of personal narratives from autobiographical or memoir-based presentations. Part of what makes personal narrative a "controversial" technique in sociological research is that it is not one of the traditional methodologies in either of the conventional metanarratives. Abbott's (2007) work carves out a variety of important studies in the field that could be classified as lyrical sociology—that is, studies that exist outside of the dominant metanarratives—and he makes the case for making room for this type of work. It is in this context that my work may best be placed, although my study has also been influenced by Patricia Hill Collins's (2000) push to establish a black feminist epistemology.

## Overview of the Book

I have written this book from three distinct narrative stances: what I saw happen as a reporter, what I thought about it at the time, and how I have subsequently analyzed it as a sociologist. In Chapters 2 through 6, the three voices are much more distinct, because these chapters include the periods when I still worked on the story or still lived as a practicing journalist. Thus, these chapters include sections that take the reader back in time and space to those moments in my life. In Chapters 7, 8, and 9, the first two voices are more muted, and the voice of the sociologist dominates throughout. My goal is to take the reader on the journey of my developing consciousness as I examined the events of the time through a sociological lens.

Chapter 2, "A Jogger Is Raped in Central Park," is largely an autoethnographic report in which the voice of the journalist dominates. The first-person narration tells the reader about me and other journalists learning of the attack on Trisha Meili and responding to the early news reports of what had happened. It introduces the reader to newsroom dynamics, how race operates in that environment, and the constructed nature of race in our culture.

Chapter 3 is titled "The Position of the Black Male in the Cult of White Womanhood." At the outset, I employ autoethnographic research and my voice as a journalist to present the mainstream press-constructed image of Meili as the "idealized" woman. I also incorporate my assessment of that image at the time. Then, relying primarily on my voice as a sociologist, I next examine the image of Meili in the context of the history of the construction of race, class, and gender in the United States, showing that the press needed to construct such an idealized image of Meili because mainstream society classifies only some rapes as worthy of attention and prosecution. I begin the incorporation of the content analysis here. I argue that the construction of race in the United States is tied to the symbiotic relationship between the growth of capitalism and the mainstream media. In other words, the development of the mainstream press appears to be a historically situated racial project.

The relationships between the police and the media—and how these relationships impact the framing of issues of race—are addressed in Chapter 4, "Salvaging the 'Savage': A Racial Frame that Refuses to Die." This segment of the book shows the close association between the police and the media contemporarily and how that relationship impacts the portrayal of African Americans in the press today. Readers are plunged deeper into the race, class, and gender dynamics of the newsroom and are provided with a more detailed description and analysis of the impact of these dynamics on crime coverage. I describe how I learned the agenda-setting priorities of the city desk and the significance of these priorities in a city such as New York, which has a large multicultural population and which includes tremendous race and class barriers that are physical (geographic), literal (the resources and jobs people have access to by virtue of their skills and their pocketbooks), and figurative (how people see themselves). These race and class barriers were being redrawn in the 1980s and 1990s by a new service economy that divided the city into two main classes: those skilled and affluent enough to participate in symbolic production[20] (e.g., working in mass media, law firms, and finance) and consumption and those who support the affluent.

Chapter 5, "A Participant Observes How Content Emerges," closely examines the internal organizing structure of the media and the impact of that structure on newspaper content. Primarily through the voice of the journalist, I recall for the reader the blow-by-blow coverage of a story that is intended to be part of the jogger coverage. However, this story challenges the narratives being used to cover blacks, in general, in relation to the police, and most egregiously—from the point of view of the news managers—in relation to the jogger coverage. By watching a story move around the newsroom, the reader develops an understanding of how the components of a newsroom's organizational structure function.

Chapter 6, "The 'Facts' Emerge to Convict the Innocent," deconstructs media language and its role in creating meaning. Through a sociolinguistic examination of the construction of the narrative of the jogger coverage, particularly the trials, I demonstrate how information in the outside world becomes "facts" in news media content and how meaning is constructed. In this chapter, the voice of the sociologist dominates.

Chapter 7, "The Case Falls Apart: Media's Brief Mea Culpa," continues the sociolinguistic analysis of the overall role of media in society as an institution that serves elite interests (Herman and Chomsky 1988; van Dijk 1993b). It uses the unraveling of the convictions to ask the question, What interests were served by the way in which the jogger case was handled by the press?

Chapter 8, "Selling Savage Portrayals: Young Black and Latino Males in the Carceral State," assesses the cultural significance of the case. The coverage is contextualized in the ongoing moral panic focused on crime and drug abuse in black and Latino communities that has identified young black and Latino males as the new "folk devils." I argue in this chapter that this moral panic contributed to the sensationalized coverage, making it easier to sell to the public the idea that young black and Latino males were hyperdeviant. To combat this perceived threat, society would require extreme measures, including nationwide changes in juvenile justice laws that would draw juveniles into the adult criminal justice system.

Chapter 9, "They Didn't Do It!" is a denouement. It wraps up the current position of the Central Park Five in their quest for justice, discussing the significance of their marginalization in the context of the construction of the unique social location that has turned young black and Latino males from low-income communities into a new "caste" (Alexander 2010).

# 2

# A Jogger Is Raped
# in Central Park

## Assigned to the Story

**I STOOD** at my closet door that morning in April 1989 distractedly rummaging through my clothes. A local radio station provided the morning news roundup; this occupied another part of my mind. Some care had to go into the selection of my work outfit. I always strove for a pulled-together, businesslike—that is, conservative—look. White men made up the largest portion of the *Daily News* staff, followed by white women, then blacks and Latinos. Many of the white journalists I worked with tended to be more casual in their appearance. With my dark-chocolate complexion, I would have stood out even without the distinction my clothing provided. Unsure of which aspect of my identity would be used to judge me, I played it safe and tried never to be too casual in this professional environment. I had long ago developed the expectation that I would be judged by a different standard, and my experience over my time working at the *Daily News* pretty much matched that expectation. I joined the paper's main news gathering desk, the city desk, after working for the business section for the better part of my first year. Working for the city desk was a coveted position. Landing regular assignments from city desk editors was that much more desirable; those stories dominate the first eleven pages of the paper. Reporters regularly featured in those spaces become prominent. Despite the treatment I anticipated, I had made up my mind that would be my goal. But it is funny what can trip one up along the way.

A report on the morning news got my head out of the clothes closet: An unidentified woman had been found raped and beaten near death in a section of Central Park bordering Harlem. I waited for the stories to cycle so I could hear the report again. *An unidentified woman had been found raped and beaten near death in a section of Central Park bordering Harlem.* Was it me, or did I sense anxiety in the news announcer's voice? Is she white? Did he say she was white? I could have sworn I heard that. Maybe it was the way they kept repeating the story to establish its importance. My guess was that the story's significance came from the victim being white. I had two private pleas. The first, shared with many blacks, was the secret plea that arises upon hearing the news of any awful crime: Please let the person who did this *not* be black. My other plea was much more specific to my own situation: Please let me have a chance to work on the story. This already had the earmarks of a big story: White woman raped near Harlem. That was all my editors would need to hear.

I hurried into work, listening for updates on the car radio during my commute. This woman had been badly beaten, her face no longer identifiable. Friends wondering about the whereabouts of their colleague showed up at the hospital and surmised it was her from a butterfly ring she always wore (Byfield 1989c). Upon hearing this, a Stevie Wonder melody drifted through my mind: the tune of the song "Lately." Only my mind twisted everything. Instead of the original lyrics, the words coursing through my head were "What their heart can't let them see, their eyes won't let them hide." The image of that butterfly ring and the thought that for even a moment such an incidental piece of jewelry would be the only thing that could connect a person to her life before a destructive random incident would haunt me for months.

Thoughts of how my editors would react to the plight of this woman—this white woman, if in fact she was white—numbed my senses. I knew it would be bad; I just did not know exactly what bad would mean. My head instead filled with the calculus of my work world. I became consumed with questions about my job. It was my ritualized preparation for disappointment. If she was white, this would be a big story. Would I receive an assignment? If so, how would the staff of largely white editors handle my contribution? Would it end up a separate story with its own byline? Would the information I gathered be folded into some larger story with my name in a credit box along with many others? Would the editors use any of my information at all? The editors and I did not always share the same perspective on events unfolding in the world. Getting your work in the paper regularly—in other words, becoming a star—often boiled down to having a world view congruent with that of the editors. As a reporter, I had to give them what they thought they wanted. I had already put in two years at the paper, including a year on the city desk, but my value to the newsroom—if it could be called that—seemed to come from the color of my skin and not from my skills. My desk's location in the outermost orbit of the city desk in the wide-open newsroom added to my sense of detachment and separation from the main flow of things, from the newsroom's mainstream. Often race[1] appeared to be the reason for the disparities I sensed. Avoiding this conclusion proved to be impossible no matter how much some people wanted to believe that the United States in 1989 was irreversibly moving toward racial equality, whatever that meant.

The police version of events quickly spread throughout the newsroom. It came from the Associated Press wire service and our own reporters. The previous night, April 19, an unidentified white woman, an investment banker, went about her regular nightly jog in Central Park. She started out late in the evening, before 10:00 P.M.,[2] a small, lone figure amidst the high-rise buildings of Manhattan's Upper East Side. Her run took her to the northern section of the park. Adjacent to her neighborhood sat Harlem, one of the country's most famous African American and Latino communities. Somewhere close to the 102nd Street transverse, near the Fifth Avenue entrance, beyond the ornate wrought-iron fencing in that area of the park, down a wooded path, an attack ended her jog.

Press reports note that earlier that same evening, a very large group of African American and Latino teenage boys was seen gathering at the park entrance at 110th Street and Fifth Avenue. Press accounts of witness reports claim that a small group of black boys was running through the park physically assaulting joggers and bike riders, many of whom were white. Whoever attacked this particular jogger raped her and severely beat her about the head, smashing one of her eye sockets. She was bound and gagged; her legs and arms were badly cut, it was presumed at the time with a knife. Law enforcement officials quickly drew connections between the black and Latino teens seen gathering at the park entrance and those witnessed running through the park allegedly attacking and harassing people jogging and biking. The picture for the police added up to the group of African American and Latino boys culminating their night of rampage in the park with the attack on the jogger.

Left for dead, the jogger lost 50–75 percent of her blood. About 1:30 the next morning, passersby found her in the undergrowth, comatose, swollen, and caked with blood and mud and with no identification on her. An ambulance transported her to Metropolitan Hospital Center at 96th Street and First Avenue. Metropolitan is one of the smaller health-care facilities in the city's public hospital system. It is situated on the edge of East Harlem, a predominantly Latino neighborhood, and serves a regular spate of patients who reflect its low-income environs and who themselves are often victims of violence. Upon the jogger's arrival in the surgical intensive care unit, the doctors and nurses who treated her in the early morning hours questioned the unidentified woman's chances for survival. News outlets were informed of the incident. By the morning rush hour, the local commercial news radio stations were repeatedly running the story.

The distribution of assignments on the Central Park rape story spread across the *Daily News* newsroom, even reaching the outer perimeter where I sat. Every available body was called into service. The news managers handled the story as if it were a major disaster such as a plane crash, for which they would assign a number of reporters to cover different angles. Reporters were sent to Metropolitan Hospital; some were sent to the area in Harlem the suspects were said to be from; some were sent to the investment bank Salomon Brothers, where the jogger worked; and some worked the police angle. Information poured in quickly about the jogger's background. This was blanket coverage. A story such as this could be an opportunity for someone outside the newsroom's mainstream.

I thought the rape would be a big story, but I had miscalculated just *how* big the editors would play it. Had I admitted this in the newsroom, my colleagues would likely have interpreted it as a shortcoming in my news judgment. For me, a woman was raped and beaten nearly to death; it was indeed horrific. Rape is a unique crime because it targets an element of the victim's identity (Lizotte 1985). But, as journalists, we had to select from among 3,254 rapes reported in 1989[3] to decide which ones to cover, the appropriate depth of coverage, and the length of coverage. Reports about sex crimes and gender issues were not excluded from the *Daily News*'s coverage of New York City. The paper had run stories highlighting violence against women, and the previous year I had received permission to cover a big story about the problem during Women's History Month. Discussions about this particular rape, however, were different. The context that quickly emerged focused on the races of the suspects and the victim and allegations about the supposed unique features of this rape that had nothing to do with the woman's gender. This was an *interracial* rape.

## Race in the *Daily News* Newsroom

I landed the assignment covering the hospital. Hospitals are controlled areas, and I did not expect to get much for my efforts. But at least I had an assignment. My fears of not having a role in the coverage were not simply feelings of insecurity in a young journalist. The history of blacks working in mainstream media is much like the history of racial segregation in the United States at large. It is littered with experiences that range from total separation to incorporation at a glacial pace. Between 1987 and 1993, when I worked at the *Daily News,* the number of black journalists working for the paper's main news desk, the city desk, could be counted on two hands.[4] The period in which the *News* hired me saw a flurry of hiring of black journalists at the paper—in preparation for a lawsuit brought by four of its African American journalists.

Protecting the paper from this legal action was a concern at the highest levels. I first contemplated a job at the *News* around December 1986 while attending a jobs fair promoting "minority" hiring. At such events, newspaper representatives from every corner of the nation scooped up rookies and veterans alike without the traditional filters of previous recommendations from trusted associates. I pushed my clip file and resume across the table to a long-faced, middle-aged white man with salt-and-pepper hair. He sat in a wide-open conference room that was abuzz with similar scenes playing out at other tables scattered across the room. Unlike those other exchanges, the representative of the *Daily News* was its editor-in-chief, Gil Spencer. He was a long way from his cloistered office on the seventh floor of the gleaming art deco building at 42nd Street and Third Avenue in midtown Manhattan.

The quick once-over he gave my resume and clip file elicited comments about my education. Without someone to vouch for me, he fell back on one of the standard employment filters—the "right" educational pedigree. He asked about the schools I had attended. I had received my bachelor's and master's degrees from elite schools, Princeton and Stanford, respectively. Three years earlier, the movie "The Big Chill" had portrayed graduates of these schools as the new "it" group, one no longer concerned about 1960s goals of transforming the world and instead set to grab society's reins and lead themselves to economic and social success. Except my case was different: I was black and female. Despite the civil rights movement, my inclusion in the mainstream was not a foregone conclusion. While I had become accustomed to the surprised response to my education, I would never grow used to the sense of curiosity with which I was perceived. I never knew if it was my looks—the close-cropped 'fro and dark complexion—combined with interests like studying ancient and medieval political theory that exoticized me in the minds of so many of the middle-aged white men I encountered—or something else. What did they see when they looked at me? It was 1987. The nation was nearing the quarter-century mark after passage of the Civil Rights Act of 1964 that had guaranteed equal employment opportunities. Here I was still worried about stereotypes old and new, from the mammies of slavery to the welfare queens of the Reagan revolution; after all, Reagan had mounted an effective challenge to gains made during the civil rights era. All told, it was enough to make some of us conclude that claims of a new racially integrated America were largely overblown. Getting the job and achieving acceptance into the mainstream could not be equated. Spencer drew me into conversation. He wanted to talk about an interest one of his relatives had expressed in attending Stanford University. After we chatted about the university, he offered me a word of warning or advice.

"The newsroom is divided down the middle by a racial discrimination suit. You think you can handle that?"

"Yes!" I answered emphatically. Whether I could or I could not was irrelevant to me. I wanted the job. He invited me to come by the newspaper and meet the other editors. At that point, I knew I was seriously in the running. So began my life as a mainstream journalist.

## My Early Moments Reporting the Jogger Story

I was not thrilled about being assigned to cover the hospital. That is a place where it is hard to get information other than the standard releases. Reporters are not exactly allowed to roam the hallways and chat up the staff. My job was to attend any press conferences held about the jogger and call in or "dump" the information to a rewrite person, who would write the piece and hand it in to the city desk. Assigned to rewrite my story that first day was a white male veteran reporter who sat next to the city desk. He was well respected in the newsroom and known as someone who could put together a story quickly under deadline pressure. I wondered why the editors did not have me come in and write the story. What did that mean?

Held in a relatively small room of Metropolitan Hospital, the first press conference included all the major news outlets. They told us about the jogger's condition. My notes take me back to that moment: "Critical. . . . She has not revived." She was in a coma in the surgical intensive care unit. I called in to the city desk with my information. With much of the workday still ahead, the editors asked that I stay at the hospital to see if I could come up with something else. An editor said the jogger's family was expected. I tracked down hospital spokespeople a couple of times. At 12:05 P.M. one told me, "She still remains in critical condition." I do not know what I expected, but I was not taking any chances on something getting by me. I asked if anyone was with her. The spokesperson responded in the negative. As a reporter, you often contemplate the degree to which people think you are harassing them with nonsense. I decided to cool my heels for a while. To pass the time, I hung out with a group of reporters from the *New York Post* and *New York Newsday.*

Later in the afternoon, sometime closer to deadline, a couple in the hospital lobby caught my attention. I was alone at the time. They looked so out of place that I could not help but notice them. Metropolitan Hospital is located on the edge of East Harlem, and the patients and visitors that walk in the doors reflect the neighborhood. Most of the people milling about the lobby or seated in the chairs that day were Latino or black. An older white couple stood in the middle of all this, looking lost. Their whiteness, their clothing that represented a patrician style and seemed to mark their class background, and their demeanor stood out in the lobby. A pall of grief seemed to surround them. The combination highlighted them in the way a spotlight defines a character on stage while dimming the background. I noticed a hospital administrator approaching them, and I knew instantly. They were her parents. The administrator led them toward the elevator. No other journalists were around, and I was not wearing my press pass. So I simply joined them for the ride up and immediately became invisible in a Ralph Ellison kind of way.[5] In this context, as I saw it, my race more than anything else rendered me inconsequential. No one imagined me to be one of the journalists wandering around the hospital in search of news on the jogger.

On the elevator, the administrator began to fill in the jogger's parents on what to expect when they saw her. I stood behind and to the right of them; the administrator was directly behind them. The information they received had to be horrible for anyone, especially parents, to hear about a loved one: She had been badly beaten about the head and face, and she was swollen beyond recognition. I committed to memory the administrator's comments and what I could gather of the parents' reaction. When I called in the information, I knew my editors would love it. They did; they even complimented me. It appeared the racism in that environment had benefited the reportage. I spent the rest of my shift at the hospital and called in before I ended the day. It was the end of my work week. For my contribution that day, my name ended up in a box along with the names of nine other reporters. And so it went for about two months, with me generating a few more scoops during that time. On some of my days off, my replacement at the hospital was another female dark-complexioned African American reporter who wore her hair in a style similar to mine. That could not have been a coincidence.

## Early Lessons about Racial Boundaries

It became clear fairly quickly that the hospital would be an important area for coverage as the story unfolded. That assignment placed me in a vortex of office and city politics, both of which were sites of racial contestation. I felt as if all eyes were on me: everyone on the newsroom floor and all 1.1 million readers of the *Daily News*. Two years earlier, in 1987, the paper had lost a racial discrimination lawsuit from which it still labored to recover. The racial tension in the office remained palpable. The plaintiffs had been victorious, and the settlement included an agreement that placed the Equal Employment Opportunity Commission (EEOC) in a position to regularly measure the *News* administration's fulfillment of its diversity plan. My hiring in 1987, along with the hirings of other black editorial employees before the lawsuit went to trial, seemed to me to have been part of the paper's effort to forestall the suit or at the very least show a willingness to diversify. It did not work. The case went to court, and the *Daily News* lost the suit anyway. With this, I earned my introduction to the 1980s version of integration. I was not called nigger in the office, although some of my contemporaries were. I did not have to walk through a phalanx of angry whites yelling slurs and epithets at me. Instead, I met the double-speak of a more sophisticated racism.

It was the age of color-blind racism. "Come in," these new-generation racists said, claiming not to see your race and to welcome you with open arms. But it was not so much a welcome as an invitation and an order: Learn what they mean by diversity and get with the program. Unfortunately, I wanted more than anything else to believe that civil rights—no, *equal* rights—had arrived. When my family migrated to the United States twenty years earlier, my parents had insisted I buy into the dream. America was full of possibilities. I wanted to feel that "I, too, am America."[6] I expected, as Langston Hughes prophesied, to eat at the dining room table when company came.

Near the beginning of my tenure on the city desk at the *Daily News*, Samuel Hitchens, one of the paper's long-time black journalists and a plaintiff in the lawsuit, warned me that the administration would view my elite education cynically. To them I represented "affirmative action run amok," he said. Hitchens was tall, well over six feet, and handsome. As one of the four black journalists who had sued the paper, I had the impression that he was feared by the *Daily News* administration. The newly hired blacks had underground conversations among themselves about the terms of the settlement. The success of the lawsuit meant not only financial awards for the plaintiffs but also administrative requirements that the *News* management had to fulfill to stay on the right side of the law. Failure to live up to the agreement meant that the plaintiffs could haul the paper back into court. Sealed court papers left us able to do no more than speculate on what the management would be required to do. Some things we could surmise from the nature of the lawsuit: They had to hire and promote black editorial employees. In our whispered conversations, we wondered how assignments for the black reporters and photographers would be handled. It was no surprise to me that some of the white employees feared or despised the plaintiffs. And while Hitchens was not necessarily feared by some of the black employees, he was not always referred to fondly either.

I neither feared nor disliked Hitchens. I wanted to engage him and was curious about the *News'* racial history. He willingly talked to me in the way of an older mentor. I noticed that, while he had a brilliant smile, his eyes remained sad and his words often seemed bitter. I witnessed some of his rancor erupt one night in the midtown Manhattan newsroom. Also there at the time was another of the newly hired black female reporters, Gloria Sterns. Hitchens entered the newsroom yelling and cursing, walking along the outer perimeter of the open room looking out across the mostly empty desks. It was the night shift, and somehow this was the shift that many of the newly hired blacks populated. Working the night shift meant haphazard opportunities to get stories in the paper, because by then the day's paper was largely set.

"These motherfuckers better . . . ," Hitchens went on.

Gloria and I looked at each other. The air was filled with electricity. I looked at the city desk and watched the agitation of the editors. As Hitchens approached us, we saw that his eyes were red and realized he was drunk. I no longer recall who said it first, but we recognized that we had to get him out of the newsroom as soon as possible. I felt the need to protect him despite some off-color remarks he had made to me previously. He seemed to think it complimentary to tell me that the *News* knew what it was doing when it hired black women with beautiful legs. But I neither hated him nor disliked him because of such comments. In many respects, I felt I owed my job to him and the three other black journalists who had brought the lawsuit, forever putting their emotional health and peace of mind at risk for the sake of people they would never know. Other people— women and men, including my future husband—would find my position on Hitchens very confusing, but I did not feel excluded from the *News's* mainstream simply because of my gender. My race also contributed to my marginalization among the group of reporters and among female journalists.

Yes, I wondered why my editors gave me the hospital assignment and why they allowed me to keep it after it became clear that the hospital coverage would be important. I never doubted my abilities to do the job, but I suspected my race was the important factor in this case, masking all other aspects of my identity. Regardless of their reasons, the hospital was where I was. A lot rode on my work covering the story and I could not afford to mess up. The problem was that the story was a racial minefield inside and out. Ironically, the tone and nature of the case did not make me feel connected to the jogger because of our common gender. The main feature of the case seemed to lie in the history of the way American society constructed this thing called "race."

## Reacting to the First Day's Coverage

Spending the first day of coverage at Metropolitan Hospital meant that I missed the office scuttlebutt about the information I had dumped from the hospital and the gossip surrounding the stories coming in from other reporters. The headlines from the first-day stories startled me. Page one of the *Daily News* blazoned "Wolfpack's Prey: Female Jogger near Death after Savage Attack by Roving Gang."

Several smaller stories accompanied that big headline: "'She Put Up Terrific Fight,'" "Lived a Dream Life," "Why Jog at Night," "Running, a Risk North of 90th Street," and "Teen Gang Rapes Jogger." Singleton and Gentile (1989) opened their story with the following:

### 'She Put Up Terrific Fight'

A 28-year-old investment banker who regularly jogged in Central Park was repeatedly raped, viciously beaten and left for dead by a wolfpack of more than a dozen young teenagers who attacked her at the end of an escalating crime spree.

After savagely assaulting the woman about 10:00 P.M. Wednesday, the gang left her bleeding, bound, nearly nude and unconscious in a remote area at the north end of the park where she was found by two other joggers at 1:30 A.M. yesterday.

"She put up a terrific fight," said Chief of Detectives Robert Colangelo. (p. 3)

The story was just so awful. "How could the boys have done this?" I wondered. Wolfpack! Prey! Savage! I had long ago stopped getting angry at these kinds of references to black people. I would just grow cold.

How can someone stand on the inside of things and still be on the outside? From a racial point of view, some white people have found a way to make this happen, to make black people appear to live in two spaces at once. No wonder everyone thinks whites are so powerful: They can defy the laws of physics and get everyone to accept their version of reality. Black people can live in white spaces every day with white people—doing the same things whites do, reading the same books, watching the same television, doing the same jobs—yet not exist *in* their world. What does it mean to really exist in their world? The whites running the show can make the mental leap from knowing black people who do the same kinds of things whites do to seeing black people in terms like "wolfpack," "predator," and "savage." Yes, blacks are in the world of whites, but they are not *in* their world. Whites have made blacks *appear* to occupy two spaces at once. This may be the ontology of categorical group membership and marginalization.

Forcing those in power to see themselves as the perpetrators of so much harm could be nothing less than earth shattering. The only way to protect their own positive sense of themselves is to construct "others" as a negation of themselves. As I read the words wolfpack, prey, and savage in the coverage, I had no choice but to elide my feelings. Like Captain Marlow in Joseph Conrad's *Heart of Darkness* ([1902] 2008), I began to peer behind the ideological narrative of my day, this color-blind narrative that cloaked the system of racial domination.[7] It was finally beginning to sink in that maybe, just maybe, many whites could not allow themselves to see blacks as equal human beings. It occurred to me that this was an idea I had always resisted. I wondered what it would mean if I accepted this notion. I naively thought, "If only this jogger thing hadn't happened." But, I was beginning to see that if this had not happened there would have been something else.

Among most white journalists I spoke to, the suspects' guilt was not in doubt. Many black journalists, however, questioned the story coming out of the police. "How do the police know for sure the kids they're picking up had anything to do with the jogger's rape?" they asked. I had developed a close friendship with one of the black photographers on the night shift. Sometimes after my work day I would hang out with him in the darkroom as he "souped" his films and made prints. He worked constantly at his craft. As a gifted artist, his eye was finely developed. He expressed skepticism at the information unfolding in the papers.

"I don't believe half this stuff," he said.

"But they confessed," I added. He was mostly commenting on the reports from the police. But I took pride in my work. I felt torn. I was now in part responsible for some of the coverage. I did not want my work discredited too.

"I'm working on this story. Are you suggesting I would lie?"

"I'm not saying you would lie. Where's the information you're getting coming from? Things get twisted. I grew up in Harlem; the police were always framing people. . . . Something doesn't feel right here. There's too much hype. There's always a problem when there's so much hype."

I wanted to shut out his words. They stopped my mind from flowing naturally where it would. My job was to get information out of the hospital about the jogger, the kind of material the editors would want. I felt secure in this task. My friend's words did not elicit a yearning in me to talk to the boys' lawyers. Nor did they pique an interest to talk to the suspects. My blinders were up. My part of the story would not insert me into the vortex of the racial dynamics of the case, right? I wanted to believe that the jogger's status as a victim was related to the crime, the rape, and not her race. Since I was just reporting on how the jogger was doing, my stories would be read with sympathy, right? They would stand apart from the rest of the madness, right? I wanted so badly to believe that if harm was being done I would not be a part of it that my friend's words angered me. "He can be so difficult to deal with." I wanted to blame him for how complicated all of this was. But, deep down I was beginning to understand that he was probably right.

I had already witnessed the police breathing down a community's neck to find suspects. Before the jogger story, when I was still on the night shift, I drew the assignment of working with another photographer, Joseph Richards, to cover the aftermath of the murder of a rookie police officer named Edward Byrne. That night I left the Manhattan office with Richards to drive to South Jamaica in the borough of Queens. I did not know what to expect because we had been simply told to check out what was going on. Richards knew how to get to South Jamaica; I knew the area a little bit because it was a few communities over from St. Albans, where I grew up. South Jamaica resembled a typical Queens neighborhood: neatly aligned two-story, nearly identical homes with postage-stamp-sized lawns in front. South Jamaica's heyday had been many decades earlier. By the late 1980s, the whites had long ago abandoned the community, and South Jamaica had developed a reputation as a tough area with an entrenched drug problem. Some of its dilapidated homes and broken sidewalks fit the bill for an area in need of resources and attention. By this time, South Jamaica had also experienced an influx of immigrants, largely from the Caribbean. It was one of these immigrants, a Guyanese man named Arjune, who was at the center of the Byrne murder. Arjune had agreed to serve as a witness in a drug case. Assigned to protect him, Officer Byrne sat alone in his patrol car outside Arjune's home early one February morning in 1988. Armed gunmen walked up to the car and shot Byrne to death. Police alleged that this was part of a plan to intimidate Arjune.

After a year on the paper and only a few short months on the city desk, what I witnessed in the Byrne case took me by surprise. The first night on this assignment Richards chased police cars around the neighborhood to get a picture—not just any picture, but the picture that would tell the story. The police radio blared in the car. The police spoke in a code I could not understand. The scratchy, staticky sounds punctuated the air, becoming noise and adding to the confusion of the moment. Why was I here anyway? There was no one to interview. Periodic communiqués from the radio led Richards to pull out of one parking spot and zip around a few corners and park again. Then he would do it again, and again. Finally, Richards found his quarry. It was not a person or persons; it was a picture. Richards screeched to a stop shortly after the car in front of us halted. The whole thing unfolded like a slow-motion scene in a movie. The unmarked police car up ahead had suddenly turned diagonally in the street and jumped the curb to block the passage of a young black male—maybe only in his late teens—walking down the sidewalk. I was as startled, as he must have been. All four doors of the police car flew open. The men were yelling, "Police! Police!" Were guns drawn? What was going on here? As we approached the action, the young man was searched and patted down in front of the fence where they had stopped him. Richards led, with his camera drawn and snapping. We had our *Daily News* press passes out, or at least I did. I was too surprised to be scared. Richards and one of the officers exchanged a few words. I do not recall now if I was close enough to overhear him tell Richards that our presence was okay as long as we kept our distance or if Richards told me directly. My eyes probably looked liked two orbs in my head.

The seemingly random stopping and searching of young black males walking down the street went on all night. Some would be thrown up against fences and walls and after the search released like that first young man. Others would be tossed in the back of an unmarked van. At one point, we were close enough to the van to see it shaking and hear thumping noises coming from inside. Our presence did not draw further inquiries. The police treated us as if we were part of their team, inside some categorical boundary. After witnessing the first few stops, I asked Richards what they were doing.

"You know," he said casually. "They're just stopping any LeRoy right now." I let his words glide over me. I had gone cold again.

"Doesn't he have the faintest clue that I might find that comment offensive?" I wondered. Should that have been the least of what bothered me? Or should I have been more concerned with the police stops? What made these police actions seem okay, so much the norm, to Richards? Possibly the values behind his comment gave a clue. All I could do was shake my head. This guy, Richards, seemed like a cowboy out in the Wild West enjoying the hustle and bustle of a chase, the rounding up of animals. All I could think about was what was happening to those guys in the back of the van—and that any one of them could be one of my brothers. But, that was not the story; the story my editors and the police alike wanted was the one telling the world that the NYPD was doing its job. The question was which world they were talking to.

I do not recall if the paper ran a picture from that night. I am pretty sure I filed a story. I do know that neither Richards nor the police I encountered showed any sign that they thought I could be troubled by what I saw or that any of their behaviors could be problematic in any way. Maybe that was because I had gone cold again or maybe it was because the mantle of the *Daily News* said to them that "we" were all part of the same group. I talked about what I saw with other black journalists and my family, but it was only much later that I came to comprehend the scope of what I had witnessed. In the wake of Byrne's murder, the New York Police Department created the Tactical Narcotics Team (TNT), first in South Jamaica and then across the entire city, for the purpose—they claimed—of addressing street-level drug activity. The TNT program, along with other antidrug measures, across the city so thoroughly filled the jails with mostly young black men that the NYPD had to scale back its operation a few years later.[8] Illegal drugs were certainly a problem, but poor blacks and Latinos were being painted as the major element in this societal challenge.

## Some Early Training in Police Reporting

Why would the police not think that we, the press, were part of their team? When I got the chance to work on the city desk, I was so happy. I had clearly begun to advance at the paper, I thought. During my first month or two on the city desk, I worked a daytime schedule. I was sent to cover a variety of bureaus to, as Gil Spencer said, get my feet wet in all the areas under the purview of the city desk before I took my position on the night shift. At the start of this tour of duty, I spent about a week fielding general assignment stories—that is, anything that came up that no one else was working on. After that, I worked in the courts. Then I moved on to the shack, the press office for reporters at police headquarters. The police and press physically work closely together. Police headquarters is located at One Police Plaza in Manhattan. The office of the Deputy Commissioner for Public Information (DCPI) is the NYPD division that deals with the press; this section has an array of officers at police headquarters who answer questions from local, national, and international journalists.

One Police Plaza is a tall but squat-looking modern building. As the new kid on the block, the first thing each morning I had to travel from the shack (which is located on one of the lower floors) up into the tower to go over "the sheets." I remember chuckling when I glanced at the sheets the first time. The sheets, I realized, were simply that: sheets of paper held together on a clipboard. They are one of those little things in the world that stand for so much. I was being "instructed" by a veteran police reporter on how to go through the sheets and cull the relevant information for my editors. He came with me the first couple of times I did this job.

"You just go through it. Then call the stories in to the city desk," he said.

"How do I determine which story to call in?" I asked him.

"Well, if you think the editors will be interested in it you give them that one. . . . You know," he chuckled, "they don't want some cheap murder."

I decided not to ask him to define "cheap murder." I was afraid I would appear stupid and inexperienced. But I was beginning to get the picture. This was all about one's "news" judgment. That unidentified body of the twenty-year-old black male would be seen as "run of the mill"—no real story there, maybe at best relegated to a "small box"-sized story secreted in a corner of the paper that needed filling. My tutor continued. "The guys up here are really nice," he said, referring to the police staff. "Sometimes they'll let you know when a big story is going on." I began to dread the moment when I would be on my own and have to call in stories from the sheets. After the city desk editors get the call, they decide which of the stories they want us to follow up for the next day's paper. This is a part of the routine for all the local papers. So, if I were to miss a story the competition had decided to run with and it turned out to be a really "good" story, the *News* would have egg on its face and the blame would fall in my lap.

The first time I did this job on my own I felt a great deal of trepidation. I stood staring at the sheets struggling to recall the earlier instructions I had been given.

"Oh, God I don't want to call in the wrong thing," I thought. They were too many entries to call them all in. The slot for each entry was standardized. There was a space for which precinct the incident occurred in, a space for what had happened, and so on; for example, "33 Pct. Unidentified body found; black, male, approx. 20 years old."

The knot in my stomach grew as I contemplated deciding what was "news."

I do not recall what I called in from the sheets that first time I did the job solo. But I grew more comfortable with the task with every passing day. I dallied longer over the sheets each morning, studying them. Noticing a greater frequency of reports from precincts that were predominantly African American and Latino, I pondered the significance of this. What would I find if I were to check the sheets in the local police precinct in areas like Bay Ridge or Bensonhurst in Brooklyn, which were then primarily white neighborhoods, or Middle Village in Queens, which also was largely white? Would all of their local crimes be on the sheets here at DCPI? I remember looking at community newspapers from white areas and noticing many police blotter reports that did not make the major papers in the city, when comparable crimes in black communities would show up in the main city papers fed through the DCPI system. Why would people not assume there were more crimes in African American and Latino communities if this was what they were presented with? A thought crystallized in my mind during those early days at DCPI: The police were the first editors.

## The City Erupts after the Early Jogger Reports

In the wake of the attack on the jogger, nearly forty young black teens were picked up for questioning. The police and the district attorney's office quickly settled on six or seven suspects, all of whom lived in Harlem near the park's

entrance. Most lived in the Schomburg Plaza Houses, a private high-rise housing complex. Despite their young ages, their names were quickly turned over to
the press: Steve Lopez, age fifteen; Antron McCray, fifteen; Kevin Richardson,
fourteen; Yusef Salaam, fifteen; Raymond Santana, fourteen; Clarence Thomas,
fourteen; and Korey Wise, sixteen. The second-day stories about the rape carried the boys' names. When I first read those names and ages, my cheeks grew
flushed, the warmth spreading across my face as a feeling of sadness overtook
my whole being. "What will happen to them?" I wondered. I thought about
their families—mothers, fathers, sisters, and brothers—walking through the
courtyards of the Schomburg Plaza complex, going up the elevators to their
apartments, feeling the condemning eyes of the city, the nation, and the world
piercing their souls. But, the story my editors wanted from me lay in Metropolitan Hospital. Convinced that my focus had to be the hospital and the
information I could get out, I wanted to believe the other aspects of the story
would be carefully told. But the pending mayoral race with the city's first serious black candidate for mayor seemed to be providing the context for how all
parts of the story would be rendered. Major elected and community leaders in
the city found their way to Metropolitan Hospital to walk across the lobby and
be whisked up the elevator, presumably to the jogger's bedside, so they could
then come downstairs and make a statement about the case to the press. Many
wound up giving a statement to me. Much of what transpired was being viewed
through the prism of race—the jogger's race and the race of the suspects. How
could I think otherwise? Plastered in big, bold type across the *Daily News* front
page on the second day of coverage was the word "wilding."

My days off work started right after the first day of coverage, so I watched
the city brew from a vantage point away from the newsroom. I percolated with
everyone else. What does the word wilding mean anyway? It was supposed to
be some new fad for kids. Black kids? The paper claimed it was the word, the
symbol, for the fun pastime of wreaking havoc. There is a feeling of familiarity
in the expected order of events: A crime happens, people are arrested. Stories
appear about the incident. Stories appear about the arrests. But this time it was
different. What would happen next? The story would not or could not subside.
The audience had to have more.

Reading the stories from the third day of news reports, I prepared for my
assignment on this new workday. I noticed additional sets of lenses applied to
the coverage. There was an extended focus attempting to penetrate the surface
of our complex and diverse metropolis. The story had captured the *Daily News*
front page for the third day in a row. On the cover was a near full-page picture
of fifteen-year-old Antron McCray, his head hanging as he was taken into the
24th Precinct. The headline next to his image read, "Rape Suspect's Jailhouse
Boast: 'She Wasn't Nothing.'" On the inside, the other big headlines were "One
Big Joke for Teens" and "Rape Suspects Laugh over Attack." Mike McAlary

(1989), the most prominent columnist at the *News* and one of the most important in the city, weighed in with his first commentary about the park incident:

## One Big Joke for Teens

### A Song that Didn't Make Hearts Sing

The noise came from the holding cell in the back of the squad room. This was right after 2 A.M. in the 24th Precinct, the moon still high over Central Park. The teenagers were together again, the videotapes already made, confessions gory and complete.

They had been joking and laughing together all night. They had talked to detectives for hours, explaining everything about the gang rape, without ever offering an explanation. Not one had used the word "sorry."

"Hit the beat," a cop heard one of the kids say suddenly.

And then it began, a sound from the street corner, taking over the room. Two of the kids became human beat boxes, supplying the rap rhythm.

"Boof, Boof, boof," they sputtered. "Boof, Boof, boof."

And then the teenagers were all in on it again, the cell filled with singing.

*That's what happens when bodies start slapping*
*doing the wild thing.*                                              (p. 3)

I read McAlary's description and interpretation of the boys' behavior in the holding cells. What did the bass line, the rhyme, the syncopation, the virtual call and response from another world tell him? If McAlary's account was accurate, these children had not only done the unspeakable, they had also committed the unthinkable. His rendition gave the appearance that the boys relished the attack and acknowledged their group act as a type of ritual with a festive and triumphant song. McAlary (1989) offered his own words of explanation about the significance of the song.

The song is called "Wild Thing," and [it's] all the rage of tough street corners. The song, made famous by a rapper named Tone Loc, is a celebration of carnal knowledge, the so-called wild thing.

*I get paid to do that wild thing.*

Any kid worth his "wilding" knows the words to "Wild Thing." So when nine suspects were thrown into a cell together early yesterday they sang the song. (p. 3)

"This is it," I thought. "People are going to be furious." Mixed in with the image of the jogger's body lying broken and beaten in a pool of blood, amidst the vegetation in a remote corner of the park shrouded in darkness, were the echoes of a celebratory song with a bass line reminiscent of a drum beat from a distant past. "White people are going to be *really* angry," I thought. McAlary ended his column with a scene whose significance has echoed throughout European systems of knowledge since the sixteenth century, when Europe penetrated Africa. McAlary's unspoken question was one that the nations of Europe and their descendants have debated and dissected ever since.

> Eventually, [in that precinct house,] between the jokes and the singing, a demand was made:
> "Yo," McCray had announced. "I'm hungry."
> This, at least, showed some need. The kids were given sandwiches from Blimpie's, quickly devoured. They wiped their mouths cleanly with crisp yellow napkins. Mothers came and went carrying in fresh clothes for prison. Finally, after the white legal pads had been filled with confessions, the videotapes removed, the second-floor cell grew oddly quiet.
> A cop looked in and was surprised to see the kids sleeping. A few of them jerked fitfully in sleep, guilt working hard on the body. The cop was glad to see this.
> "Look," he recalled saying to a detective. "Humans." (McAlary 1989)

That the conclusion about these children's humanity was in dispute, waiting for some sign, makes it easier to understand why, in 1989, it became easy to contemplate, to believe the improbable—a group of as many as fifty black and Latino boys could run chaotically through Central Park, New York City's playground for the affluent, searching—no, "hunting"—for a white woman to attack. The whispers I heard in the office among the black journalists made it into print a few years later. The police had misunderstood the boys talking about the song "Wild Thing," and with that misunderstanding, a new social activity among black children was born: "wilding" (H. A. Baker 1995).

Back at work on Sunday after my days off, the latest installments of the story changed the contours of my assignment. "Give us an update on the jogger. And, get a reaction from the visitors about their feeling about the suspects being so remorseless." I was in the thick of it now, I thought.

During my shift at the hospital, I cannot say I was surprised at the comments from the jogger's visitors. One person I interviewed—I will call her Marlene—told me that the Church of the Heavenly Rest, an Episcopal church on 90th Street at Fifth Avenue, had held a huge vigil for the jogger the day before. Founded shortly after the end of the Civil War in memory of soldiers who had served and died, the church (in its second location, across the street from Central Park) occupies a huge gothic building with a venerable history and has a largely white congregation.[9] At the time, I was not aware of the church's history. But later, after I learned about its Civil War origins, I wondered if the jogger was seen in some small way as yet another victim of that seemingly endless conflict. My interviewee Marlene did not know the jogger personally; she was just the friend of a friend of the jogger. She told me that some 150–175 people had turned out for the service and vigil the previous night. They had spent thirty minutes holding hands and praying. Then they had all lit candles and carried them away. It must have been a sight to behold, so many dots of light illuminating the cavernous art deco chamber, these people hoping their good will could make things better. Marlene was at the hospital that Sunday to drop off a list with the names of the people who had attended the vigil. The list was tied with a yellow ribbon. That so many strangers would be moved by another's plight—the beauty of the image, the beauty of the sentiment—touched me deeply. With another part of my mind, I wondered what would have happened if it had been me. Would there have been a vigil? Would they have come to pray for me?

I do not remember now what Marlene looked like. She did not look like me; she was white, and she looked the way one would expect someone from Wellesley to look. Then her words made all the beauty evaporate, like the thin wisps of dark-edged white smoke swirling away from the candles of the previous evening.

"Now I'm angry and I want be positive," she said. "Was she angry at me too?" I wondered.

She went on, "I went to positive when we found out it was someone we knew. The Wellesley grapevine is very tight. We started calling everyone we knew. Everyone wanted to get together, even Wellesley alums. We've got people. Tons of people came and signed their affiliation as 'runner,' 'a stranger who cares,' 'a feeling citizen,' 'you'll be okay, hang on.'" Like Marlene, some of these people did not even know the jogger. They just cared so deeply. Someone in their circle had been felled. My eyes moved up from my pad and I looked in her face. There was more there than compassion and pain.

She continued, "Now goddamn it, the anger kicks in. The hate kicks in."

"She's a wonderful, wonderful person," was how Marlene described the jogger. "She's one of the people who would have contributed to society."

And what about her thoughts on the suspects and what they had allegedly done? "I have no pity. I would have no mercy. It's incomprehensible. It's unforgivable." Marlene was not unique in her sentiment; members of her circle of friends and contacts were equally outraged. "I was really shocked. The people I called about this, how angry they are; really bitter." It seemed all us reporters were on the same mission that evening. Another reporter from a competing newspaper was present during my interview with Marlene. The reporter showed her a copy of the day's paper with the headlines about the boys singing in their cells. She could no longer hold it together. She burst into tears and ran from us, from the hospital. We had our reaction story.

# 3

# The Position of the Black Male in the Cult of White Womanhood

## Tears and Fears

**MARLENE WAS NOT** the first and will not be the last white woman to be reduced to tears and fears based on the alleged actions of black men. Her emotions were not simply related to issues of crime and violence. Those fears and tears are related somehow to the ways in which we socially construct the meaning of people's race, class, and gender categories. On that first day when I heard the news of the attack on the jogger, I knew right off the bat that the story of a white female possibly raped by black males would resonate differently than a story of a white female raped by white males, or of a black female raped by black or white males.

A week after the city awoke to news of the attack, three of the accused teens went before Justice Carol Berkman, a no-nonsense, Harvard-educated white woman. At an arraignment hearing the *New York Times* described as "raucous," the prosecutor stood before the judge and argued that what had happened to the jogger was the "'most vicious and brutal assault' ever committed in New York City" (R. Sullivan 1989a). In the prosecutor's estimation, the suspects should be denied bail. Whether the prosecutor spoke with an eye on the long lens of history or was simply comparing the attack with more recent events, it appears she found that the assault represented some extreme event in the city's history.[1] The teens' attorneys countered that in the 1986 murder case involving the infamous Robert Chambers—the white, preppy-looking youth who eventually pled guilty to strangling Jennifer Levin in Central Park, supposedly during "rough sex"—the defendant still managed to get bail (R. Sullivan 1989a). Chambers's case remained part of the context of the period, because it had drawn to a close only about a year earlier. The defense attorneys also referenced the notorious 1986 case in which a black man had died after being chased onto a highway by a group of white youths from Howard Beach, a white ethnic enclave in the city's borough of Queens. In that case, the court had also granted bail to the accused teens. It is possible that the prosecutor's words were court-room theatrics, but what is clear is that there was a disparity in treatment. No death occurred in the Central Park attack, yet the suspects were denied bail. By this time, vigils were being held across the city with white and black partici-pants. Everyone, white and black alike, wanted to make clear that they too were outraged—everyone, that is, except some supporters of the suspects who report-edly behaved "raucously" at the hearing. With rancor, some mainstream press reports noted, the supporters questioned the veracity of all that was being re-ported by the media—the rape, the beating, the jogger's reason for being in Central Park late at night—all of it.

## Reporting in the Middle of a Feeding Frenzy

The media competition to get information about the jogger and about what had transpired in Central Park could be summed up in a word: fierce. The blanket coverage meant that reporters had been dispatched to find out about the jog-ger's personal life back home in Pennsylvania and in the places she had been educated, her life in the city, her family's background, anything that could help to paint a picture of this person. My assignment, working out of Metropolitan Hospital and contending with the competition, was difficult on its own. But I also had to deal with the reactions from various quarters in the city, some of whom I had not encountered before.

Some members of black communities across the city developed a growing distaste for the approach of the mainstream press to the coverage of the case. The *City Sun,* a Brooklyn-based weekly newspaper that served the black com-munity, termed the mainstream media coverage an "outrage." They charged that the mainstream media were exploiting the beating and rape of the jogger "to accomplish their own base agendas" (*City Sun* 1989). Some of the support-ers of the young suspects were quoted in the mainstream papers questioning just about everything about the case. "Has anyone seen the jogger? How do we know she actually exists? How do we know if she was, in fact, raped?" some would ask. The doubts about the very existence of this woman echoed in my ears as I went about the business of reporting from Metropolitan Hospital. I found those types of questions a little embarrassing. To me, such questions came from a bygone era. Did people actually think someone in this day and age could *get away with* making up a story like this, whole cloth, just to make peo-ple classified as black appear in a negative light? I did not know what to think. But, I could not squelch the charge of exploitation made by the *City Sun* as eas-ily. In fact, I agreed that the case was being sensationalized. I tried to hang on to my naïve notions that, despite the seemingly exploitative use of the case by the press, my behavior could and would be perceived differently. So I hunkered down and focused on my basic assignment: Stay at the hospital, cover the goings-on, and stay out of the many lines of fire.

My reporting on the goings-on was as imprecise as that, no specifically planned story that I knew of, no conspiracy. I was not privy to the discussion among the editors in the morning meeting, in which they planned the day's paper. I only knew what marching orders I got from my city desk assignment editor after the meeting. They just wanted some story, any story featuring the jogger. I also knew that before 3:00 P.M. I needed to have some new piece of information that could constitute a story to call in to the desk. This would ensure that when my editor sat in the afternoon meeting with other editors to finalize the list of events reported as news in the following day's paper, he or she could ostensibly argue for space for my story. Furthermore, I knew in my bones that if I had a story, it would make the paper. But the assignment was essentially a stakeout. Had the jogger been at home, we, the press, would have camped out in front of her door. Stakeout stories are just that: journalists planted somewhere watching time pass. In this case, how does one build a story when the subject is comatose? As I roamed the hospital lobby, outside environs, and sidewalk, I observed a storm of grief, anguish, love, and resentment intensely swirling around the image of this woman called the jogger. Meanwhile, she lay in bed upstairs teetering on the edge of life, unaware of her position in the eye of that storm.

The winds swirling around her appeared to result from a community coming together as if to offer her the protection that ought to have been hers that night in the park. By then I had spent twenty years in the United States, thirteen of those in New York, and I had never seen a reaction like this to a rape. Was it all women who had been let down by society, or just this one in particular? It was the late 1980s, and feminists (Brownmiller 1975;[2] A. Davis 1981; J. D. Hall 1983) had made strides in this regard; rape was more and more being viewed as a "crime of gender oppression" (Benedict 1992; Lizotte 1985) with its roots in the common law principle that women are the property of men (Galvin 1985). Women had had to march in the streets of New York City and across the nation in "Take Back the Night" protests to draw attention—in the general public and in the press—to the problem of rape in our culture and to reinforce women's rights to walk on the streets at night without fear of attack. The 1970s in many states across the country had been a decade for the reform of rape laws (Galvin 1985). No woman should ever have to deal with rape, and over the previous two decades women had fought loudly to make this point. Then suddenly the mainstream press and prominent people across the nation singled out this particular rape for special treatment. Why?

The case likely started out as a police blotter item—white, female, with a catalogue of injuries, found in a section of Central Park near Harlem. But once the press picked up the item from the sheets or other police sources, something else happened. As the jogger remained comatose, her survival in doubt, I along with many New Yorkers read with interest those early stories about her life before New York City. One of the first-day stories in the *Daily News* captured the image that would be nurtured throughout the coverage. Reporter Mark Kriegel (1989) summed her up as follows:

### Lived a Dream Life

. . . The young woman whose life was jeopardized by marauding teenagers lived the way most of us dream.

She grew up in Upper St. Clair, Pa., an affluent suburb of doctors, lawyers and professionals, 10 miles south of Pittsburgh, far from the steel mills.

Her mother is a member of the school board and former Republican committeewoman. One brother was said to be a lawyer in Hartford, another an assistant district attorney in Dallas.

After graduating from high school, in 1978, she headed east for Wellesley College, an exclusive women's college near Boston.

She majored in economics and graduated Phi Beta Kappa. She was much more than a brain.

In her yearbook photo she appears as a pretty blond in a turtleneck sweater with an engaging smile and eyes gleaming with promise.

By September 1983, when she attended her first graduate class at Yale, she had worked for the State Department in Zimbabwe, for Braxton Associates and for former Rep. James Shannon, who went on to become attorney general of Massachusetts. . . .

She was headed for the big time: New York, Salomon Brothers, Wall Street. (p. 2)

Whether or not one bought the media renditions of the jogger's life seemed irrelevant; a human being had been very badly hurt. One could not help but care. I saw the press accounts of all these people commenting about the case—religious leaders, elected officials, and citizens from all backgrounds who did not represent a position in officialdom. Many simply expressed sorrow and shame; others talked about retribution, what should happen to the young boys suspected of raping and beating this young woman.

My initial focus at the hospital was to get comments about the jogger's condition from the medical staff and to try to get a statement from her family. Her mother, father, and brothers sat daily vigils by her bedside in shifts, so I was told by one of my sources. They entered and exited the hospital blankly staring ahead, silently walking past me and other members of the press with no comment. But, much to my dismay, the focus of my reporting had to expand to include the growing numbers of people coming to the hospital and its environs to see the jogger or to wish her well. During the early days of her hospitalization, with still no really clear sign that she would survive, these visits picked up quite a bit. The coverage distinguished the jogger as a special person.

As I stood in the lobby on her first Sunday in the hospital, the Archbishop of New York, John Cardinal O'Connor, walked through the entrance. He traveled with a few others. I do not recall now whether the city desk had alerted me about his visit or I had told them about his presence. But it was easy enough to figure out that he had come to visit the jogger. Cardinal O'Connor had led the archdiocese for the previous four years; when in the past I had covered minor stories involving the archdiocese, I had only ever gotten access to the cardinal's spokesperson. This would be my first time meeting the cardinal himself.

I vaguely recall a minor exchange with him when he first entered. But it was understood I would wait for him to leave and get his comments after the visit. I do not remember what I asked him, but I spoke only once. His comportment when he gave his comment suggested someone making sure to recall all he had to say. Although he looked in my direction, his eyes were not specifically focused on me. His statement was measured, predetermined; its length suggested I had asked a series of questions. But, in fact, I had asked only one.

"I talked to her mother and father. I'm here as a priest. I offered them whatever assistance I could." He noted that he gave them his home phone number and said they could call anytime of the day or night.

"I'll be praying every day," the cardinal said. "I said that at my mass this morning. . . . We prayed for the girl, for her parents, for the parents of all those involved and those themselves." He seemed to cover everyone with that comment. Were these incarcerated teens "those themselves"? Sometime afterward, the cardinal received criticism in the press and from New Yorkers for visiting the young suspects at Rikers Island jail more than once (Santangelo 1989). Years later, I would see the cardinal's visits with the jogger and her family and with the suspects and their families as the cardinal possibly stating in his own way that choosing between sympathy for the jogger and support for the rights of the accused teens is a false dichotomy.

That day after the cardinal's visit, the jogger's parents made some of their first comments to the press. When her father came through the lobby that afternoon, I asked him about her condition.

"It's very hard to tell [if she's responding] . . . her condition is about the same," he said. He did not address my question about the suspects, skipping over that to make a comment possibly about New Yorkers. "The response from everybody has been fantastic; it's been outstanding. Every kind of support helps."

A hospital press conference held the next day, following the cardinal's visit, had a more upbeat prognosis for the jogger. It was the first clear statement that her life was likely no longer in jeopardy. Although her medical team no longer viewed her death as imminently possible, my assignment did not change. I do not recall any discussions about pulling back on the volume of coverage from the hospital. In fact, the community of well-wishers surrounding the jogger continued to swell. People from her apartment building and neighborhood and some strangers—fellow joggers—continued to stop by the hospital. They brought flowers, cards, and kind words of support. By Tuesday of that week, residents of Schomburg Plaza, the Harlem housing complex where four of the young suspects lived, and students from a local high school held what *felt* like an impromptu vigil on the sidewalk outside the hospital. I did not know whether or not the desk would want a story from me, because a female columnist from the *Daily News,* Gail Collins, showed up to cover the vigil.

Television journalists also showed up. I watched this, contemplating the message that could be relayed to the public from the whole event—a vigil spontaneously organized by a group of teens, black and Latino girls and boys. I wandered among the kids gathered on the sidewalk by the hospital fence, asking a few questions. They were from a new high school, Manhattan Center for Science and Math, which had a reputation for academic rigorousness. I was given the impression that the purpose of the vigil was to show that the kids wanted to offer their support, care, and concern for the jogger, as well as to challenge the idea that the attack was racially motivated. I cynically wondered whether the students had really done this on their own or had been spurred by school administrators or others who wanted to fight the negative definitions assigned to the category "black" by placing "good" black and Latino kids in the public eye. Everyone saw that this was a huge story and that the press was seeking comments from everywhere. Why not use this opportunity to dispel the notion being reinforced by the coverage that black and Latino youth regularly engage in violent behavior? (See Gitlin 1980.) Whatever the case might have been, I thought it sad that these children had to worry about coming up with strategies to circumvent being lumped together with kids who might have attacked the jogger, simply because they all shared the same race.

The journalists circled the students. I stood with a group of African American girls in the vicinity of *News* columnist Gail Collins. She asked them questions about how they were treated by their male peers. The girls told stories of derogatory treatment at the hands of their fellow black male teens. I cringed while listening to their comments. In the following day's paper, Collins (1989) wrote:

## Gifted, Black & Angry

. . . "All the guys have the attitude that girls are dogs," said Roberta Yates, 18, who wants to be an accountant. "We don't mean anything. We're just here to give them sex."

A quarter of a century of civil rights and women's rights, and we now have the beautiful sight of young black women from hard neighborhoods who feel no dream is beyond them—except perhaps a young black man who will treat them with respect. (p. 5)

I stood there divided down the middle—black and female. Part of me wanted to scream out to the girls, "Don't tell her that. Those comments will only make things worse, 'things,' like the assumptions that all black males have no respect for women. And, they're the only ones who have no respect for women. They're the only ones who rape." Collins's gender analysis masked the racial hierarchization of the society. In her interpretation of the life experiences of people classified as "black," black females were singled out as a group that does not get respect from black males. It suggested that males from other racial categories treat black women, or women in general, with respect. History has proven otherwise. The consequence of the categorical life experiences of gender/womanhood masking those of race is that the unique social location that is created when race and gender intersect goes unnoticed or is treated as insignificant.

But another part of me joined Gail in the questioning, knowing full well that these girls, these budding young women, needed to be supported and protected, because there was a greater likelihood of them being raped than there was for white females (J. D. Hall 1983: 334). And, there was a greater likelihood that the rape of a black woman would not garner the same type of public attention and outcry as would arise in the case of a white woman. I liked that Gail had asked questions about gender equality and gender oppression and that she had linked the tone and the intensity of the coverage to class. Further down in the published column, Collins (1989) stated:

Almost everyone in front of the hospital felt the story would not have made such a splash if the victim had been black.

This is the single point on which I part company with the kids from Manhattan Center. I think the outcry would have been exactly the same if the victim had been black, as long as she was a black investment banker who lived on the Upper East Side.

The rape in the park shattered the myth that middle-class New Yorkers use to comfort themselves—that the violence pulsing all around us will not hit home if we live in the right neighborhoods and send our children to the right schools. (p. 5)

I agreed with Collins that in addition to gender, class and race were also operating here. But I also disagreed with her racial analysis. I felt certain that even if a middle- or upper middle-class African American woman had been raped and beaten in the same manner as the jogger, the press and everyone else would *not* be clamoring to show their concern and support. Typically, women of color who have been sexually assaulted have been treated as "unworthy" rape victims (Lizotte 1985). In a case of rape, whether these girls were poor or upper class would not matter as much as their race. That day, that moment, standing there with Gail, listening to those girls while a number of internal conflicts swirled within me, I just wanted to be someplace else. I walked away from the scene thinking that despite the good intentions of these teenagers, their comments would be used to advance the historical construction of black males as sexual predators.

## Identifying Mainstream Sensibilities about Rape

The discomfort I felt as a black female journalist working for a mainstream institution translated into a constant feeling of anxiety over whether or not I belonged. Mainstream is one of those words that I had known and used for a very long time without a full sense of its meaning or possible implications. I now see the mainstream as a site for corralling support for the dominant forces in our world. As an instrumental entity, the mainstream includes and excludes categories of people, cultural symbols, forms of meaning making, forms of expression, and forms of interaction in society based on the needs of the dominant groups.[3] One's possession of attributes of the mainstream determines how easily one gains right of entry to navigate its institutions. The mainstream is that "it" we are all drawn to, yet only some ever experience. Belonging to the mainstream is that feeling one gets from looking at television commercials depicting the norm and learning the story of what you *should* look like, how you *should* dress, what your home *should* look like, and how you *should* interact with others. Then, upon turning away from that manufactured image to review everything in the vicinity, one sees a reality that is a reasonable approximation of the constructed image. That is the feeling of belonging to the mainstream. My consciousness of the mainstream and how it functioned began to really develop while I worked at the *Daily News*.

My job at the *News* gave me working knowledge of how many institutions functioned. I got a taste of what it meant to be inside or outside of the mainstream. As I cranked out story after story and had to deal with a myriad of editors reviewing my work to make sure that the audience got the "right" perspective and was provided with the "necessary" facts, I realized that all information deemed "appropriate" fit into the mainstream. The mainstream, in general, brings together the currently dominant ideas about race, class, and gender. In the current period, the prevailing ideas are based on the ideology of color blindness. The mainstream filters allow in "appropriate" categories of things, people, and behaviors based on hegemonic ideas. By excluding or devaluing others, the mainstream shapes our race, class, and gender hierarchies.

In the case of the jogger coverage, the knowledge or facts the editors privileged to identify the jogger as a part of the mainstream included details about her class, such as her father's job at Westinghouse, the fact that she attended Wellesley College and Yale University, and the fact that she worked in a professional position as an investment banker on Wall Street. Such class markers intersected with race as well as with notions about gender. These intersecting ideas about the jogger's race, class, and gender serves as indicators of how her rape was regarded in the mainstream. A study of rape cases in the period leading up the 1980s highlights the importance of class status in cases of sexual assault. Lizotte (1985: 172) found that rape is a unique type of assault because of the "censoring bias" practiced by the criminal justice system and by the victims of rape when it comes to reporting sexual assault—that is, getting these assaults on the books and in courts. Female rape victims and police tended to report cases they believed would lead to prosecution—"worthy" cases. They used both cultural and evidentiary standards to determine whether or not they had a "strong for prosecution" case. These cultural and evidentiary standards served as types of mainstream filters. The factors used to define a rape case as strong for prosecution, according to Lizotte (1985), were the woman's white racial classification, the woman's lack of a criminal record, the woman's positive marital status, the unquestionable sexual virtue of the woman, an unknown offender, the use of weapons, the occurrence of medical injuries, and the woman not being identified as a prostitute. The first criterion mentioned by Lizotte (1985) is white racial classification. The second, third, and arguably the fourth criteria are indicators of status or class.

Years after my involvement in the coverage of the jogger case, while studying to be a sociologist, I conducted a content analysis[4] of fourteen years of press coverage of the case. I measured the occurrence of words and terms used in the articles in my study sample that served as an indicator for categorical life experiences such as race, class, and gender. My premise was that the frequency of use of certain words and terms would indicate the importance of these categorical life experiences in the coverage. The results of the content analysis initially suggested that in 1989 race was not an important criterion for determining which rape cases were worthy of extensive reporting. Figure 1.1 shows that indicators of race were used less frequently than those for class, gender, and age. The jogger's white racial classification was mentioned in about 10 percent of the articles, while her classification as a jogger was mentioned in 95 percent of the articles. But no one is defined by only one of their categorical memberships. The question remained: How do class and race intersect in the mainstream in the context of cases of rape?

For my content analysis, I read through a data set of about 500 articles to determine the often-used words and terms that were indicators of categorical life experiences such as race, class, and gender. From a randomly selected sam-

**TABLE 3.1**   Frequencies of Articles that Included the Listed Indicators for Race (in percent)

| Race Indicators | Time Periods 1–4: Apr 21, 1989– Dec 31, 2003 | Time Period 1: Apr 21, 1989– Jun 9, 1989 | Time Period 2: Jun 10, 1989– Mar 14, 1991 | Time Periods 3 and 4: Mar 15, 1991– Dec 31, 2003 |
|---|---|---|---|---|
| Wilding | 17.9 | 20.0 | 15.8 | 19.7 |
| Predator | 2.8 | 1.8 | 0.0 | 7.9 |
| Wolfpack | 6.8 | 25.5 | 0.8 | 2.6 |
| Savage | 5.2 | 12.7 | 4.2 | 1.3 |
| Hunt | 0.8 | 1.8 | 0.8 | 0.0 |
| Pack | 8.0 | 14.5 | 4.2 | 9.2 |
| Black suspect race | 11.6 | 9.1 | 9.2 | 17.1 |
| Latino suspect race | 7.2 | 3.6 | 5.0 | 13.2 |
| Jogger white race | 9.6 | 9.1 | 6.7 | 14.5 |
| Harlem | 19.1 | 23.6 | 5.8 | 36.8 |
| Upper East Side | 6.0 | 12.7 | 0.8 | 9.2 |
| Racial tension | 6.0 | 5.5 | 1.7 | 13.2 |
| Northern Central Park | 22.7 | 32.7 | 19.2 | 21.1 |
| Source black race | 3.2 | 3.6 | 0.8 | 6.6 |
| Source Latino race | 0.8 | 0.0 | 0.0 | 2.6 |
| Animal | 2.0 | 1.8 | 1.7 | 2.6 |
| Feral | 0.8 | 1.8 | 0.0 | 1.3 |
| Sample size | $N = 251$ | $N = 55$ | $N = 120$ | $N = 76$ |

ple of half of the articles, I measured frequencies of the words and terms I had identified from my initial review. I found seventeen racial terms, only one of which signified white racial classification (see Table 3.1). For class, I determined frequency of use of fifteen terms (see Table 3.2). Ten of the class terms were related to the jogger, such as universities she and her family and friends had attended or institutions in which she and her family or friends worked. These sites—elite universities, major corporations, and investment banks—are not racially diverse; therefore, it is logical to assume that people in those institutions are most likely members of the white racial group. It appears, based on my content analysis, that depending on the social context, class can act as a stand-in for race. While the jogger's white racial classification was rarely mentioned in the press coverage, her class—mentioned in 95 percent of the articles—served as an indicator of her racial group membership. This finding suggests that even within the context of interlocking systems of oppression and privilege, one categorical life experience can mask another. But that does not make the one being masked irrelevant. The aspect of one's identity doing the masking takes on the role of the identity feature being masked.

**TABLE 3.2**  Frequencies of Articles that Included the Listed Indicators for Class (in percent)

| Class Indicators | Time Periods 1–4: Apr 21, 1989– Dec 31, 2003 | Time Period 1: Apr 21, 1989– Jun 9, 1989 | Time Period 2: Jun 10, 1989– Mar 14, 1991 | Time Periods 3 and 4: Mar 15, 1991– Dec 31, 2003 |
|---|---|---|---|---|
| Runner | 7.6 | 14.5 | 4.2 | 7.9 |
| Jogger | 95.2 | 90.9 | 95.0 | 98.7 |
| Avid runner | 0.8 | 3.6 | 0.0 | 0.0 |
| Jogger's universities | 4.0 | 14.5 | 1.7 | 0.0 |
| Jogger's family and friends' universities | 0.0 | 0.0 | 0.0 | 0.0 |
| Jogger's family and friends' jobs | 3.2 | 9.1 | 2.5 | 0.0 |
| Jogger's non-Salomon job | 1.2 | 1.8 | 0.8 | 1.3 |
| Salomon Brothers | 8.4 | 18.2 | 8.3 | 1.3 |
| Investment banker | 37.8 | 69.1 | 35.0 | 19.7 |
| Jogger middle class | 4.0 | 9.1 | 3.3 | 1.3 |
| Schools suspects attended | 1.6 | 7.3 | 0.0 | 0.0 |
| Suspects' family and friends' schools | 0.4 | 0.0 | 0.0 | 1.3 |
| Suspects' family and friends' jobs | 0.4 | 1.8 | 0.0 | 0.0 |
| Suspects' moderate income | 0.8 | 3.6 | 0.0 | 0.0 |
| Suspects' middle-class lifestyles | 2.0 | 3.6 | 1.7 | 1.3 |
| Sample size | $N = 251$ | $N = 55$ | $N = 120$ | $N = 76$ |

Without a detailed analysis of the articles in the coverage, it might appear that in the world of the new color-blind narrative, the jogger's race was not singled out as an important factor. But the media did follow the cultural and evidentiary/juridical cues identified by Lizotte (1985) for selecting the jogger story for the prominent treatment it received. While the stories do not appear, on the surface, to place any significance on the jogger's race, they actually privilege her race through the emphasis placed on her class. Her white racial privilege is maintained without being overtly articulated in the text. The attack on the jogger was one of 3,254 reported rapes in New York City that year. She was also one of fourteen individuals who was reportedly raped in Central Park in 1989 (Purdum 1990). There was another equally disturbing and brutal rape in the city shortly after the jogger's rape, but it received relatively scant attention.

The coverage of this other rape shows how race, class, and gender come together in the assessment of the significance of rape by mainstream media producers in ways that marginalize some categories of individuals. An African

American woman in a poor black community in Brooklyn was gang-raped by a group of nonwhite teens and young adults (Arce 1989: 7). She was stripped naked and thrown off a rooftop. Her life was spared only by the cables attached to the building, which stopped her fall and left her dangling for a resident of the building to find (Newkirk 2000: 28). From the point of view of my editors at the *Daily News,* that story did not warrant much coverage. In addition to this rape, and while the jogger's rape was being covered, a teen named Matias Reyes had been raping women on the Upper East Side, where the jogger lived and ran. Labeled in the press as the "East Side Stalker," Reyes would later be discovered to be the person who had actually raped the jogger. But the coverage of these other rapes was paltry compared with the number and intensity of reports about the jogger. Nor were there more generalizing reports addressing the problem of rape in society.

To justify the selection of the Central Park jogger's rape for sensationalized treatment, media producers created an image of the jogger as an upper-class, virtuous white woman, without a questionable or criminal past, who also suffered numerous injuries during a sexual assault by an unknown offender(s)—that is, this was a "worthy" rape. To construct the jogger's image, stories about the incident in the mainstream media focused on descriptions of her life that reinforced the accepted definition of the idealized woman and on depictions of the attack that itemized her injuries. (See Table 3.3 for the frequency of use of indicators of violence in the reports.)

This was primarily a gender story for me; a woman had been raped. Therefore, I initially expected to have gender terms be the ones used most frequently in the coverage. However, to my surprise, I found that class terms outpaced gender terms and far outpaced race terms. (See Figure 1.1.) While this result may appear to fit journalist Gail Collins's idea of why the story was so salient to news producers and audiences, it does not address the likelihood that the jogger's race—like anyone else's—could not be separated from her class. There were very, very few black women who had an educational, professional, and social background like the jogger's. The likelihood of her being black was negligible, because in the United States, class acts as a stand-in for race (Gans 2005). Thus, in the media content, as in the larger contemporary society, racial factors can be hidden in plain sight.

Race and class were not the only cultural concepts that intersected in the coverage. Class and gender also intersected. Categorical life experiences related to class helped to define the jogger as a woman who could be a "worthy" rape victim. Table 3.4 shows that while 84 percent of the articles in the sample used the term "rape," only 53 percent of the articles used the noun "woman" and 27 percent used the pronoun "she" or "her." The woman attacked in Central Park was primarily "the jogger." With her race/class/gender status—white woman—helping to distinguish her rape as one worthy of prosecution, the media renditions

**TABLE 3.3** Frequencies of Articles that Included the Listed Indicators for Violence (in percent)

| Violence Indicators | Time Periods 1–4: Apr 21, 1989– Dec 31, 2003 | Time Period 1: Apr 21, 1989– Jun 9, 1989 | Time Period 2: Jun 10, 1989– Mar 14, 1991 | Time Periods 3 and 4: Mar 15, 1991– Dec 31, 2003 |
|---|---|---|---|---|
| Left for dead | 14.3 | 10.9 | 13.3 | 18.4 |
| Beat | 55.8 | 58.2 | 55.8 | 53.9 |
| Brutal | 16.7 | 16.4 | 14.2 | 21.1 |
| Gang | 12.4 | 21.8 | 7.5 | 13.2 |
| Attack | 72.5 | 72.7 | 67.5 | 80.3 |
| Terror | 4.0 | 5.5 | 3.3 | 3.9 |
| Rampage | 15.9 | 27.3 | 9.2 | 18.4 |
| Assault | 31.9 | 32.7 | 16.7 | 55.3 |
| Harass | 4.4 | 7.3 | 0.8 | 7.9 |
| Maraud | 4.0 | 10.9 | 1.7 | 2.6 |
| Blood | 15.9 | 20.0 | 15.0 | 14.5 |
| Knife | 4.8 | 5.5 | 2.5 | 7.9 |
| Size of "gang" | 14.7 | 21.8 | 15.0 | 9.2 |
| Rock or brick used as weapon | 27.5 | 34.5 | 28.3 | 21.1 |
| Hold down | 11.6 | 10.9 | 15.0 | 6.6 |
| Hit | 11.2 | 16.4 | 10.8 | 7.9 |
| Strike | 6.8 | 5.5 | 8.3 | 5.3 |
| Rob | 11.2 | 7.3 | 9.2 | 17.1 |
| Kick | 5.2 | 0.0 | 8.3 | 3.9 |
| Cripple | 0.4 | 0.0 | 0.8 | 0.0 |
| Sample size | N = 251 | N = 55 | N = 120 | N = 76 |

**TABLE 3.4** Frequencies of Articles that Included the Listed Indicators for Gender (in percent)

| Gender Indicators | Time Periods 1–4: Apr 21, 1989– Dec 31, 2003 | Time Period 1: Apr 21, 1989– Jun 9, 1989 | Time Period 2: Jun 10, 1989– Mar 14, 1991 | Time Periods 3 and 4: Mar 15, 1991– Dec 31, 2003 |
|---|---|---|---|---|
| Rape | 84.1 | 81.8 | 81.7 | 89.5 |
| Sodomy | 1.6 | 1.8 | 2.5 | 0.0 |
| Gang rape | 15.1 | 14.5 | 10.8 | 22.4 |
| Female | 12.7 | 7.3 | 11.7 | 18.4 |
| Woman | 53.4 | 74.5 | 53.3 | 38.2 |
| Pretty | 1.2 | 0.0 | 2.5 | 0.0 |
| Attractive | 0.4 | 0.0 | 0.0 | 1.3 |
| Bubbly | 0.4 | 0.0 | 0.8 | 0.0 |
| She/her | 26.7 | 56.4 | 20.8 | 14.5 |
| Breast | 8.0 | 7.3 | 11.7 | 2.6 |
| Sample size | N = 251 | N = 55 | N = 120 | N = 76 |

cast her as the idealized woman. In fact, the headline on that first-day story about her said it outright: "Lived a Dream Life."

Later on in the coverage, media producers worked to keep that dreamy image alive. After the trials began, courtroom supporters of the teen suspects wanted the media spotlight turned on another individual, the jogger's boyfriend. DNA analysis revealed that his seminal fluid was on her jogging pants (Alvarez 1990b). Some of the supporters of the boys questioned why the boyfriend too had not been identified as a possible suspect. The mainstream press treated as ludicrous the idea that the jogger's white boyfriend—someone known to her—could possibly have done such a thing.

This reaction reflects the propensity of the mainstream to assume that white men cannot be rapists and to privilege the notion of the stranger-rapist. There are deeply rooted historical reasons for the disconnect between the notions of white male and rapist. (This topic will be discussed in more depth later in this chapter.) In thinking of the context of that period, this kind of disconnect allowed white Robert Chambers to use "rough sex" as a defense in the death of Jennifer Levin (Benedict 1992). It is also necessary to further examine the inclination to more readily expect rapists to be strangers. Lizotte's (1985) study notes that the rape cases that go on the books are the ones that both the police and the victim deem to be "strong for prosecution." One of the defining features of a strong rape case is an "unknown offender." This type of selection bias in even the victim's reporting of rape likely helps to fuel the myth of the stranger-rapist. As Angela Davis (1981: 180) points out, "In much of the contemporary literature on rape, there is nevertheless a tendency to equate the 'police blotter rapist' with the 'typical rapist.' If this pattern persists, it will be practically impossible to uncover the real social causes of rape."

Why is the "unknown offender" rape easier to prosecute? People are less likely to believe a woman's accusation of rape if she knows the offender. This reflects common expectations regarding the exercise of male sexual dominance. In fact, most rapes are not committed by unknown offenders (Benedict 1992: 13). Also, people more readily call the woman's reputation into question when she knows the rapist. If the press had taken up the boyfriend issue in the Central Park jogger case, it could have sullied the jogger's reputation. Thus, no questions were raised about the jogger's virtue despite contemporary sensibilities about premarital sex. I raise this not as a criticism of the jogger but instead to note a seeming double standard here: Often in rape cases, albeit unfairly, when the victim is a member of the working class or nonwhite, her social life or sexual history becomes an issue. The jogger's class status as an affluent woman, with all its imputed virtue, may have worked to protect her in this regard. There were some initial stories questioning her decision to jog late at night in Central Park, but those dried up quickly under criticism from feminists on the grounds that women should feel free to run anywhere at any time.[5] Outside of making sure that the coverage did not disrupt traditional delineations of gender roles, the mainstream media had no grand gender concerns—not those of sexual oppression and definitely not those of gender violence.[6]

At the time, I had many reservations about the mainstream framing of rape, because only the rape of a woman who fit a man's idealized definition of womanhood would be considered "worthy." In our private conversations about the coverage, some of the black journalists pointed to this culture's particular reluctance to accept that a black woman could be raped. Despite the disparity in treatment meted out to black women, I identified with the jogger as another woman and I would have considered it oppressive to put her, the victim of a rape, on "trial" for questions about her sexual virtue. My objection was that the foundation of virtue was used by the mainstream media to build her image. This worked to continue breathing life into nineteenth-century notions of the "cult of true womanhood" (J. D. Hall 1983). As historian Jacquelyn Dowd Hall (1983) notes in her groundbreaking essay "The Mind that Burns in Each Body," these ideas of womanhood come with a downside: They support the notion that women's sexual/gendered expressions could be a threat to society in general and to men in particular.

The only issues deemed appropriate by my editors were how badly the jogger had been victimized and the unlikelihood that anyone other than the apprehended boys could have been responsible. Media producers did not mind sensationalizing the case and exploiting everyone within reach to make this point. The jogger's long list of injuries seemed to be a testament to the "savagery" of the black male. I had no choice but to wait until the trial to see how the defense attorneys would proceed. But, as the narrative for the story was being constructed in the early days of the coverage, about twenty different words or terms for violence were used in the articles, with "attack" being the one most frequently incorporated (see Table 3.3). All of these indicators represented acts committed against the jogger, allegedly by the young suspects. In the sentences of the newspaper articles, the words and terms indicating the violent acts perpetrated against the jogger were not structurally divorced from words representing the black and Latino suspects/subjects who supposedly committed those acts. "They attacked." "They raped." "They beat." One early press report stated, "The teens used the pipe and a brick to bludgeon her when she tried to fight them off, police said" (Clark and Landa 1989). Compounding the inflammatory impact of this use of language, the term "alleged" shows up in only twelve articles in my sample of 251 stories. Thus, the media language created an indisputable association between the black and Latino male suspects and the violent acts that had been committed. In this case, the violence-related words and terms also served as a stand-in for words expressing race. Therefore, in the coverage, violence became assimilated into the meaning of the racial category known as black/Latino.

J. D. Hall (1983: 332) argues that in most studies of racial violence, rape is traditionally overlooked as an "aspect of sexual oppression" and is instead interpreted as "a transaction between white and black men." If, as Hall suggests, rape has been used by white men to send a message to black men, and white men interpret the rape of a white woman by a black male as a message being delivered to them, it is important to ask how the white male definers of the mainstream (among them the press) read the rape of this white woman allegedly committed by black and Latino youngsters.

## Constructing White Male Privilege in the Mainstream

One of the marks of power in American society has been the ability to define meanings for everyone else. The people running mainstream media institutions often get to determine the significance of our everyday interactions, because they are the ones who determine what should be elevated to the status of news and, consequently, what is construed as important. These institutions are dominated by white men, who have been privileged in this society from its inception because they were able to define everyone else's rights and privileges relative to their own. The white men who determined this at the outset were European Americans. But as the category of people known as "white" coalesced, the media played an important role in normalizing the concept of "the white race." The development of shared identities—a type of nationalism—occurs discursively, and the media supplied the discursive incubator that supported that development in the United States.

Early American culture was being constructed around a system of racial categorizing that incorporated heredity, group affiliation, and group hierarchy. These were some of the first attempts to establish the racial categories that would eventually allow America to arrive at the point where elite, moderate-income, and poor Europeans could share a hegemonic position over blacks. Descendants of these Europeans would be able to unite into a group known as "white" (Allen 1997; Roediger 1999).[7] This racialized system served as a form of social control for issues revolving around freedom, slavery, and labor. Historian Theodore Allen (1997: 248) argues:

> Instead of social mobility, European-Americans who did not own bond-laborers were to be asked to be satisfied simply with the presumption of liberty, the birthright of the poorest person in England; and with the right of adult males who owned sufficient property to vote for candidates for office who were almost invariably owners of bond-laborers. The prospects for stability of a system of capitalist agriculture based on lifetime hereditary bond servitude depended on the ability of the ruling elite to induce the non-"yeoman" European-Americans to settle for this

counterfeit of social mobility. The solution was to establish a new birthright not only for Anglos but for every Euro-American, the "white" identity that "set them at a distance," to use Sir Francis's phrase, from the laboring-class African-Americans, and enlisted them as active, or at least passive, supporters of lifetime bondage of African-Americans.

Europeans—particularly those who were not owners of large tracts of land and who were not in possession of enough capital to be independent merchants or businesspeople—were actively differentiated from blacks, with whom they had much in common from a class or social status perspective. Allen (1997) asserts that this occurred in order to create a buffer between the lower and higher strata of people to reduce the likelihood of systemic revolt. He notes:

> Thus was the "white race" invented as the social control formation whose distinguishing characteristic was not the participation of the slaveholding class, nor even of other elements of the propertied classes. . . . What distinguished this system of social control, what made it "the white race", was the participation of the laboring classes; non-slaveholders, self-employed smallholders, tenants, and laborers. In time this "white race" social control system begun in Virginia and Maryland would serve as the model of social order to each succeeding plantation region of settlement. (Allen 1997: 251)

Legal scholar and Critical Race Theory proponent Derrick Bell contends that America's racial history, which in large measure was constructed during centuries of slavery, does not completely explain the persistence of racism in the United States. Instead, he says, the unflagging racism in U.S. society can be explained by the "symbiosis" between racism and American liberal democracy (Bell 1992: 10). In this system, some people's freedom is based on the oppression of others.

With the establishment of racial categories came the policing of racial boundaries. Central to sustaining racial borders were regulations against interracial sexual interaction that would prevent the development of a group of "mixed race" people who could challenge the traditional racial/labor/class order. Thus, interracial sexual interactions were thrown into the middle of issues of freedom, slavery, and labor, forever commingling concerns of race and class with gender. The rules about interracial sexual interaction were designed and managed to maintain existing race and class hierarchies.

The wide-scale acceptance of these types of legal and sometimes extralegal social practices elevated elite white males into a position of sexual dominance over all others—white women, black men, and black women. The sexual boundaries these white males legislated for other groups did not apply to them. They normalized their sexual freedom to such an extent that behavior that constituted rape for others was not defined as such when *they* (the white men) did it. And their white wives and the rest of the community went along with this charade (White 1999). The sexual domination of the master class over female slaves was viewed in the context of property rights; in legal terms, black women's status as property precluded defining sexual exploitation by their masters as rape (Bardaglio 1994; A. Davis 1981; Ferber 1998). This notion became so ingrained in the culture that up until the eve of the Civil War even the rape of a black female slave by a black male was viewed as "a mere assault and battery."[8] (Bardaglio 1994: 759). The law simply did not recognize the rape of black women; by definition, all female rape victims were white. But it is important to note that during this period not all white women who accused a man of rape—even a black man—could be sure the accusation would be viewed as legitimate. The white woman had to come from a particular class *and* be virtuous (Bardaglio 1994: 765; Hodes 1997).

The societal consequences of the laws and social practices around interracial sex were severe for all women—black women in particular—because these conventions institutionalized rape, especially the rape of black women (A. Davis 1981). To justify the rape of black women, society created the cultural myth of black women as being "oversexed" (White 1999). In the process, black males were emasculated because they could not protect their mothers, wives, daughters, sisters, or other female members of their communities (White 1999). In this formulation, white men would not be defined as rapists. Further, the white female/black male relationship was marginalized and stigmatized in the mainstream. Society made white female/black male sexual liaisons the focus of negative attention because they disrupted the system of racial oppression (Allen 1997; A. Davis 2000; Ferber 1998). The social order was established with elite white men at the top.

## The Mainstream and Media Converge

Although elite and middle-class European American males had sought common bonds before the American Revolution, the war and the post-war period created new opportunities for middle-class whites, particularly men, to come together as a group in their quest to share power with elite whites. The middle-class white men who had been indentured before the revolution gained their freedom after fighting in the war. Within fifty years of the war, under Jacksonian democracy, opportunities for these individuals to improve their status increased greatly. Many gained capital, elevated the social prestige of the fields of work they typically pursued, and developed an interest in the press. It would be through the field of publishing that the middle-class whites would see tremendous political gains. One of the most important of these benefits came in the ability to consolidate power with elite white males. The early history of middle-class whites as publishers, coupled with the role of the press and the discursive nature of the construction of whiteness, allowed the publications owned by these individuals to likely serve as a site for the consolidation of whiteness.

The fusion of this group of independent, free whites in post-revolutionary America developed discursively, as Roediger (1999) points out. This coming together reached new heights fifty years after the war, when the group established its own press system—the Penny Press—which would eventually become the precursor of our contemporary media. Named after their one-cent cost, these new-style newspapers represented a break from earlier journalistic publications, or the "blanket sheets,"[9] in terms of political affiliation, business model, and focus of coverage. Equally important, the Penny Press put the growing group of middle-income whites in a position to eventually share the hegemonic position of the elites as whites ruling over blacks.

Building the newspaper readership of the nascent Penny Press meant using all of the organs of the newspaper—editorial content, advertising, production, and distribution—to meet the needs of the audience the publisher wanted to attract. Historian Alexander Saxton argues that the initial success of the Penny Press came from changes in format, price, distribution, and content. In contrast to the blanket sheets, the format of Penny Press publications was much smaller; they were printed on 8½- by 11-inch sheets. These newspapers went for a penny a copy, and they were sold by street vendors, as opposed to subscription (Saxton 2003: 97). And their subject matter was not politically neutral—they reported on crime, violence, humor, and sex (Saxton 2003: 97–98). Thus, the features of the developing Penny Press in the 1830s, along with its new advertising system, suggests, at the very least, that the people being amassed into an audience had fewer financial means than the traditional readers of the blanket sheets.

The first Penny Press publications started by the new classes of whites grew out of the expansion of the free market system. These individuals disagreed politically with the outgoing national leadership and hailed the rise of Andrew Jackson and his brand of democracy, which increased rights for men of European descent in the middle classes, voting rights in particular (Roediger 1999). Saxton's research grounds the socioeconomic and political background of the Penny Press founders with this emerging group of middle-class white males:

> Of the seven men identified as founders of pioneer penny dailies, available biographical data indicates that six began as artisans—five printers and one cabinetmaker. . . . The seventh . . . like the others . . . was a wage earner. . . . Men such as these—on the basis of their journeyman's and editorial skills—might have had access to working credit, scarcely to large capital. One reason for the affinity of their newspapers to Workingmen's and Jacksonian politics was the anger many of these editors

felt at seeing upper-class blanket press dailies subsidized by bank loans
. . . while they themselves were starving for capital. (Saxton 2003: 99)

Many of the early Penny Press publications were essentially labor papers
that supported a growing labor movement. A number of graduates from the
Penny Presses served in the Jackson administration; Jackson is said to have
"appointed more than fifty [editors] to posts in his administration" (Pasley
2000: 52).[10]

The new business model of the Penny Press changed the economic foundation of journalism; it required owners to, in effect, sell their audience to adver-
tisers. Wilson and Gutierrez (1995: 39–40) tie the development of this new
business model to modern mass media systems, which are supported by adver-
tisers seeking the largest possible audience:

> The first "penny press" took on a new form that was uniquely adapted
> to the free enterprise system. The newspaper sold for only a penny,
> but its primary income did not depend on subsidies from a political
> party, a government in the form of public notices, or the subscription
> of readers. Instead, the newspaper's revenues and profits were to come
> from advertisers who would pay for the space in the *Sun* [the first
> penny paper] to place commercial messages to reach the large reader-
> ship attracted by the low price. . . . Mass society in the United States
> did not necessarily mean a society of the masses, but a society in which
> the people were amassed into an audience for the messages of the mass
> media of communication.

Wilson and Gutierrez (1995) also establish connections between the Penny
Press's new economic model and the need to maintain an audience by appeal-
ing to their likes and dislikes. The positions taken by Penny Press publishers on
issues in their news coverage, in part, reflected their competitive need to amass
the largest possible audience. While some Penny Press publications were inclined to support the old elite, Saxton (1984) notes that for the bulk of these
papers, the coverage supported the rights of working men. The Penny Press
papers' support for the new classes of whites, who emerged with the changing
status of labor categories, entailed reinforcing the elevation of these whites into
middle-class positions above those occupied by the free blacks.

The ability to bring this audience together was doubly important because
media serve as the "connective tissue" in society (Ewen 1996). The Penny Press
papers did not simply connect economically. Through the stories they covered
about race, such as the nation's westward expansion and removal of Native
Americans from their land, these papers united readers discursively and philosophically on issues of race. In this context, such coverage was used to build
group loyalty among whites and thus represented a type of nationalism.

As Duara (1996: 163) notes, "Nationalism is best seen as a relational identity. In other words, the nation . . . is hardly the realization of an original essence, but a historical configuration which is designed to include certain groups and exclude or marginalize others—often violently." Duara argues that national identities are relational: There are times when some people will feel connected as a group and other times when this feeling of connection will be submerged and a sense of connection with another group will be privileged (p. 165). Thus, he defines identities as being in flux: "forged in a fluid complex of cultural signifiers; symbols, practices, and narratives" (p. 165).

Duara's (1996) argument is similar to the idea espoused by Durkheim and articulated by Karen Fields (2002) about the shared identification developed through common totems (as discussed in Chapter 1). In the case of the development of the Penny Press, this media form created shared identities through the creation of common totems—such as the white male as the symbolic head of white racial group classification. The interests of the symbolic head became the vehicles used by the mainstream to distinguish the privileges accorded one group relative to another—white to black, white to Native American, men to women. With these interests grounded in the definitions of white racial group classification, a common identity could be forged between the non-elite and the elite European descendants. Oftentimes the narrative used to articulate the group interest was the narrative of citizenship—whether that narrative was framed in terms of citizenship as a social practice or as a legal notion (Glenn 2009). As such, the development of the modern mass media occurred as a type of racial project.

## Framing Blacks in the Press: The Nascent Mainstream and the Abolitionist Media

The abolitionist newspapers and the black press were the sites that framed black concerns independently from mainstream formulations of white nationalism found in the Penny Press publications. Abolitionist newspapers have not been treated by scholars and others as if they were part of the same society in which the Penny Press operated, although they were interacting with roughly the same set of social forces (within the context of their own limitations, of course). Journalism historian David Mindich (2000: 15) makes a strong argument for synthesizing the scholarship on the birth of the Penny Press with that on the abolitionist press:

> To discover how much the field of journalism history is in need of a fundamental revision, thumb through the indices of all the usual suspects and look up references to Frederick Douglass. It is no exaggeration to say that you will find that nearly all the standard journalism histories fail to place him in the context of nineteenth century politi-

cal reality. The corollary is true, too: mainstream histories can help us understand his politics but fail to explain his journalism.

However, the politics and journalism of the abolitionist press went hand in hand because these papers often practiced advocacy journalism, openly advocating for political positions that supported black rights. There were approximately 500,000 free blacks in the United States during this period; however, the black communities across the nation had tremendous difficulty financially supporting a black press (Rhodes 1994). About forty black-owned newspapers were started in the antebellum United States, but only six were able to survive for more than two years:

> Poverty, illiteracy, competing political agendas, and the social effects of racism and discrimination contributed to the creation of an audience that could not support—financially or otherwise—a single vision of one newspaper. African American publications played a vital role in galvanizing the abolitionist movement, encouraging education and racial improvement, and disseminating the news, yet nearly all operated at a loss and most were short lived. (Rhodes 1994: 95)

The white-owned abolitionist press took both moderate and more radical positions concerning the future of slavery in the United States. The more moderate abolitionists took the position of "the American Colonization Society, which was formed in 1816 to promote the colonization of free blacks in Africa" (D. B. Davis 1975: 33). Radical abolitionists included Quakers Charles Osborn and William Swain, Elihu Embree, and William Lloyd Garrison, one of the most famous and radical white abolitionists and publisher of the *Liberator* (Franklin 1980: 180–185). Journalism historian Jane Rhodes distinguishes pro-abolition Penny Press publications from white-owned abolitionist papers. Like the black-owned abolitionist press, the white-owned abolitionist press had trouble gaining subscribers (Rhodes 1994). These papers did not reach the types of circulation numbers that the Penny Press, in general, achieved. "In reality, most anti-slavery and other associational newspapers had circulations that rarely reached in the thousands. William Lloyd Garrison noted that even ten years after he began publishing the *Liberator,* the paper never had more than about 3,000 subscribers" (Rhodes 1994). While the abolitionist press likely influenced the coverage by the Penny Press, that influence was not reflected in circulation of the abolitionist papers. The publications that used the new mass media business model were the ones to thrive.

In his research on the Penny Press, Saxton (1984) found that both pro-abolition and anti-abolition Penny Press papers used the same types of pejorative language to describe blacks and Native Americans. Synthesizing the historiography of the Penny Press and of the abolitionist papers makes the socioeconomic divisions and the diversity of ideas among whites more accessible because we get to see them as part of one society.[11] It also makes it easier to see how many antislavery whites joined in the racial agenda of proslavery whites to "otherize" people of color. Journalism historians (Mindich 2000; Rhodes 1994) argue that divided positions on race were evident between even the white radical abolitionist press and the black abolitionist press. In the antebellum North, Frederick Douglass wrote for one of the most renowned white abolitionist newspapers, William Lloyd Garrison's *Liberator*. Often described as extremely nonpartisan and radically abolitionist, the *Liberator* was not aligned with Douglass's political vision (Mindich 2000). Based on his own brand of radicalism, Garrison did not want to be subject to the U.S. Constitution. But Douglass did not want to be divorced from the American political system; quite the contrary, he wanted party affiliation (Mindich 2000). Regardless of the political positions Douglass shared with Garrison around abolition, Douglass saw the mainstream—the construct that determined the right to belong, or citizenship—as an existential necessity for blacks in America. Douglass imagined that it would be through the political system that blacks would gain any rights. Thus, he started his own paper, the *North Star* (Mindich 2000).

If the views of Douglass are used as a stand-in for the position of the black abolitionist press, at the time what these papers wanted was full inclusion—citizenship. If the views of whites are judged from the positions of the moderate abolitionist press and the Penny Press, what emerges is that the very humanity of blacks was being debated and the public discourse was strongly in favor of the exclusion of blacks from the system—noncitizenship. Such was the discourse framing blacks in the press in the nineteenth century. The 1856 Supreme Court decision in the Dred Scott case essentially rendered blacks noncitizens and clearly indicated which faction among the whites had become dominant. For a brief moment after the Civil War, during Reconstruction, blacks made significant inroads toward exercising their rights as citizens. But looming equality for blacks put African Americans in direct competition with non-elite whites. Thus, Reconstruction ended with a white backlash that included solidifying the hegemonic position of the white race and destroying the image of black men in American culture by rendering them as a threat to the broader society (Fredrickson 1971a).

## Ida B. Wells: Reframing the Black Male Image in the Media

In the post-Reconstruction era, publisher and editor Ida B. Wells (also known as Ida Wells-Barnett) challenged the construction of the black male image as a threat to white society and to white women in particular. Ida B. Wells was one of the first female journalists in the United States; she also happened to be black. In the 1880s, at the beginning of her period of fame, there were only forty-five black female journalists in the United States (Bay 2009: 44). As the first black female editor and publisher, she held an unusual position in society, particularly for a woman. She made a name for herself as a journalist, though today she is not as well known as Frederick Douglass. A bit younger than Douglass, Wells was still somewhat his contemporary. They worked together briefly and were personal friends, and Douglass served as one of Wells's mentors as she navigated white and black social movements that demanded equality for blacks and women. Wells often found that although her work and her choices challenged racism and patriarchy, her colleagues in these movements were sometimes less than supportive.

Wells lived in one of the most revolutionary periods in American history, and she embraced the spirit of change. The story of her life demystifies the fable often used to explain the Reconstruction era and stands in graphic relief against the dominant ideas of the period—which portrayed blacks as immoral, depraved, less than human, unable to rule themselves, akin to animals, and a weaker species destined for extinction. These were essentially ideas of biological determinism. Historian Mia Bay (2009: 16–17) puts it this way: "The myth of Reconstruction that emerged after the North and South reconciled in the late nineteenth century cast Reconstruction as a scandalously corrupt period of 'negro rule,' in which unscrupulous 'carpetbaggers' from the North collaborated with self-serving Southern 'scalawags' to turn the government of the South over to ludicrously inept freedmen."

Born as a slave in 1862, Wells came of age during the most radical stage of the period, when blacks, after having been subjected to two centuries of slavery, finally had the opportunity to grab the reins of freedom. Bay (2009) notes that the social, economic, and political transformations of the age loomed large in Wells's life, and she imbibed the revolutionary fervor of the moment. Learning at the knees of her parents, former slaves who strove for economic and political independence, Wells clearly understood the promise of freedom in the air and she did not intend to squander it.

When she was sixteen, Wells's parents died and she was forced to provide for herself and her four siblings. Infused with personal pride and likely the pride of the moment, Wells's parents had ensured that she learned how to read and write. The conditions of her life were such that they seemed to have aided in her development of sensibilities about race, class, and gender. As a single young woman, she had to be independent enough to find a way to provide for her siblings while simultaneously maintaining the decorum expected from women. For a while, Wells worked as a country teacher. This helped her to learn the conditions of postslavery African Americans. Later she developed as a journalist, writing for a variety of papers in the South and pushing for equality for blacks.

After she moved to Memphis, Wells became an editor and a publisher. She had been aware of lynchings but had not taken them up journalistically as a cause because she had largely accepted the dominant culture's explanation that the black men who were lynched had committed the crime of rape (Bay 2009). But her personal experience with lynchings in 1892 opened her eyes to the reality of the matter: Black men were being falsely accused of rape as justification for lynchings that were largely being used to subvert Reconstruction efforts and the growing demands by blacks for equality. The particular incident that turned Wells's attention to this subject was the lynching of three of her friends, black businessmen in Memphis who had tried to defend themselves from attacks by whites that arose out of the economic competition the black men's businesses posed (Bay 2009). Wells denounced the lynchings in a vigorous editorial in her newspaper. In response, whites burned her paper to the ground, just as abolitionist papers had been attacked during the Jacksonian era. Wells was away while this happened, and she was threatened with death if she returned to Memphis. After this incident, she lived in exile from her home and led an antilynching crusade that grew to national and international scope (Bay 2009).

As part of her antilynching activities, Wells published *Southern Horrors: Lynch Law in All Its Phases* in 1892. This piece was essentially an investigative report in which Wells examined previous accusations of rape and lynchings to expose the myth of the black male propensity to rape white women and to draw attention to lynchings occurring because white women had allegedly been raped by black men. She spread her message to numerous papers across the nation. Ferber (1998: 38–39) cites Wells (1892) and the work of Hazel Carby (1986) to make the point that "lynching and rape both served as economic and political weapons against the black community and at the same time defined black men and women as outside of the ideological construction of manhood and womanhood. Wells's *Southern Horrors* exposed the hypocrisy of the rape charges and the lynchings, noting that if whites kept at it they might overplay their hand and expose the truth that some white women in fact found black men desirable. Revealing this truth would have undermined the period's carefully constructed notion of white womanhood. In *Southern Horrors* Wells reported the following:

> What is true of Memphis is true of the entire South. The daily papers last year reported a farmer's wife in Alabama had given birth to a Negro child. When the Negro farm hand who was plowing in the field heard it he took the mule from the plow and fled. The dispatches also told of a woman in South Carolina who gave birth to a Negro child and charged three men with being its father, *every one of whom has since disappeared.* In Tuscumbia, Ala., the colored boy who was lynched there last year for assaulting a white girl told her before his accusers that he had met her there in the woods often before. . . .
>
> Hundreds of such cases might be cited, but enough have been given to prove the assertion that there are white women in the South who love the Afro-American's company even as there are white men notorious for their preference for Afro-American women.

> There is hardly a town in the South which has not an instance of this kind which is well-known, and hence the assertion is reiterated that "nobody in the South believes the old thread bare lie that negro men rape white women." (1892: 56–58)

One can only imagine how despised Wells was for having the temerity to lay bare American sexual politics for all to see. She incorporated in *Southern Horrors* the mainstream newspaper accounts of these so-called rapes and attacks on white women. Wells noted in her research that part of the purpose of the southern press in spreading these myths was to get sympathy from northerners and the concomitant freedom for southerners to do as they liked with blacks—institutionalization of Jim Crow segregation. "With the end of Reconstruction, white Southerners campaigned for segregation and black disenfranchisement by questioning not only the racial character of black people, but their gender characteristics—often construing black sexuality as a racial threat to the white race" (Bay 2009: 74). Feminist writer Valerie Smith (1998) critiques Wells, arguing that in the journalist's work, race masked gender because she failed to acknowledge that some white women were indeed raped by black men. Early in this chapter I noted that when one categorical life experience masks others, the one doing the masking takes on the role of the experiences being masked and hides the other. As in the case of the Central Park jogger, where the woman's class privileged her race, in the case of black men—throughout American history—their race has been used to determine their marginality in all other areas of their lives and prevents us from understanding the significance of their gender marginalization in their interaction with others.

## The Black Male in the Mainstream Media: The Framing that Stuck

Ida B. Wells's attempt to reframe the black male image in the press was not successful. Forces such as social Darwinism and Negrophobia conspired against her. The latter followed the former as the nation moved out of the Reconstruction era (Fredrickson 1971a). By the beginning of the twentieth century, the "black brute" and the "black beast rapist" image of the black man had stuck. Journalism historian Jane Rhodes (2007) notes that northern newspapers had sided with southern white lynch mobs. The language employed in their stories to describe blacks continued the use of pejorative terms, and they regularly ridiculed blacks (Rhodes 2007). Even the more liberal press of the era—the muckraking press that challenged government and business malevolence—neglected to criticize Jim Crow segregation or lynching (Rhodes 2007). Mostly there was fear and loathing for blacks, and for black males in particular.

It is no wonder the media—and the rest of society—reacted with such hatred when black boxer Jack Johnson beat a white opponent to win the world heavyweight title in 1908. When Johnson successfully defended his title in 1910 by beating a previous white champion who had initially refused to fight any black, race riots broke out. Johnson, who had never placed any limits on himself as a result of his race, did not live within the boundaries set for blacks. He traveled with white women, some of whom were prostitutes. He eventually married a white woman, thereby openly competing sexually with white men. The 1910 Mann Act, which banned crossing state lines with women for the purposes of prostitution, was used to bring Johnson down. He was tried and convicted in 1913 of violating this law.

All forms of media during this period were rife with negative representations of black males. The D. W. Griffith film *Birth of a Nation* is an example of motion pictures during this era that contributed to the propagation of this negative image. The film, released in 1915, is often hailed as a piece of landmark cinema because of the novel film techniques it incorporates. But its racist depictions make it a milestone in that regard also. The story rewrites history, casting southern whites as suffering at the hands of lascivious blacks during Reconstruction. Blacks protested the film's release. The NAACP, then only a six-year-old organization, held protests in Los Angeles and New York in an unsuccessful attempt to prevent release of the film.

Under white male patriarchy, black males have never shared in the power and privilege assigned to the male gender. They had no power over white women, only over black women; thus, interactions with white women represented a boundary transgression that could easily be denoted as rape or equated with rape even when no actual rape had occurred, as in the cases of Jack Johnson, the Scottsboro boys, and Emmett Till.[12] "Racism is above all a social relation—'systematized hierarchization implacably pursued,' in Fanon's words—anchored in material structures and embedded in historical configurations of power" (Shohat and Stam 1994: 19).

Coverage of black life in mainstream media in the second half of the twentieth century moved from omission to selective inclusion. Carolyn Martindale's longitudinal study of the coverage of African Americans in four leading newspapers from the 1950s to the start of the 1980s found that since the civil rights movement began in the 1950s, the coverage of race in mainstream papers had been transformed from widespread omission of African Americans "both in column inches and as a percentage of their available news space" to some inclusion, albeit still stereotyped (Martindale 1986: 79). As a result of civil rights activities, coverage of blacks increased significantly during the 1960s (p. 79). One unexpected finding was that during the 1970s, despite the reduction in strife as compared with the previous decade and continued racial stratification in housing, coverage of blacks continued to increase in two of the four papers Martindale examined; the other two papers experienced only a slight decline (p. 80). She states, "This unexpected finding of continuing newspaper attention to news about American blacks during the 1970s suggests that the events of the

1960s . . . produced among the managements of the newspapers studied an increased awareness of blacks and, perhaps, a desire to cover them more extensively and realistically than they had in the past" (p. 82). The elevated levels of coverage carried on into the 1970s despite the continued lack of diversity in newsrooms. Martindale found that during the 1970s, the subject matter switched dramatically from the civil rights story. For example, during the 1960s at the *New York Times,* 74 percent of the coverage of blacks was related to civil rights; during the 1970s, only 23 percent of the coverage of blacks focused on civil rights. In that same period, coverage in other areas increased; for example, stereotypical coverage of blacks in entertainment or of black crime made up 14 percent of the *Times'* coverage of black people. That represented a 9 percent increase over the previous period. Additionally, Martindale found that throughout all three decades, but particularly in the 1960s, the newspapers' coverage of black protest activities vastly outpaced their coverage of the causes of the protests (pp. 86–87).

   Well into the twentieth century, the media still operated as an arena for the positive articulation of whiteness and the negative articulation of blackness. After the urban unrest in the 1960s, the media were severely criticized for the role they had played in supporting a racially divided society. The criticism came from the Kerner Commission, a group appointed by President Lyndon B. Johnson and charged with studying the causes of the riots. The commission, which was headed by Otto Kerner (governor of Illinois at the time), researched various aspects of the television and newspaper coverage of "Negro ghettos" in the three days before, during, and in the three days after civil unrest in fifteen different cities nationwide (U.S. Riot Commission Report 1968: 362–367). The report overall concluded that white racism was responsible for a deeply divided society: "Our nation is moving toward two societies, one black, one white— separate and unequal" (p. 1). The media were harshly criticized for exacerbating this problem. The study concluded that media reportage came from a "white" perspective. While the media may not have been the cause of the disturbances, the researchers concluded, the virtual segregation of mainstream media and racial stratification in the country at large created a major problem for the entire society (pp. 382–387). Specifically,

> The problem of race relations coverage goes beyond incidents of white bias . . . the news media must publish newspapers and produce programs that recognize the existence and activities of the Negro, both as a Negro and as part of the community. . . . The full integration of Negroes into the journalistic profession is imperative in its own right. It is unacceptable that the press, itself the special beneficiary of fundamental constitutional protections, should lag so far behind other fields in giving effect to the fundamental human rights of equality of opportunity. (pp. 383–387)

# Coda

What erupted in the courtroom on the day of the bail hearing for the Central Park jogger's accused attackers had been bubbling beneath the surface all along. No one had seen the jogger. And, as a rape victim, her anonymity was being maintained by the mainstream press. The supporters of the suspects were not only defending the innocence of those charged, they were also questioning whether or not a rape had even occurred. And why not? Doubting the authenticity of a story about black males raping a white woman was not a knee-jerk reaction seeking to protect the boys involved. It was a political position born out of a shared history since Europeans had encountered Africa, out of African enslavement in the New World, and out of the position of white women in American society. Through this shared history, blacks and whites alike have come to live confined within the structures of race, gender, and class.

Doubts about the case had been building up from the very beginning, as soon as word of the incident had begun to spread. Members of the press, among them columnist Mike McAlary at the *Daily News,* quickly moved to discredit those doubts, mocking the sketchy parallels being drawn between the early reports and the false accusations of rape against the Scottsboro boys in the 1930s.

My own rejection of the doubts did not come from an abjectly naïve place. It was deeper and more profound than that. It meant that behind the veil of my post–civil rights—color-blind—world lay a different, ingrained, and indelible reality that could be traced back to Captain Marlow, to the conquerors and colonialists who saw blacks as little better than animals—those whose messages of domination that, as Richard Wright ([1940] 1993) suggested, created a Bigger Thomas in some blacks.[13] I would have to see the world that was approaching the twenty-first century through the veil of that double-consciousness[14] W.E.B. Du Bois (2003) had articulated early in the twentieth century. I would have to see myself stuck at the bottom of race/class/gender hierarchies. As Derrick Bell (1992: 6) notes, constantly deciphering possible racist intentions "breeds frustration and alienation—and a rage we dare not show to others or admit to ourselves." Once the dominant position of the racial oppressor is normalized, the oppressor finds it difficult to contemplate reality from any other position. Since the history of the United States taught in classrooms across the nation often left out details germane to those occupying the black racial space, it is no surprise that the suspects' defenders came across as kooks in the mainstream press. I for one read about their denial of the jogger's rape in the coverage and thought it would be better for the suspects, the jogger, the city, and everyone involved if they would just remain quiet. But silence had been the problem for far too long. It was only after historians had unearthed the voices of women—particularly black women from the eighteenth and nineteenth centuries—that we gained greater understanding of how race was intertwined with gender, sexuality, and class.

# 4

# Salvaging the "Savage"

*A Racial Frame that Refuses to Die*

## Life on the City Desk before the Jogger

**I BEGAN WORKING** for the city desk about a year after I started at the *Daily News*. After my transfer there from the business desk, I did a tour of duty at major bureaus in the city. The purpose of this rotation, according to the editor in chief, was to familiarize me with the network of offices that fed the main section of the paper. For a month or so, I spent time at the police headquarters bureau—called "the Shack"—and at one of the court bureaus; I also worked general assignment on the day shift for the city desk. The plan was to put me on the night shift after my initial tour of duty, where I would wait my turn like everyone else until I "earned" a position on the day shift, the space occupied by the city desk's main reporters. The bylines of these individuals appeared regularly in the front section of the paper on or close to page one, which was referred to as "the wood." My goal was to become one of those reporters. Wooden plaques displaying famous front pages lined the walls of the city room.

My first assignment at the paper was on the business desk. Professionally I did well in that department. In my year there, I was given a weekly column that ran in the Sunday business section, I worked on another business column, and I produced daily stories. I had good sources for the subject because I had previously worked at *The American Lawyer,* a publication that covered attorneys in the top law firms and banks in the nation. Much of the work that consumed the attorneys I had covered was on Wall Street in mergers and acquisitions, an economic sector that pumped new capital into the city's and the nation's economy. This was the era of the "Go-Go '80s," a return to prominence for Wall Street,[1] as the country dragged itself out of one of its most devastating recessions and New York City was working its way back from its near-bankruptcy of the 1970s. The financial sector (Wall Street) was one of the legs on which this recovery stood.[2]

Signs that the recovery was not assured—such as the Wall Street crash of 1987—only added to the salience of business news during this period.

The economic rebound from the 1970s was not only good for the city's overall economic forecast; it was also good for the media. The media world was being transformed in the 1980s. Wall Street had discovered that many newspapers were cash cows as they transitioned from private hands to publicly traded companies (Bagdikian 1983; McChesney 2008). This discovery helped to fuel a never-before-seen consolidation of media companies that concentrated control of the companies into fewer and fewer hands. Commensurate with this and other growth in the business world, general-interest newspapers increased the number of pages devoted to the coverage of business news and more reporters were being hired to cover this area (Williams 1988). Business and government leaders, as well as their lieutenants, were sometimes regarded as celebrities, enjoying frequent coverage on the regular news pages and in the growing number of gossip columns in the local papers. During this period, real estate developer Donald Trump often made the front page of the *Daily News.* Fascination with this business figure/celebrity became so extreme that on the day after Nelson Mandela's release from Robben Island on February 11, 1990, after twenty-seven years of incarceration,[3] it was a story about Trump's marital problems that dominated the front page in one edition of the *Daily News.* The other city papers made Mandela the biggest story of that news cycle.[4]

After spending a year on the business desk, I asked to be transferred to the city desk. The work in business could have sustained me professionally for a while, but the tension that existed with one of my coworkers there did not seem to be worth it when opportunities for advancement were already so limited. Although I found the idea of working on the city desk quite intimidating, I decided to attempt the move, because regardless of my comfort level with business news, being a reporter on the city desk was infinitely more prestigious. I approached the paper's editor in chief, Gil Spencer, and requested a transfer. I was at ease turning to him because I felt a sort of bond with him had been established when he plucked me out of the minority jobs conference and hired me. Some years later, when I looked back on my transfer request, I recall thinking that I had stepped outside the chain of command. But who else was I going to ask? I still had few contacts at the paper or in journalism in general, for that matter. Working in the business section separated me from the other departments—it was like a distant satellite of the city desk. It was a position that did not provide a bird's eye view of the decision-making process at the paper.

When I met with Spencer, I could not tell whether or not he was surprised that I was there making such a request. He heard me out and finally said, "There is a man working the night shift for the city desk who wants very badly to be on days. Maybe we can make a switch." If I had not known it before, I learned it then: The day shift on the city desk is the plum assignment and it is one that is very difficult to get. Spencer went on to explain about making the tour of duty for about a month and then switching to nights. I was sold on his plan instantly; he would talk to the business and city desk editors about the swap. I met with the city editor to be schooled on the department's expectations. He told me to anticipate having to push the envelope to be successful on the city desk. True to his word, Spencer made the transfer happen. Once I had completed my tour of duty and my time on the night shift began, I met a bunch of other black people working nights, including Gloria Sterns. We would all jokingly call that slot "the black shift," and that was where I would really learn the ropes at the *Daily News*.

We worked from 5:00 P.M. to 1:00 A.M. I soon discovered that before the arrival of two black women on the night shift, the white women who had worked nights previously had been on a 3:00 to 11:00 P.M. shift. Management thought the later hours were unsafe for women. However, we black women did not get the same treatment the white women had received.

I was told right off the bat that I could not expect many bylined assignments. The people on the night shift served a particular function and rarely got to "own" their stories. Instead, they updated stories produced by a staff member on the day shift that had run in an earlier edition of the paper; the editor would decide, depending on the level of contribution, whether the night person would get his or her byline added. The night shift covered breaking news— oftentimes a fire, shooting, or murder that typically ran as a fat box[5] unless the story was considered extremely big and required more space. A big story was generally picked up the following day by a day-shift reporter, who would continue working it and get any future byline credit. The night shift was essentially support staff. Once I learned the set-up, I understood why it was so difficult to get off nights: It was extremely hard to get your own bylined stories.

Because it was my goal to get onto the day shift, I came up with a strategy: find stories independent of the desk that I could "own." This was possible for me, because I had sources independent of the general card file of sources the city desk made available to its reporters.[6] When things were slow, and they were slow a lot, I used the time to dig up my own stuff—what is called in the business "enterprise" stories. I thought this would be a good way to show that I merited being on the day shift. However, it created a problem for my editors: I wanted my stories to run in the paper like any other reporter's stories and I considered them *my own* stories that I should be allowed to follow up. This approach disrupted the new racial hierarchy developing in the newsroom in the wake of the lawsuit—one that left quite a number of new young black reporters in supporting roles. The *News* had lost the lawsuit, in part, due to the racial bias reflected in its hiring and promotion practices. As with most mainstream papers, there was already a dearth of black and other minority journalists. Promotions were typically helped along by getting regular assignments that featured one's work—and one's byline. Typically, editors made story assignments unless the story was an enterprise piece. Therefore, if the editors did not regularly assign a reporter significant bylined stories, it was harder to get promoted.

The paper's loss in the lawsuit seemed to indicate that there was a racial bias in the distribution and management of assignments. By the time the *News* had lost the suit, it had already hired a group of new black staff that consisted primarily of young reporters and a photographer in an attempt to diversify. Had the administration hired primarily older, more seasoned black journalists who would have expected to be treated as peers of the established white journalists on the day shift, this could have exacerbated the racial tensions that historically existed in its newsroom and that had been heightened by the lawsuit. Instead, the bulk of the new black hires were young reporters like me, with minimal experience, and we automatically fell to the bottom of the newsroom hierarchy. Employing us seemed to be part of a strategy by the paper to defend itself against the lawsuit while creating the least disruption of the existing racial order. Distributing us to the night shift would ease the racial tensions if we kept our place there and did not push too quickly to be moved to the day shift. However, this dynamic was not part of the calculus of *my* planning for the development of *my* career.

I was aware of the setup, but I never prioritized it in my thinking. I recognized the night shift as a "black space," a place with boundaries that could become very difficult if not impossible to cross. At the time, my approach was a combination of chutzpah and naïveté. I believed in my abilities and more importantly I believed that the articulated desire for racial equity on the part of some leading whites was largely sincere, even if it was not shared by all. Implicit in my interpretation of the management's stated desire for racial equity was the notion that the mainstream would or could be fundamentally transformed. As a sociologist, I can now look back on this period and see how woefully I lacked knowledge about how institutions operate to create hierarchies of race, class, and gender in the larger society, and I now understand the significance of individual and group interactions in the reproduction and entrenchment of these hierarchies.

## The City I Called Home

By this time in my life, the perspective I had developed about New York City had been shaped not just at home but also by the experiences I had had living in "black" Queens and attending predominantly black elementary and middle schools and a predominantly white high school in Manhattan. I was still immigrant enough to think of Queens as part of "the city" and to chuckle inside when people I knew said things like, "I'm going to the city" to refer to a planned trip into Manhattan. But, really, I got it. The city in which we lived was "black" Queens, and it existed worlds apart from Manhattan and even from other parts of Queens that were not predominantly black. The city I came to know growing up in the 1970s was a city of neighborhoods—areas defined culturally by the racial or ethnic groups that populated them. And these neighborhoods were balkanized.

When I invited a white female friend from my high school to visit my home in St. Albans, she expressed fear that she would be beaten up because she was white. I had never heard anyone in my neighborhood convey such a desire nor had I seen anything like that, but no amount of reassuring could convince her otherwise. Instead, she extended an invitation for me to visit her in her neighborhood, an area that years later I heard people refer to as a "white ethnic enclave." I tried to use logic to break through her insistence that she would be unsafe in my neighborhood.

"Shouldn't I also be afraid of being beaten up in your neighborhood?" I asked.

"No," she said. "You're a girl. Black *guys* might get beaten up, but people will just think you're a maid." Unbeknownst to her, that tidbit of information gave me mental pause. I quickly processed the significance of her words; the comment was just offensive, insulting in a way she could not really understand and that I deemed then not worth the time it would take to explain to her. I was an immigrant from a black nation who still found it hard to imagine not being allowed into a space because of my race. But I also learned another lesson about race in America that day. The existence of racial group boundaries did not mean that they were not supposed to be breached by blacks. They were permeable, but only in certain ways—in ways that did not disrupt the existing norms defined by the mainstream. As long as people thought I was a maid—that is, as long as I kept my place—it would be safe for me to enter "white spaces." I did not think my friend's experiences would allow her to understand why I found her comment offensive. I sensed then that it would be upsetting to some whites, my friend included, to have to contend with my perspective on the world because it would disrupt their understanding of the fairness and lawfulness they believed to be intrinsic in their world. Like me, she too believed that she lived with racial boundaries, but those borders were not necessarily bad—they were meant to protect her. Likewise, I did not understand her sense of inherent danger in my black community.

Shortly after this incident, I left the city to go to college and on to grad school. While away, the New York I thought of was the one in the magazines and newspapers. This was a habit I picked up at the universities I attended, where some of the friends I made came from different areas of the country and knew the city only as it was represented in the mainstream press. These media had the habit of universalizing the qualities of Manhattan—white, upper-class Manhattan—by applying them to the whole city. New York City was the city of museums—the ones on Fifth Avenue. It was the city of music and theatre—Lincoln Center and Broadway. It was the city of universities—Columbia and New York University. It was the city of great job opportunities—Wall Street and law firms. It was the city of great architecture—such as the Chrysler, Pan Am, and Flatiron buildings. It was the city that signified the ultimate modern urban space; it had both the World Trade Center and Central Park. The people who controlled these spaces—upper-class or upwardly mobile whites—were better educated, which implicitly served as an indicator of their racial tolerance.

The rest of the city—lower-class whites, blacks, Latinos, Asians—existed on the margins, forever having to prove their worth, their significance as a part of humanity. The spaces they occupied in New York—their neighborhoods—were marginalized in the media; only periodically were they the subject of media attention. Network television in the 1970s brought forth the television sitcom *All in the Family,* a representation of a working-class white ethnic enclave in Queens. But the racism of the show's lead character, Archie Bunker, was presented as something benign, because he was stupid and the presumption was that everyone recognized his stupidity. It was no accident that *All in the Family* writer and producer Norman Lear did not target corporate America in this critique of U.S. society. Likewise, it was no accident that a black version of the Archie Bunker character was soon produced in the form of George Jefferson, the main character in the sitcom *The Jeffersons* (another Norman Lear production). This program was the story of a successful black owner of a dry cleaning business who moved his family to the Upper East Side, a quintessential upper-middle-class, white Manhattan neighborhood—the jogger's neighborhood.

In *The Jeffersons,* this elite New York neighborhood of the 1970s was portrayed as having not completely impenetrable racial boundaries despite intense racial segregation. Yet, like Archie, George was marred by his own stupid bigotry. The show used one of the typical frames of color-blind racism in its regular narrative. It presented the United States as a meritocratic society in which race-based structural hierarchies were being eliminated.

Norman Lear created a type of sameness in the ways in which whites and blacks lived race within their boundaries and a sameness in their experiences when they crossed those borders. There were no ongoing story lines about George or his son being regularly stopped by police or being constantly fearful for their lives for crossing racial boundaries. One of the running commentaries in the show was the racialized insults George directed at his white neighbors. These became equated with the racialized insults Archie directed at blacks. The show ignored the history of white attacks on blacks for crossing borders and the society-wide denigration of blacks led by the people who had enslaved them.

I knew that George's and Archie's experiences were different, but at the time I did not have the vocabulary to articulate the falsehood created by neutralizing the racial disparities between the two subjects. Racial disparities are anything but neutral. This was not news to any of us in balkanized New York. My high school friend had articulated the potential danger for black males coming into her neighborhood. She had made mention of the violent response their crossing of racial boundaries could fuel. I knew this to be true; certain things were just a given.

While I was away at school, the city seemed to grow edgier, more racially tense than I had ever known it to be. This aspect of life in New York was not incorporated into the representations of the "universal" city my friends in college and graduate school knew. But those living on the margins knew a different city. When I returned to New York in late August of 1983, I heard my father express concern for my brothers' safety because he feared retribution for black male violation of racial boundaries. His fear was not amorphous. He thought even a minor wrong move on their part could incur a lethal reaction. It could come from white youth or police if my brothers traveled in the "wrong" neighborhood. So, in my home, as in the homes of many black families with teenage males, there were conversations about how the police or others might respond to them. Then, in September, shortly after my return to the city, graffiti artist Michael Stewart lost his life and the term "chokehold" became part of the public lexicon. Transit police had allegedly caught Stewart tagging (spray-painting a street alias) in a subway station about 3:00 A.M. and beaten him when they apprehended him (Roberts 1983). Stewart died thirteen days later. During the trial of the six officers charged in Stewart's death, a witness said Stewart had been placed in a chokehold (Gross 1985).

In the late 1970s and early 1980s tagging became a popular activity among young urban black males. Graffiti appeared everywhere, but it generated the most desired effect when the young men (and women) who created it left their communities and spray-painted their tags in forbidden zones (Chang 2005). It appears that the ability to articulate their subjectively developed identities in areas outside the boundaries of their daily world was important to them. According to press reports, Stewart, age twenty-five, allegedly stopped to tag in the First Avenue and 14th Street subway station on his way home to Brooklyn after attending a party (Roberts 1983). This Manhattan station was a stop on the LL subway line, which also ran into Brooklyn and Queens. But this Manhattan stop served Stuyvesant Town, a private housing complex for middle-class and upwardly mobile whites, a place where few, if any, blacks resided at the time.[7] I knew the station and the neighborhood well. My high school friends and I would catch the LL train there on the way home from our school, which was just two blocks away. The Stewart incident frightened me in a way I had never before felt in New York. The change in climate was palpable, and I sensed that if Stewart had been tagging in his Brooklyn neighborhood, he would still be alive.

After Stewart's death, charges of police brutality ensued. Thus, much of the press coverage of the incident became contextualized as a case of police brutality.

I would learn that Stewart's case was one in a long history of police violence in the city and that in the 1970s and early 1980s there had been a series of "controversial shooting cases involving white police officers and young black males" (Johnson 2003: 282).

At the time of the Stewart incident—prompted by an earlier case of police brutality involving a young black male theology student—Congressional hearings were held on the subject of New York City police brutality (Johnson 2003: 282). The House Judiciary Subcommittee on Criminal Justice, chaired by U.S. Rep. John Conyers, raised ninety-eight cases—most involving blacks, Latinos, and Asians—that had occurred over the previous twenty-five years. Fifty-two of those incidents occurred during the administration of Mayor Edward Koch, which began in 1978, the year after I went away to college (Roberts 1983). Those fifty-two incidents during the Koch administration resulted in twenty-five deaths; "prosecutors and grand juries found criminality in one of the 25, and in that one the officers were acquitted by a judge" (Roberts 1983). Historian Marilyn Johnson's (2003) documentation of police violence in the city notes the high level of distrust for police in black communities during this period. She points out that even black police did not trust their white counterparts:

> As in past investigations, hundreds of black citizens turned out to recount their stories of police abuse, expressing bitter disappointment with the ineffectiveness of the CCRB [the Civilian Complaint Review Board] and the police disciplinary system. Some of the most persuasive testimony came from members of the Guardians Association who recounted recent cases of shooting of black plainclothes and off-duty officers by their white colleagues. When the House Subcommittee issued its report the following year, it concluded that "racism appears to be a major factor in alleged police misconduct." (Johnson 2003: 282–283)

The Civilian Complaint Review Board (CCRB) was unfamiliar to me at that time. But its significance for me would grow as my career as a reporter unfolded. The CCRB was first established in 1953 in response to complaints from African Americans and Puerto Ricans about police abuse of power.[8] It initially consisted of three deputy police commissioners whose purview was investigation of civilian complaints. Minority communities had long criticized the board for its biased assessment of police brutality cases, and political leaders from communities of color in New York City regularly called for civilian representation on the board. This had occurred briefly during the administration of Mayor John Lindsay, who served as mayor from 1966 to 1973. But the police union (the Patrolman's Benevolent Association, PBA), which vigorously opposed civilian representation, challenged Lindsay's board and won. The configuration of the board did not change again until 1987. This time, civilians were allowed to work alongside police in the investigation of abuse cases. However, the Tompkins Square Park incident in 1988, which I discuss later in this chapter, swung public momentum in favor of an all-civilian board.

Two of the popular ways in which the press framed police brutality obscured the racial dynamic frequently inherent in these cases. One favorite motif was to represent the brutality as the behavior of individual rogue police officers or officers exercising poor judgment. Another media rendition of possibly inappropriate police behavior was to use language that blamed the victim by way of questioning the victim's actions as much as or more than those of the police officers. At the time, I saw the role of the police and other parts of the criminal justice system as the keepers of mainstream boundaries, particularly race, class, and gender boundaries. For me, what was obviously missing then from the mainstream press discourse on police brutality was questions about the fairness or justness of those boundaries, the methods used to enforce them, and other people's rights to question them. Within that logical framework, Stewart had contributed to his own demise because he had committed the crimes of graffiti writing and resisting arrest, thereby forcing officers to hogtie him and put him in a chokehold. Thus, the underlying boundaries that the police were so vigorously enforcing were not called into question. However, if the boundaries had been acknowledged and questioned, the possibility existed that Stewart's initial infraction had been simply the crossing of a racial border, to which police responded in a lethal manner.

Three years later, in 1986, a more clear-cut case of fatal boundary crossing emerged with the death of Michael Griffith. Shortly before Christmas, a car carrying Griffith, age twenty-three, and two others broke down on Cross Bay Boulevard near a predominantly white ethnic enclave in Queens, an area in the margins. The three young black men, who were from Brooklyn, left the car and walked in search of help in the community of Howard Beach. Griffith and his friends encountered a group of white male teens, angry words were exchanged, and the white teens left to round up friends and associates. The original young whites, along with reinforcements, returned with baseball bats and tree branches. They were reportedly led by one who had gathered them with the charge, "There's niggers on the boulevard! Let's go kill them!" (Mooney 1996). In his attempt to flee, Griffith ran onto the Belt Parkway and was struck and killed by an oncoming car.

The story spread like wildfire. People from all communities across the city were angry. For blacks, the incident collapsed past and present into one and left us skeptical about the future. When I heard the reports that these young men had gone in search of help in Howard Beach, I knew they could not have been from Queens. From the earliest days of my teenage independence I had been warned: Avoid Howard Beach; it is dangerous for blacks over there. This was information I always kept in the back of my mind. Howard Beach seemed worlds away from my life. Living within racial boundaries does that; it keeps you in your own world physically and mentally. Griffith's death, only a few miles from where I lived, was a jarring reminder that at the end of the day I had very little protection from whatever forces official (the police) or unofficial (a mob) might seek to maintain racial boundaries. I had a palpable sense of personal vulnerability because of my race and my gender.

While as a teen I could not articulate many of my thoughts about the ways in which I lived race, I knew then that my white high school friend and I did not experience racial boundaries in the same way. And I knew that New York City was not a race-neutral space. Many blacks who lived in the marginal zones of this sprawling city expected to spend the remainder of their lives in those margins. While I had never been convinced that my race should prohibit or limit my existence in other spaces, the Stewart and Griffith incidents made me question that feeling. A deeper understanding of what it means to be a black American grew inside me. I used to wonder whether some people, black people included, refused to adjust to the changing world and thus stayed within their designated spaces. But, one thing was sure: Incidents like the deaths of Michael Griffith and Michael Stewart affected members of the black community in much the same way as the lynchings of earlier eras. They determined future interactions; in essence, by design, they reinforced both physical and mental boundaries.

My intention, upon returning to the city after graduate school, was to live in Manhattan, the universal representation of New York City, and to get a professional—read that white-collar—job. I wanted to live my life as if I could make any space in New York City I could afford my home, be it Manhattan or "black" Queens. As I said, I had picked up this idea from some of my friends at school. But the palpable fear blacks felt in the city, and the limitations on where they could go physically and within the social structure, provided a rude awakening for me. This time, unlike my high school years, I came to understand in no uncertain terms that, for blacks, the crossing of racial boundaries was still a life-and-death issue. Because the schools I had attended and the companies I worked for responded in some small degree to the push toward integration, those institutions in my life aimed to give the appearance that America was becoming a racially mixed society. This was part of the perspective of New York as the "universal" city. However, my early professional years taught me that while blacks could occupy a space in the "universal" city, their roles would be limited, their choices circumscribed, and their positions fraught with risk.

## The "Universal" City of the 1980s

Thus, I joined the reporting staff on the city desk night shift with an awareness of the racially balkanized nature of my city and a developing sense of the people, places, and perspectives that really counted in this "universal" city. Growing up in a balkanized community means that there are limited opportunities to interact with those from other communities, except possibly at school[9] or at work. In the work environment, one's job position often determined the degree to which one interacted with those who were part of that "universal" city and those born and raised in other areas. Being a reporter—as opposed to a member of the mailroom staff, for example—in a major media corporation put me in the position to interact with those from the "universal" New York.

The *Daily News* had positioned itself as the paper for strap-hangers, the workers from the margins of the city who rode buses and subways and stood hanging onto metal straps as they read the paper while traveling to and from work each day. This accounted for the choice of the tabloid-sized paper used by the *News* (as opposed to the "broad sheet" used by the *New York Times,* with its target audience of more affluent readers). The *Daily News* readers were people who used words like "dem, dese, and dose," according to one of my editors. Just as the physical size of the Penny Press and "blanket sheet" papers indicated class position in the nineteenth century, so too do the sizes of their twentieth-century counterparts represent the class of their own audiences. In essence, the *Daily News* audience was the people being marginalized in the city. Like many of the early Penny Press publications, the *Daily News* focused on street crime and scandals. The poor and racially marginalized were often the subjects of stories about street crime—sometimes as victims, but primarily as perpetrators (Dorfman and Schiraldi 2001). Scandal—sexual, criminal (white collar), or political—was the typical route through which members of the "universal" city became the subjects of stories in the *Daily News.* If one were the victim in a street crime, that incident would have a greater likelihood of being covered if the perpetrator belonged to another race. At the *Daily News,* details about the structures and institutions of society and how they worked were not typically presented as fundamental, necessary knowledge for an informed public; for the *Daily News* audience, bits of such information simply helped shape the context of reports about street crimes and scandals.

Like the conversation with my high school friend and the Norman Lear juxtaposition of the Archie Bunker and the George Jefferson characters, the press created a moral equivalence between the crimes of the poor (such as street-level drug dealing) and the scandals of the affluent (such as insider trading on Wall Street), treating them as comparable, as possessing a type of "sameness," as if the two groups had equal footing in society. The enormous power differential between the two went unacknowledged—presumably by the editors and the readers alike. While it was understood that the members of each group had different choices, there was a sense that choices *were* present in their respective worlds and that the mere existence of these choices "balanced" the two worlds. Such is the nature of the ideology guiding a market-based society—equality simply meant the equality to have choices. Having come from the racial borderlands of Queens, I saw "equality" just a little differently. By the time I completed my initial tour of duty learning the workings of the city through the lens of the *Daily News* city desk, I had learned the distinctions between my perspective and those of my editors. I thought this power disparity should be reflected in our coverage of New York City. They saw it differently. They viewed their representations of the polyglot from the margins placed alongside images of the "universal" city as balanced coverage.

When I joined the city desk staff, yuppies from the "universal" city were the big thing. News magazines touted yuppies as the nation's new educated elite (McGrath and Fineman 1984). They worked primarily in the rebounding sectors of the city's economy—finance, insurance, and real estate. I did a fair amount of eye rolling at the attention lavished on them; I derided the focus on them because I did not initially understand their source of power. After the 1970s, urban areas were being transformed into sites of symbolic production, a shift from the previous economic era, which had privileged the manufacturing sector and its production of tangible goods. This new economy—labeled "the service economy"—provided jobs in areas such as advertising, mass media, management consulting, finance, and legal services (Ford 1992). By this time, the ranks of those working in manufacturing had been on a long decline. In their stead, the new service economy divided people into two groups: "affluent symbol manipulators," who are the new consumers, and "low-income, unskilled laborers," those locked out of the consumer market and trapped at the bottom (Bauman 1998; Ford 1992).

The 1988 movie *Working Girl,* starring Harrison Ford and Melanie Griffith, presents a quintessential example of the new service economy. The Melanie Griffith character, with her big hair, rides the ferry daily from the margins of Staten Island to her secretarial job in the finance industry of Manhattan. By virtue of her origins and her persona, she is essentially locked out of opportunities for advancement in that world. She tries to get her ideas—which she hopes will lead to a promotion—taken seriously by her boss, an affluent woman played by Sigourney Weaver. But the boss steals her ideas. Her only chance for advancement is if she can assume a more yuppified identity, one that would signal an elevated position in the new consumer economy. She does, and she succeeds.

Yuppies in New York City often came from out of town, and they lived mainly in Manhattan in certain—white, upper-class—neighborhoods. They were more than an economic and social force. They represented a new lifestyle, young people with a lot of disposable income. In my previous job reporting on lawyers, the need to cover the work of "lawyering" masked the implications of the attention yuppies received. When I started working on the city desk night shift, their importance seemed completely contrived from my vantage point, given the balkanized city I called home and the day-in, day-out struggle for survival in the marginalized quarters. But the yuppies—who were government officials, up-and-coming corporate leaders in the new business sectors, and the media workers who tracked their activities—were part of the newly ascendant ruling elite in the "universal" city.[10] As an investment banker for Salomon Brothers, one of the most important investment banks on Wall Street, the Central Park jogger was one of these elites.

This service economy that supported the yuppies was all the talk as I began working at *The American Lawyer* and while I covered business at the *Daily News*. The yuppies were both a component of and a support for the new economy. Their power came from their "ability to . . . consume . . . [and also] the[ir] ability to choose and deploy cultural symbols that are the technologies of power" (Ford 1992: 119).[11] Their education and skills enable them to fill the jobs that organize and distribute the cultural symbols that are consumed by everyone to define who they are (Bauman 1998). For example, they work in the finance industry, which backs the builders gentrifying a community. Those who can afford to, because of the skills and jobs they have, buy into this new, upscale version of the community. The upscaled community then attracts other cultural products associated with its new, higher-class position—for example, premium ice cream parlors, trendy cafes, and expensive restaurants. Those who live in these areas are defined as belonging to the higher classes.

In this postindustrial, postmodern society, conceptions of even an individual's race are similarly fungible or redefinable; that is, one is able to "buy" one's race through the purchase of "'culturally authentic' clothing, books, hair care products, membership in organizations and also where one lives, goes to school, works, socializes and *where one can afford to do these things*" (Ford 1992: 127). In this society, where class can often stand in for race, it is still very difficult to find blacks in the socioeconomic class position that allows them to buy into new classifications. Therefore, in the service economy, in which yuppies can buy their class position—as opposed to acquiring it through pedigree, as had been done in the past—the affluent, skilled yuppies can also buy into a geographic location that effectively defines their race. The Upper East Side of Manhattan, where the jogger lived, was a "white" space. Ford (1992: 131–135) points out that "imaginary racialized space is made real by a complex of economic, political and social forces." He notes that the city's "black" space became black in a similar way:

> The spatial demarcation of racialized neighborhoods makes politically possible, a number of regulatory activities that in turn guarantee the continued segregation of the races. Real estate brokers refuse to show property in white neighborhoods to Blacks and strongly discourage whites from moving into Black neighborhoods. Financial institutions "red line" Black neighborhoods so that real estate improvement becomes infeasible. Localities fail to provide adequate services in Black neighborhoods.
>
> A circular causation ensues in which each of the above phenomena feed on the others. (Ford 1992: 134–135)

As Jim Crow segregation became illegal and race as a biological concept lost credibility, separation of the races continued through economics and self-imposed segregation (Ford 1992: 127). In New York City, the spatial demarcation was profound. The content analysis of the Central Park jogger coverage showed that the most widely used indicator for race in the 251 articles examined was a geographic location—northern Central Park. (See Table 3.1.) This was also the most widely used term in the early days of the reporting, when the narrative was being constructed. Along with the animalistic terms "wolfpack" and "wilding," the other most frequently used racial indicator was again a geographic term, Harlem. Ford (1992) argues that in the post–civil rights era, the spatial segregation in urban areas in the United States was the most intense arena of racial contestation:

> The American metropolis is the battleground on which the war of race is now fought. Although much more is at stake than territory, it is along the spatial axis that the meaning of race is determined and enforced. We have seen that biological, economic, and socio-historical theories are inadequate to describe race as it actually operates in the minds and lives of Americans. We have also seen why this must be the case. Finally, we have seen how the very symbolic forces that seek to determine racial meaning also conspire to instate this latter's instability, fungibility, and incredibility. (p. 136)

The jogger was enmeshed in the many levels of racialization. She worked in the finance sector, which helped to organize the deployment of the cultural products that defined conceptions of race. And she jogged in an area that existed on the borders of these racial spaces—the northern section of Central Park, next to Harlem.

Reinforcement of physical boundaries occurred not only at the hands of the police—as in the case of graffiti artist Michael Stewart—but also through everyday interactions. Members of the "universal" city were taught which boundaries could be breached and how they could be crossed. In balkanized New York, those in the margins resided largely outside Manhattan—in the "outer boroughs" of Bronx, Brooklyn, Staten Island, and Queens. The margins also existed within Manhattan—above 110th Street and sections below 14th Street. Drivers in the city's fleet of yellow cabs regularly refused to go above 110th Street, the boundary for Harlem.[12] Subway riders in upper Manhattan knew the boundary. On the East Side, if you rode the Lexington Avenue express trains, a flood of whites exited at the 86th Street stop, the last stop before the train reached Harlem. And if you took the Lexington Avenue local, 96th Street was the demarcation line. On the West Side, the boundary for whites on the Broadway lines was 96th Street. It seemed that everyone who lived in the city at the time knew these race and class borders.

Yuppiedom was said to come with its own ethos (Barol, Springen, and Foote 1988; Ehrenreich 1986), and the press made this ethos scandalous in a way. The seemingly tongue-in-cheek coverage of yuppies manufactured their importance through the coverage of petty or faux scandals about who was seen with or was sleeping with whom, or about the levels of decadence yuppies could reach through the amounts of money they could afford to spent on clothes, food, nannies, rent/mortgages, or private school tuition for their children. The media presented yuppies as the manifestation of the ideal type of consumer, to which we should all aspire—for every aspect of their lifestyle was deemed significant for coverage. This fake ironic presentation of yuppies, which often appeared in the lifestyle pages and gossip columns, hid a deeper truth. The media's so-called critique of the affluence of the yuppie lifestyle was a type of advertising *for* that lifestyle, with all its products and its trappings. The constant focus on the yuppie lifestyle served to create a yen and a wanting from many of the "others." The lifestyle of the yuppies stood in stark contrast to those of the people from the margins, those who had relied on a part of the economy that would not rebound—the manufacturing sector. The people from the margins could now only survive working in jobs where they could provide support for the people who could afford the yuppie lifestyle. Among these people, there would be very little mobility from service jobs to the upper echelons and scant opportunities to increase one's economic power unless one took a second service job (Ford 1992). Yet the press maintained the position that power disparity between the groups was balanced by the existence of *choices* on both sides.

## Getting to Know New York City as a Journalist on the Night City Desk

Once on the city desk, I did not have many opportunities to cover yuppies, either as subjects of sexual, white-collar criminal, or political scandals or of the faux scandals of the gossip columns. And, until the rape of the Central Park jogger, I cannot recall ever covering a story about a yuppie who was the victim of a violent street crime. On the night city desk I was indeed steeped in stories about crime, but these were street crimes and fires, the stories from balkanized New York. Other kinds of stories that I saw with some regularity were disruption-of-life stories such as water main breaks, other types of service outages, and—dare I say it—protest marches, for it was in the context of a service outage that such protests were often perceived. And, every now and then, there was a disaster story, such as an airplane crash. All of these categories of stories put me into regular contact with the police, either by phone or on location at the crime scene or site of activity. Because I covered street-crime stories most frequently, it was in this context that I typically interacted with the police. I would come to understand how ideas about race, crime, and the role of the police were being framed in the media.

In November 1987, shortly before I began working for the city desk, the Tawana Brawley story broke. Brawley was a fifteen-year-old African American girl living in a small upstate New York town called Wappingers Falls. She had gone missing for a relatively short period and was found in a garbage bag, near a dumpster, feces smeared on her torso, and with the word "nigger" written on her body. She was found near her family's former residence, and the case was reported as a sexual assault. The story slowly seeped out to the public, as her family and advisors provided the press with information. The press initially legitimized her claims based on the family's report. But, as the investigation got under way, the tide turned. As details of the initial investigation started to emerge and advisors from New York City became more involved and demanded that Brawley's charges be examined through a lens that acknowledged the racism in the political structure in upstate New York, the media began to approach the case quite critically and to treat Brawley's claims as dubious. They cited too many missing elements in her charge of rape.

As incomplete and confusing pieces of information dribbled out to the public, from young Brawley and her family, it became clear that she had accused at least one cop from the town of being involved in her assault. Criminal investigators also cast doubt on Brawley's account of what had occurred when she disappeared. The case became a political issue in African American communities, in part because of the prominence of the family's advisors: civil rights lawyers C. Vernon Mason and Alton Maddox and the Reverend Al Sharpton, a controversial figure who served as a spokesperson for the family. Reverend Sharpton had developed a reputation as a strong advocate for racial justice in New York City. At the time, his activism around police brutality was helping make the issue part of the political agenda in the city.

The Brawley family and the advisors eventually requested that Governor Mario Cuomo assign a special prosecutor to the case. They argued that it seemed unlikely the case would be properly investigated in the small town where the incident had occurred, where equal opportunity for blacks was not a priority. Many people in African American communities were incensed that the family's repeated requests to have outside investigators or a special prosecutor look into the incident—because of possible local police involvement—went unheeded by the governor. The Brawley case eventually reached a grand jury, but Brawley never testified. The grand jury determined the case to be a hoax and the press joined in that evaluation. It seemed to me at the time that questioning the role of the police was virtually taboo. While the Central Park jogger case was unfolding, the Brawley incident remained part of the political landscape of the city. As it was *the* black issue when I joined the city desk, the case, along with questions about Reverend Sharpton, became the two things my white colleagues included in the litmus tests they gave me about my positions on the issue of race.[13] I never knew how to respond. Oddly, the Howard Beach case was not a part of the litmus test. The verdicts in some of the first trials in that case were just coming down as I joined the city desk. The case was definitely part of the political backdrop.

I had initially settled into "my place" at the bottom of the newsroom hierarchy, but those slow nights gave me lots of time to think about how to get off the night shift. I developed enterprise stories from my old sources and from working during the daytime on my own material. My plan was to use the enterprise stories as a way to move my career along. When I tried to introduce my own stories into the mix, I quickly came to understand the difference between my approach and that of my editors. I learned about their views vis-à-vis crime coverage, the role of the police in the city, and what can happen when the two come together. One big thing I learned at the time was the role of the press in the ongoing War on Drugs.[14]

In my first big enterprise story, I did not wrestle with my editors over the approach. But my work on the Willye Jean Dukes story taught me a lot about my editors' priorities. The Dukes case involved a black woman fatally shot by her shotgun-wielding estranged boyfriend on January 7, 1988, on a subway platform in Grand Central Terminal a few minutes after 5 P.M. The brazenness of pulling out a shotgun at the height of rush hour on a crowded subway platform in the bowels of the storied Grand Central Terminal captured the imagination of my editors. Compounding the sensational nature of the story was the fact that the man was black. The headquarters of the *Daily News* was only a block and a half away from the crime scene. Taking advantage of this proximity, the editors invested a lot of people in the coverage, me included. After the breaking news stories[15] about the incident had died down, I asked the city desk editor if I could follow up with a feature story about how the system of "orders of protection" issued for many women who were victims of intimate partner violence had failed Ms. Dukes. I pitched the story as something that could run during Women's History Month in March. At the time, from the *Daily News* perspective, this was an ideal way to address an issue related to the workings of our society—having it tied to a spectacular crime. The city desk editor approved the piece and allowed me to work on it. For two months, I researched the story, conducting interviews in the city and out of state to bring the article to fruition.

At the end of the day, I had major reservations about my finished piece. The Dukes story I wrote continued the sensationalizing of the shooting itself, thereby diminishing the attention paid to the broader issue—the really serious problem in the "orders of protection" system. Even in death, Dukes's position as a woman was subordinated by her male lover. His actions had simultaneously crossed a number of boundaries, which in the eyes of my editors made them newsworthy. He had committed murder, but had he shot Dukes in the black neighborhood where they lived, I doubt it would have been front-page news. It was his crossing of a racial/spatial boundary—shooting his girlfriend in Grand Central Terminal—that propelled this incident of domestic violence onto the front page. Intimate partner violence, especially in the form of a story about a black woman being killed by her estranged boyfriend, did not regularly receive front-page treatment. But the site of the shooting—Grand Central, located in the "universal" city, a zone most black workers left at workday's end to return to the margins—pushed this story to the wood.[16] Despite my ultimate dissatisfaction with the outcome of this project, working on the Dukes story helped me understand how to pitch my enterprise stories to the editors. And I learned another thing: I had to use the daytime to do the necessary interviews, and I still had to come in for my regular shift—with no overtime. In other words, if I wanted opportunities to develop a track record with my own byline, it would be largely at my own expense.

My next two major enterprise stories taught me a lot about the role of the police in the city and how the press presents that role. I had joined forces with Clarence Sheppard, an African American photographer who was also in search of enterprise stories. By working together, we supported each other's careers. We scoured the city in search of stories we thought the *Daily News* would run. Our hunt took us to the Lower East Side, which was in turmoil due to conflicts between the different groups of residents in the area. This was not your typical New York City segregated zone. The new, more affluent residents who lived in the recently refurbished, shiny condos cropping up in the community were pitted against the old-timers (who were lower income or outright poor), as well as the "squatters" and an assortment of young people (who were sometimes runaways or dropouts from society) who came from other parts of the city and the metropolitan area.

Clarence and I met many individuals from all of the groups. The squatters had converted abandoned buildings into roughly hewn "squats" that were nonetheless homes to large numbers of people and stood in contrast to the polished new condos. Some of the squatters, after investing their labor and resources in their squats, attempted to gain legal ownership. The young people, whose dress and style often elicited the label "punk," seemed to spend much of their time in Tompkins Square Park, where there was a healthy drug trade. Both of these groups slowed down the real estate–driven engine of change in the area. The new condo residents—some of them yuppies, whose relationship with the real estate industry seemed both organic and symbiotic—voiced concern about the ugly squats, the drug trade in the park, and the noisy young people, who were mostly white and were regarded by many of the new residents as avoiding their middle-class lives in the suburbs of Long Island or New Jersey. The long-term residents of the area were lower-income African Americans, Latinos, and whites. They expressed fears of being forced out by rising real estate prices. Their longevity in the community allowed them to recount the area's past as a gateway for immigrants from Europe and other parts of the world.

Tompkins Square Park, located in the center of the community, brought together this mélange of area residents. Thus, the park became a contested public space. While the spotty media coverage about the changing real estate market in the area acknowledged its effect on rising tensions in the community, I noticed that the media addressed this transformation as a given that all should accept. As a denizen of the margins in the city myself, I interpreted the gentrification of the Lower East Side differently. To me, the whole neighborhood was essentially contested territory, in which wealthy investors and yuppies were elbowing out a lot of poor people who would have to move and never be heard from again. I did not anticipate being able to get my editors to care about the impact of development on the poor, but I did think I could get a story published about the situation if I focused on the squatters and their unique dwellings and tied this element into the community's history as a strong counterculture area with deep immigrant roots. Clarence and I continued our reporting, hoping to present our editors with a completed package of pictures and stories.

In late July 1988, in the midst of our period of enterprise reporting, tensions in the neighborhood boiled over. The city began enforcing a 1:00 A.M. closing time for Tompkins Square Park. Squatters, "punks," and others protested the early park closing. The police were placed on the front lines to protect the interests of the propertied and to absorb the anger and frustration of the other groups in the area. One night, violence broke out. I received a report about the incident and went to see what had transpired. The first night of violence had dissipated fairly quickly, but another protest was planned for the following weekend. The air in the community was thick with tension. More violence seemed inevitable.

The night of the second march, a Saturday, the demonstrators coalesced in the park and moved out into the streets, where the police had set up a wall of resistance. I was off to the side but between the opposing forces when I saw a bottle lobbed into the air toward the cops. Then all hell broke loose. The police descended on the demonstrators with a vengeance I had only seen described in history books.[17] They swung billy clubs from side to side, beating anyone in their way. These officers were from every corner of the city; they were not simply from the local precinct. I saw NYPD cars with precinct numbers from Queens with officers jumping out to join the fray. Officers had black electrical tape covering their badges to prevent identification. Once I saw this, it became clear to me that this type of police response had been planned. Near an entrance to the park, a police officer approached me and Andrew Hyatt, a *New York Times* photographer who was shooting pictures of a couple being beaten. We were both displaying our press passes, but the officer wanted us to leave the area. We were attacked, shoved, and hit. Hyatt snapped a picture as I was hit in the head by the cop.

I was not seriously hurt, and then and there I decided to stay for as long as I physically could. The police would push the demonstrators back, and the demonstrators would disperse and then regroup elsewhere on the streets near the park. The conflict ebbed and flowed, staying primarily within the confines of the streets surrounding the park and erupting into sudden bursts of intense violence. Helicopters swooped over the area. Police on horseback arrived and pushed into the crowds. At one point during the night I was pinned against a building by a mounted police officer. I saw injured people all over. The riot— some later referred to it as a police riot—went on all night and into the early morning.

Throughout the night, I checked in with the city desk and called in portions of the story—the way I was supposed to. Because it was too late to capture the full scope of the events in the Sunday paper, I was not surprised that the bulk of the story appeared on Monday. What did surprise me about the *Daily News* coverage was how brief it was and how much it ignored the information I had provided in favor of the police version of events. I got a brief byline acknowl- edgment for the work I did. Then the city desk sent out other reporters—white male reporters—to cover the material I had already called in. I was left to won- der whether the night editors on the city desk simply had not trusted my judg- ment, or had preferred the police version, or a combination of both. Later the *New York Times* ran a piece providing their own blow-by-blow version of what had transpired. It was close to what I had called in. I went to the city editor and complained about how the desk had dropped the ball on the story. Because I was the only reporter from a major paper there that night, and I had been injured trying to report the story, I was angry that the *News* had blown the opportunity I had given it to beat the *Times* on a story simply because the edi- tors found the police rendition more compelling. After videotapes of the inci- dent (taken by a resident and others) surfaced, more questions were raised about police actions in the park that night.

The day after the violent clash in Tompkins Square Park, I got a call from Gil Spencer, the paper's editor-in-chief. He was phoning to inquire about my well-being. I was such a gung ho reporter at that point that I found it slightly amusing that he would call.

"Are you okay?" Spencer asked.

"I'm fine," I said. I repeated the story of getting hit over the head. To me, the best part of what I had to tell him was that a *Times* reporter had gotten a shot of me being hit by the cop.

"Can we get the picture?" I asked him. This, I thought, would be the quint- essential evidence of how out of control the police were—so much so that they would beat a reporter wearing a press pass.

"I'll look into it," he said.

Things seemed to stall after that, as far as the picture was concerned. I never got a copy and, for all I know, my paper did not even try to obtain it. The police behavior in Tompkins Square Park gave some credence with the general public to minority complaints of police abuse and put the Civilian Complaint Review Board back in the news. During the CCRB investigation of the incident, a letter from the board turned up in my mailbox at the *Daily News*. I really do not remember much of what it said; I think I was being asked if I wanted to file a complaint. By this point, I was disgusted with the whole affair. Without the photo, all I could say was that some cop had hit me. I was afraid the CCRB, with half of its members drawn from the ranks of the NYPD, would whitewash incident, and I had no wish to participate. In the end, the image of the NYPD was severely damaged by police actions in the park, creating a political opportunity to bring the issue of an all-civilian CCRB back to the top of the political agenda. Finally, in 1993, under the administration of Mayor David Dinkins, the city's first African American mayor, an all-civilian board was instituted.[18]

The Tompkins Square Park episode had certainly given me an up-front-and-personal view of my editors' priorities. From time to time, my mind would drift back to the days immediately after the incident, when I had tried to get a copy of the photo. "Was the *News* afraid to bite the hand that feeds it?" I would ask myself. I had certainly spent enough time on the city desk and on nights to know just how much the paper relied on the police as sources and for copy. I saw even more evidence of the bond between the criminal justice system and the press in an enterprise story I broke at the end of 1988. This was the story of the federal bust of a Mafia-based drug ring that allegedly smuggled heroin and cocaine into the United States from Italy (Blumenthal 1988a). The case, which was touted as a joint operation between U.S. and Italian authorities, was led in the United States by the FBI and then–U.S. attorney Rudolph Giuliani. They planned to simultaneously arrest more than 233 people in New York City, Buffalo, New Jersey, Pennsylvania, Florida, Illinois, and California, as well as in Italy. A source of mine had leaked the story of the bust to me, and as I started my shift that day in late November 1988 I was wondering if my plan to break the story myself and keep it as my own would work. Typically, night shift people dealt with the night editor. But, by then, I knew enough to go take the story directly to the main city desk editor at the beginning of my shift. At this point in the day, he was wrapping up the first and second editions of the next day's paper.

I nervously spelled out the whole thing to him. The editor listened impassively. I remember him asking one question: "Who's your source?"

"I'd rather not say," I responded. By this time I was so filled with distrust of my editors that I had never even considered giving them that information.

"Okay, you need an independent confirmation," he responded. Then he walked away. Of course, he was right. But, I could not tell if he cared one way or another, or if he thought there was no way I could have a story like this, or if he had been through so many "big" stories that he simply would not get excited about anything without an independent confirmation.

After I got the confirmation, things became really interesting. I gave the city desk's night editor the update: "I got a confirmation."

"From whom?"

"The FBI," I said proudly.

"The FBI confirmed your story?"

"Yes," I said and recounted what had taken place. The plan I had hatched to get the confirmation was to catch the FBI spokesman off guard with a ridiculous request.

"I asked the spokesman what time I could show up with a photographer at one of the New York City sites of the bust so we could get a picture, and the spokesman blurted out, 'Who told you about the bust?' That's my confirmation," I said. With that, I gave the editor the name of the spokesperson.

It appeared that my FBI confirmation was checked. By this time, the night editor had been on the phone with the city editor. One of them had spoken to Giuliani, who apparently had asked them not to run the story. I was given the impression that they had negotiated with Giuliani and, in exchange for not running the story, I would get a one-on-one interview with him after the post-arrest press conference, where he planned to announce the bust. I would also be able to cover the press conference. "Oh wow," I thought, "they let me keep my own story and sold it to me as a privilege." The next day I attended the press conference, met with Giuliani, and got a front-page story. Most important, I got to witness how the police agencies use the press to help develop and promote their image. Just like every other sector of the service economy, the police agencies have to be concerned about the image they project into the world, because that image could determine the resources they receive. The police agencies need to effectively use producers of cultural products to articulate their own significance in society. Giuliani had become a master of this dance. This particular Giuliani story was part of a larger image he had been cultivating for himself as U.S. attorney—the Elliot Ness–like crime fighter taking on the mob.

The police work surrounding this bust was part of the War on Drugs— a heavily promoted component of federal anti-crime policy—and the media played an important role in publicizing the policy. Another story I worked on while on nights significantly expanded my understanding of the outsized impact of the media in shaping public perceptions of law enforcement and justice in society. This story—also with a drug tie-in—came to me through an assignment.

In late 1988 or early 1989, the city editor came to the reporters on the night shift with a project. He was planning a week-long series of stories on what the paper termed "the exploding phenomenon of violence in New York City" (Byfield, Arce, and Broussard 1989). One part of the series would focus on the climbing homicide rate, as well as the increasing rate of violent crime in general. In 1988, 1,875 homicides had been committed in the city (Krajicek 1989). Bursts of violence had been erupting in all five boroughs with some regularity, and the police frequently described these outbreaks as being drug-related, more specifically due to crack cocaine. Innocent people were often caught in the crossfire, and this would be the focus of another part of the series.

The series represented a type of investigative reporting. It was not based on breaking news but was supposed to be a deep examination of ongoing patterns and trends in the news. In this particular case, the objective was to take a sustained look into "the margins." The series was billed as a major report, and it was designed to get readers' attention. At this point, especially in light of my recent experiences, I was more attuned to police abuse of power than to escalating violence in African American and Latino communities. If the truth be told, since I often traveled alone at night all over the city, I was also more concerned about being a victim of rape than about being caught in a random drug shootout. That perspective was not a cause for concern in this case, however. Someone somewhere in the *Daily News* management had decided that it was time to do *this* series—focused on flashier incidents of violence, with an emphasis on the drug angle.

Reporters from both the day and the night shifts staffed the project. The day shift reporters were to write the major stories about this "new phenomenon" in everyday life in New York City. Those on the night shift would review old clip files in the library—some papers called it the morgue—to find past stories, going back about a year, of innocent bystanders injured or killed when gunfire erupted in the streets. We found about thirty incidents—in which eighteen people had been killed and forty-nine wounded—that had sufficient information indicating that the victims had been caught in crossfire. Once we had amassed this group of events, the city editor wanted us to find as many people related to the incidents as possible and interview them. The paper planned to run a story consisting primarily of a chart with brief annotations listing what would be labeled "crossfire" shootings in the city. Some of the incidents in the chart would be punctuated with pictures of the victims and more detailed information from the interviews we conducted.

We spent weeks working on the project. The resulting series (which ran in the *Daily News* from January 22 through January 29, 1989) was represented with a logo that included an image from the Willye Jean Dukes Grand Central shooting with the following text: "The Meanest Streets: Your Risk Grows as Violence Rules." The headlines on the first-day reports were classic in a tabloid journalism sense. The main story from that day led with the headline "Trail of Fear and Loathing in City: A Swath of Scars Spreading Wide and Cutting Deep." Another headlined with "So How Rotten Is It in the Apple?" The second-day report featured maps and graphics showing the city divided by police precincts, demonstrating that crime had been increasing in sixty-four of the city's seventy-five precincts (Krajicek 1989). The point of this article—headlined "It's Called Spillover: Silk-Stocking Areas Share Run on Crime"—was that crime had not only increased in the margins but was also creeping into the "universal" city. The third-day report was a frightening piece about an alleged crack-addicted teenager who had allegedly gone on an eight-day crime spree that left in its wake five people dead and six wounded. The headlines on that multi-page story were "8 Days of Terror: Teen on Crack Ravages a Nabe" and "A Nabe Shattered: Crack Leads Teen to Kill 5 and Wound 6."

In the research I had done on crossfire shootings, I came across one particularly poignant story about a Queens teenager named Ghanshyam Patel who had been caught in a crossfire shooting and had been paralyzed as a result. (I will return to the details momentarily.) That piece was part of the fourth-day report, along with a story itemizing all of the crossfire shootings—fatalities and injuries—in the city over the previous year. Those headlines were "Bullets Destroy American Dream" and "Death for No Reason: In Wrong Place at Wrong Time." The fifth-day report focused on teen violence, with headlines that included "Young, Armed & Dangerous" and "The Dead-End Kids: Nothing to Lose, so They're Fearless." Here is an excerpt from the latter story:

> Like tens of thousands of adolescent New Yorkers, 16-year-old Raymond Forbes lived in a dead land.
>
> He was poor and practically illiterate. He wasn't particularly attached to his family, and he didn't go to school. His frame of reference was a ghetto area of Far Rockaway, Queens. He was drifting toward nowhere, until September 3, 1988.
>
> That was the day he decided to solve a money problem by getting a gun and attempting to rob the driver of a Mister Softee truck. (Arce and Mustain 1989)

The sixth-day report focused on the family, tying crack to domestic violence. That headline was "Child vs. Parent, Husband vs. Wife: Crack Feeds Surge in Domestic Violence." The final day's report had the following headline: "A Picture Imperfect: Need to Rock Cocaine Boat." Images of the drug addicted and the dangerous accompanied all of the stories in the series, and they all showed the faces of African American and Latino youths. One story featured a photo of a person fighting the drug problem in her community; that person appeared to be white. The message was clear.

At the time, I had been glad to work on the project. In pursuit of my research on crossfire shootings, I met with the family of Ghanshyam Patel one night to interview them all about their ordeal. They told the heartbreaking story of a family who had migrated to the United States from India to pursue educational opportunities, only to have their dreams destroyed by a random bullet. When I told the city desk editor about the results of the interview, he asked me to write a feature story on young Patel and the family's struggle to get him the services he needed and their fight to survive financially. My story really did put a human face on the growing violence in the city, which primarily affected New Yorkers living in communities on the margins, mostly poorer communities populated primarily by African Americans and Latinos. But the stories in the series were destined to do something else, far bigger.

My piece on young Patel included the following account of the shooting:

> Feb. 2 was cold and rainy. Ghanshyam left Halsey Junior High School in Rego Park at the usual time. Heading home on the F train, he realized his library card was missing.
>
> He decided to visit the library at 89th Ave. and Merrick Blvd. and report the card lost. Leaving the subway at the 169th St. and Hillside Ave. station, he could smell the spicy food cooking in Jerk Chicken, a Caribbean restaurant beside the 168th St. exit.
>
> Inside the restaurant, a member of a Jamaican drug posse—Hamton Fraser, 21—was preparing to leave.
>
> Fraser worked the nearby corner, a spot worth about $2,000 a night, Detective Jack Egan said, and that made him the target of another dealer.
>
> Ghanshyam walked by just as Fraser stepped out. A gunman fired seven or eight rounds from a .45 automatic.
>
> Fraser was fatally wounded, his own .45 still in his waistband.
>
> Ghanshyam fell, too, but with only his books. "I heard boom like a bomb," he says. And then he realized something was wrong: "Where's my legs?" he recalls thinking. "I don't feel nothing."
>
> The next day, after surgery, Ghanshyam's family was told he was paralyzed from the waist down and would never walk again. (Byfield 1989a)

The story received a lot of attention. I got calls from readers. One stood out. It came from the Governor's Office on Minority Affairs. Someone I knew worked there and called to say that people in the office had seen the piece and thought it was good writing and effective. Then one comment stopped me in my tracks. These people thought the story would help to bring the death penalty back to New York State.[19] I did not interpret the comment to mean that my one article could make the state legislators change their vote for the death penalty. But I understood the implication: Articles in a series like the one the *Daily News* had published could change public discourse around the issue of capital punishment. The series had sharply focused the problems of youth violence in the city and the drug trade as phenomena caused by blacks and Latinos that were spreading like a disease to everyone else. These were the ideas at the heart of the push against the so-called "crack epidemic," which would be the next campaign in the War on Drugs (Reinarman and Levine 2006).

The Central Park jogger was raped three months after the violence series ran. As a result of the growing importance of crime on state and national political agendas, the death penalty issue had long been simmering just beneath the surface. About two weeks after the attack on the jogger, New York real estate developer Donald Trump turned up the heat when he applied his enormous financial resources in support of the campaign to reinstate capital punishment in New York State. The legislative forces pushing for restoration of the death penalty in the state had run up against a sort of Maginot Line in the form of Democratic Party Governors Hugh Carey and Mario Cuomo. Each year, beginning in 1977, the state legislature would pass a bill to reinstate capital punishment. The governor would veto the bill. State legislators would then seek votes to override the veto. In 1989, legislative leaders claimed to need only one or two more votes to accomplish the override (Foderaro 1989). Trump spent $85,000 to run full-page ads in four of the city's newspapers calling for reinstatement of the death penalty (Foderaro 1989). The ads—which ran in the *New York Times,* the *Daily News,* the *New York Post,* and *New York Newsday*—peddled hatred: "I want to hate these muggers and murderers. . . . They should be forced to suffer and, when they kill, they should be executed for their crimes" (Foderaro 1989).[20]

## Changing Notions about Youth Violence in New York City's History

This growth in violent crime across the nation, particularly homicides, had been going on for a while—between 1983 and 1993. It had become a major topic of discussion among members of the media, government, and academia alike. The media regularly published the FBI crime statistics. Unsurprisingly, the big story coming out of these news reports was the increase in the numbers of violent incidents involving people under eighteen years old, particularly those who lived in urban areas, such as New York City. As stories go, the reporting of such crime statistics was relatively mundane. However, the very existence of such dramatic numbers within the body of knowledge about the world around us justified a journalistic focus. Media renditions of up-to-the-minute crime data went far beyond the statistical reporting in New York City's "hometown newspaper," the *Daily News.* Myriad stories (such as the violence series described earlier) portrayed the city as having its very governability threatened by a mythic type of wild west violence erupting on the streets of the city—streets that happened to be in communities that were predominantly African American and Latino (Byfield, Arce, and Broussard 1989; Vitale 2008).

The crack "epidemic," as it was then described, was credited in these media accounts as the underlying source of much of this violence, which came by way of warring factions of drug dealers (Byfield, Arce, and Broussard 1989). While studies such as *In Search of Respect,* Philippe Bourgois's (1995) ethnography of people involved in the illegal drug business in East Harlem, illustrate the notorious violence of the crack trade, some of the escalation in violence committed by juveniles between 1983 and 1993 was appreciably different from the violent activities related to drug use and the drug trade. A 2001 study of youth violence by U.S. Surgeon General Dr. David Satcher warned against conflating the lethal violence witnessed during the early 1980s and 1990s with youth violence in general. In what was the first such report by a U.S. Surgeon General, Satcher (2001) noted that no community—regardless of its regional, racial, or socioeconomic features—had been immune to the surge in violent behavior among its young people. While the violence accompanying the drug trade contributed some of the reported "youth violence," these activities were also promulgated as a result of the ready availability of guns (Satcher 2001). The report further indicated that reduction of the gun violence in the drug trade did not dramatically reduce the levels of youth violence in society (Satcher 2001). Sadly, the nature of and reasons for the different types of violent activities young people engage in has often been ignored in discussions in the mainstream media. Instead, press reports have created in the public mind images of violent, anarchic black and Latino youths in urban areas, who were a threat not only to people within their own communities but to the entire society.

The white media's rendition of youth violence in general and of the violent acts of black and Latino youths in particular was not always expressed in the negative terms that society witnessed in the 1980s. In other periods, elements of New York City press coverage of youth violence and the violent acts of black and Latino youths were framed sympathetically or even politically. In the latter cases, the press sometimes drew connections between youth eruptions and social, economic, and political inequality (Chang 2005).

For more than a century, gang violence has been documented in New York City, and since the nineteenth century the gangs themselves have been a part of the city's youth culture (Greene and Pranis 2007: 15; see also Austin 2001). From the post-war period to the mid-1960s, New York City had experienced a changing economic base, white flight, and interracial gang warfare among black, white, and Latino groups (Chang 2005; Greene and Pranis 2007). Gang activity had waned significantly by 1965 (Greene and Pranis 2007). What was left was periodic internecine strife between the lower middle-class and poor whites and the newer and economically disenfranchised black and brown residents (Chang 2005; Greene and Pranis 2007). These whites were the ones white flight had left behind. Their incomes did not allow them to buy into the American dream, or to join the burgeoning suburbs being built for the white middle class. Poorer whites had no choice but to move to the outreaches of the city, as they had to some sections of the Bronx, or to maintain their hold on areas in other parts of the city that would later be regarded as white ethnic enclaves. Meanwhile, in neighborhood after neighborhood in some areas of the outer boroughs (i.e., Bronx, Brooklyn, and Queens), the color of the residents seemed to change overnight. In other areas, new public housing developments brought black and brown people to the "inner city" spaces that formerly had been occupied by whites.

All of this reshuffling of people went on while the economy of the world and consequently the city was undergoing a major transformation. On the wings of white flight away from urban communities went the jobs, tax base, and services that had formerly supported those areas. By the 1960s, New York City's conversion from a manufacturing-based economy to one supported by financial services, real estate, and insurance was quite obvious. It was a change that moved like a juggernaut, destroying and limiting opportunity for the city's poorer communities, primarily its African American and Latino areas. Joe Austin (2001) contends that New York City held within its history a narrative in which the city itself was an internationally recognized trope for capitalist advancement and modernity. But the growth of new groups of black and brown people in the 1950s and the 1960s is part of another narrative:

> This mythic New York City is always stalked by its Other, the Naked City, the Asphalt Jungle, the Rotten Apple, where the story is one of living in the shadowy crevices of the modern metropolis. Poverty, crime, moral decay in infinite variety, claustrophobic surroundings, alienation, uncaring bureaucracies, inequality, struggle, restricted life chances, loneliness, ruin, and loss have equally long histories in New York City, but these stories are less frequently recited. The story of the Naked City is one of a fearful and inhumane present and a lack of hope for the future. (Austin 2001: 12–13)[21]

This "other" New York City witnessed a lot of youth violence and gang warfare in the 1970s, a period that experienced a resurgence of gang activity in what is now known as the South Bronx (Chang 2005; Greene and Pranis 2007). In the wake of white flight, the communities in this area were long on disenfranchisement and short on resources. They spawned youth gangs made up largely of Puerto Rican and African American teens. These gangs fought with the police and they fought with white gangs from communities that bordered their areas. Sometimes they fought with each other. Flavored as the times were by the 1960s upheavals—which included picketing, sit-ins, rent strikes, school boycotts, and mobilizations against police brutality—some gangs evolved into an "organization," at times much more than a social organization but rather a political organization (Chang 2005). They grew by forming "chapters" all over the city and into the tri-state area (New York, New Jersey, and Connecticut).

These gangs sported names such as Ghetto Brothers, Black Spades, and Savage Skulls. They rose to the fore because government officials and the police—

the traditional representatives of power and authority—held little sway in their communities. Racism and the benign neglect by those in charge gave the gangs, these symbols of an alternative system of authority, power in their communities. This power was at times legitimated in the mainstream press, further elevating the status of the gangs:

> Some residents began to see them as the real law on the streets. Savage Skull Danny DeJesus says, "Before they would go to the local police, the people would come to us to solve their problems." Even *New York Post* columnist Pete Hamill wrote, "The best single thing that has happened on the streets of New York in the past ten years is the re-emergence of the teenage gangs. . . . These young people are standing up for life, and if their courage lasts, they will help this city to survive." (Chang 2005: 49)

Chang argues that Hamill took this position because the gangs were on a "crusade to . . . rid the streets of junkies and pushers" (2005: 49). In their role as political organizations in the 1970s, the gangs made demands on the city for jobs, services, and recreational programs—demands that were never met.[22] The mainstream media had never taken up the cause of youth joblessness, particularly among minorities. Carolyn Martindale's (1986: 110–112) seminal study of stories about blacks in major national newspapers points out that in the 1970s, the *New York Times* devoted a very small portion of its coverage to the problems, such as joblessness and housing, faced by black New Yorkers.

By 1971, many of the gangs had turned on each other, which elicited stories about gang violence in the local papers (Chang 2005; Greene and Pranis 2007). The solution for ending gang warfare did not come from the conventional authority structure; instead, the gangs appeared to reach a truce when gang leadership sat down together and forged a highly publicized peace treaty (Chang 2005: 54–62). Days after the peace treaty, the NYPD set up the Youth Gang Task Force in the Bronx, which, according to Black Spades leader Bambaataa, created its own gang called the Purple Mothers that attacked and killed members of the black and Latino gangs. Within a year, the task force had jailed many of the gang leaders (Chang 2005).

The jobs and social programs some of the gangs had pushed for would never materialize. Between 1978 and 1990, the federal contribution to the city's budget, which helped pay for many social programs, dropped from 20 percent to 11 percent (Byfield 1996). Funds were diverted to the War on Drugs, whose focus on incarceration "account[ed] for two-thirds of the rise in the federal inmate population and more than half of the rise in state prisoners between 1985 and 2000" (Alexander 2010: 59). Under this federal policy, the police experience few legal constraints, Alexander (2010: 60) argues. Court rulings in their favor helped to legitimize the actions of police when they crossed constitutional lines in the War on Drugs. What the courts could not do for them the media did—elicit public support for violations of African American rights. At the time of the attack on the Central Park jogger, mainstream discourse on youth violence did not include stories of unconstitutional police actions in black communities, the history of white youth attacks on blacks and Latinos, or the history of factions of blacks and Latinos fighting *for* their communities. Instead, the media flooded the public discourse with stories about black and Latino drug-related violence using language associated with traditional discourses on race, which articulated genetic differences between and whites and nonwhites. But, in the era of color-blind racism, this language meant something different—blacks and Latinos were culturally inclined to be violent.

## The Media and the NYPD

One of the most important reasons crime stories receive the treatment they get in the press is the institutionalized relationship between the police and the media. This relationship is facilitated in part by the historic priorities of the mainstream media in the area of race—that is, the union of race and crime in the press is a long-established precedent, and the sensationalizing of race and crime has always sold newspapers. In this chapter, discussion of the workings in the newsroom has focused on how the media interact with an outside institution (the police) to meet the media's own racial priorities in a contemporary socioeconomic and political context. Mainstream media have historically otherized or marginalized nonwhites. In the 1980s, this often took place in the context of an ongoing federal-level War on Drugs, whose policies targeted street-level drug infractions in low-income, black and Latino urban neighborhoods. Thus, with the media's easy and consistent focus on police activities, the War on Drugs would serve as part of the material foundation of the new overarching narrative on race.

The inclusion of external institutional forces, such as the police, in the establishment of media priorities highlights at least two aspects of the functioning of media: (1) a relationship whereby the external institution serves as a major resource for the media institution, and (2) a feature of the external institution organized or designed specifically to promulgate institutional goals through the dissemination of symbolic information. Put simply, for most crime stories reported in New York City during the 1980s, the NYPD was the first editor of information. During that period, there were three typical avenues—standard operating procedures—for gathering information about crimes for news stories. Journalists had the option of going to (1) a civilian source or person involved in the crime incident as a participant or witness, (2) a police source who spoke directly to the journalist without going through the police department's formal system for relaying information to the media, or (3) the press relations office of the NYPD. The second and third avenues certainly offered the smoothest and quickest route to a publishable story.

The press relations office of the NYPD is the official source for information about crime in the city. Local, national, and international journalists all use the department's press office to get information and police comments for their crime coverage. Even more importantly, at the start of each day, reporters working out of the NYPD headquarters bureau go to the press office to review "the sheets," lists of crimes supposedly covering all precincts in the city. These interactions generate the media content on crime; for local papers like the *Daily News,* the police department's crime priorities greatly influence the newspaper's priorities for coverage.

The importance of the relationship between the police and the press cannot be overstated. Since 1947, when the public relations bureau of the New York Police Department was created, the police themselves have played a critical role in controlling the crime information journalists receive. Further complicating the relationship is the fact that it is the police who issue the credentials required by members of the working press to cover events in the city.

An article in the *Journal of Criminal Law and Criminology* published three years after creation of the NYPD's public relations bureau describes the relationship between the press and the police:

> Working closely with the Public Relations Bureau are between 30 and 40 working reporters who represent the eight or ten leading New York dailies and the press associations. . . . They have a direct line to the Public Relations Bureau, and when important spot news comes in, they are immediately notified. . . . The reporters make it their policy to maintain good relations throughout the police echelons, so when perhaps a spectacular arrest is made they may be tipped off where to get a good story. (Larson 1950: 368)

The NYPD's public relations bureau eventually became organized as a department headed by a deputy police commissioner. Currently the press office is run out of the office of the Deputy Commissioner for Public Information (DCPI).

As the first editors of the city's crime news, the police are likely to share crimes with the press that reflect the department's internal policy priorities as well as what the police think the press wants to hear. During the 1980s, the police in New York City and in other parts of the nation wanted to communicate to the public that they were seriously engaged in the War on Drugs. No doubt many of the stories my fellow journalists and I were fed during that period contributed to highlighting the role of the police in that federal initiative.

# 5

## A Participant Observes How Content Emerges

### The Tip That Could Change the Framing

**I THOUGHT OF** my time spent at the office during this period as just visits. I had a sense of freedom that was unusual for me in this job. As I spent days at a time working on my own without constant oversight, or should I say surveillance, from an editor, I started thinking, "So this is what it's really like to be a reporter." The ways in which I experienced the world underwent a transformation. I existed at once as a part of the everyday world and removed from it. I filtered the things I saw everywhere in terms of potential stories and the different ways in which to tell those imagined stories. There was my editors' way and there was my way. It had come to that.

I remember once attending a reading by Walter Mosley[1] and listening as he read a scene in which he portrayed what in media language would be referred to as a "devastated urban neighborhood" because some the buildings were dilapidated and uninhabitable. Mosley described the sidewalk and the glass embedded in the concrete refracting the rays of the sun as jewelry or gems sparkling in the streets. It hit me then. I thought Mosley's use of a word like jewelry or gems to represent something in that community was a synecdoche for the neighborhood precisely because he could still see the beauty and humanity in the inhabitants despite the state of their area and despite the fact that some of the residents sometimes did bad things, even really bad things. The point of reference from which my editors viewed blacks and other non-whites informed their whole world view and provided the basis for the type of coherence they gave all of the pieces of the phenomena unfolding in front of them.[2] They could not or would not see any organic beauty or truth or goodness anywhere. Black communities, when refracted from the point of view of these editors, were dark, dangerous places awash in ignorance, with the few good people living there largely overwhelmed by welfare dependence and outsized numbers of depraved criminals.[3]

The coherence or frame I applied to all of the observable facts I encountered originated in a different place. My black, female body told that story in part. My operating simultaneously with these two different frames at times seemed to split me in two. But that was not the worst thing. My bifurcation came from a particular state of awareness; it was Du Bois's (2003) double-consciousness all over again. Uncomfortable as this situation might be, it certainly beat being a porous vessel for the world view of my editors. And it put me in a position, I thought, to maneuver around their epistemic point of departure. On one of my visits to the office I received a fax from a youth center located at 110th Street and Fifth Avenue in Manhattan, right across the street from the northern entrance to Central Park. The flyer promised a press conference organized by young people who wanted to talk about the coverage of the jogger case. This was obviously not a professional press release, but it got the message across. Upon seeing the location of the youth center, I wanted to attend. It was only moments away from the Schomburg Plaza apartment complex, where four of the suspects in the Central Park jogger case lived. No one challenged my decision to go.

The site of the press conference, Youth Action Program (YAP), was a jobs and leadership training center for youth between the ages of sixteen and twenty-four years old. That twenty-four-year marker, which often served as a boundary for youth, always seemed odd to me, but it turned up a lot in government statistics. In the world of the mainstream white middle class, it was an abnormal range for defining youth; in that world a twenty-four-year-old would have already graduated from college and begun to make his or her way in life. The presumption at YAP, however, was that the youth being served were neither white nor mainstream nor middle class. (In the debate on welfare and crime, liberals would argue that such a center is necessary, while conservatives would call for the money to be spent fighting crime.)

The short, squat building housing YAP and a number of other youth programs was in the shadows of the Schomburg towers. YAP's goal was to empower youth while providing them with job skills. Some of the organization's work included preparing these budding adults for jobs in the construction industry. The site was structured for the organization's needs, with offices and a central meeting space. Young people were clearly being pushed to the forefront.

I followed a group of people into the central meeting area, the site of the press conference. There was only one other media person there, even though press releases had been sent to all of the major New York City television news outlets and newspapers. I was not surprised at the turnout. I had not expected that most of those journalists would see this as a news story, much less something worth sending a reporter to. The conference started shortly after I was seated, with the appointed spokesperson at the front of the room. Other young people, mostly black and Latino, joined us in the seats for the press. A few words into the discussion, it was clear the black and Latino youths were unhappy about the coverage the jogger case had been receiving.

"Is it really necessary to describe the suspects with words like 'savage'?" the speaker challenged. "You all report the stories as if everyone in the community is responsible, as if we're all bad people." There are many positive things that young people like us do, he said, as his eyes surveyed the room. This very center was a prime example of those positive things. "If only the young people here knew how the media worked," I thought. I wondered if they knew how many people in the mainstream viewed such tax-dollar-supported job-training and development programs. YAP appeared to be well established, but I had never heard of it; it was not exactly one of the sites in Harlem regularly highlighted by the mainstream media.

I sat there chagrined. I had never once written words like "savage," "animal," "hunt," "wolfpack," or "predator," I thought defensively. "Maybe I could do a story to fix this. But my editors won't run a story about these kinds of complaints, especially from children. Maybe a story about the center would be a good idea."

I sat there thinking that even if YAP had been covered by the media, chances were it would have been a one-time story about the center's various programs. Even within the context of a so-called positive article about a black community, stories about places like YAP highlight negativity, because the special programs provided by YAP to serve the community are often patronizingly cast: "We have to offer these programs for these people because they need our help, especially our tax dollars, because they can't manage for themselves." As the subjects of such stories, blacks are drawn as lesser Americans, people unable to fit into the role of the mythologized super-independent rugged individualist. These faux positive stories are presented as if only blacks or other minorities benefit in any way from programs supported by tax dollars. Everyone else is miraculously able to thrive independently. "These [jogger] stories have made things so bad we can't even use the park anymore," said someone sitting close by. The voice came to me from what seemed like a distance. I had been deep in thought contemplating the real-life consequences of our coverage. I turned to the young man who had raised the question and said, "What do you mean you can't use the park anymore; you mean Central Park?"

"Yes, the police are kicking black and Latino kids out of the park." Maybe I had found another way to provide concrete evidence of what people in black and Latino communities experience.

"We went on an Outward Bound Center course in Central Park," he said. "As we were sitting in a group wrapping up our day," the teen recalled, "the police came over and inquired what we were doing there."

"Were you with adults?" I asked, as if that should matter.

"Yes," he said, "we were sitting in the Conservatory Garden writing about our experience in the course."

"We told the cop we were in an Outward Bound course," the boy said, "but he demanded that we show him ID. He told us that if we couldn't produce identification, we should leave the park. He also told us that if we didn't leave, he could lock us up for 72 hours." I later learned the significance of the time period; police could hold someone without charges for a maximum of 72 hours.

"They can't do that," I said.

"There he is—the leader of the Outward Bound Center group," the teen said. "He was with us." The Outward Bound instructor had been listening to the press conference wind down. In the meantime, I had started mentally reporting this story on the side. It often worked that way, that a press conference led you to another story. But when the teen pointed out the Outward Bound leader, I could not believe my luck. I could get adult confirmation, coming from a "reputable" source. I started thinking about all the pieces of information that would make the story credible to my editors: the presence of an adult and the name "Outward Bound Center." The Outward Bound Center conducted outdoor adventure courses for youth leadership development. I thought it was something middle-class white people would find relatable. I was not sure if my editors would find the Outward Bound Center instructor I interviewed credible, because he was African American. But they had been in the park with another Outward Bound instructor—one who was white. With this interview confirming the story, I could not wait to return to the office and tell the city desk editors. I thought they would surely see the news value in the story.[4] After all, the press had been steadily covering reactions to the rape.

## Pitching the Story

I pitched the Outward Bound story to a city desk editor the moment I walked into the office that day.[5] The story really excited me. It represented a reaction story in the universe of the jogger coverage, it was a response from members of the black community and the geographic community the suspects were from, and it was being advanced by black and Latino male teens. It also represented another salvo in the ongoing conflict between minority communities and the police. "It's a no-brainer," I thought. I rattled off what had transpired at the meeting to an assignment editor, hoping the story would run the next day. I had gotten used to anything I had to say about the jogger running, and running the next day. But, this time, my pitch did not connect with the editor.

"Nah," he said, with a bit of indifference. "Why don't you try the suburban desk?"

"The suburban desk?" I wondered. "Is he out of his mind? This is a great story." The suburban desk was located toward the back of the newsroom, close to where I sat. So I knew the people who ran that desk. I also knew the perceived unimportance of that desk relative to the city desk. The name "suburban" desk was a bit of a misnomer. Composed of a variety of editors, including a main editor, other subordinate editors, and a team of copy editors, the suburban desk managed the stories produced by the bureaus for each of the boroughs of the city and around the metropolitan area—the Bronx, Brooklyn, Queens, Staten Island, Long Island, and New Jersey bureaus.

The purview of the suburban desk was not the suburbs in a literal sense. It also managed, under a title of "Metro," the stories coming out of the Harlem bureau and the city desk's unwanted stories from other parts of Manhattan. The suburban desk also got the stories produced by a variety of the paper's other bureaus—for example, City Hall and the Courts—that were deemed not strong enough from a news value point of view to be "up-front." The city desk controlled the "up-front" stories, which dominated the first eleven to fourteen pages of the paper. Suburban stories were compiled in pull-out sections geared toward individual boroughs[6] and suburban geographic areas. Therefore, papers sold in Queens contained the Queens pull-out section with stories specific to that borough. In terms of newsroom prestige, the suburban desk was a second cousin once removed from the city desk. Excellent journalists certainly worked for the suburban desk, but they were not the favored journalists within the power structure of the newsroom.

The position of the suburban desk within the newsroom power structure and the organization of its jurisdiction reified or made concrete the binary nature the "universal" city and "margins" in two important ways. First, the suburban desk existed as a division of labor in the newsroom that reinforced the physical boundaries of the "universal" city discussed earlier. Second, the geographic areas covered by this so-called suburban desk made clear that its "suburban" terrain was imagined. The desk's territory had been constructed more around power, class, and race than around any real topographical boundaries. This imagined province was representational of the power divide in the city. The divide between city desk and suburban desk mirrored the separation between the yuppies or symbolic elites of the "universal" city and the relatively powerless white ethnics and minorities who existed outside the "universal" city, in the margins.

The rationale for Long Island's inclusion under the suburban desk surpassed simple reasons of geography. Issues of race and power were palpable there too. A significant part of Long Island has long been a more affluent region than the outer boroughs of New York City—the Bronx, Brooklyn, Queens, and Staten Island. Since the geographic boundaries of the desks were imagined, why not place the more wealthy Long Island counties under the purview of the city desk? Long Island also represented the zone that received white ethnic flight from New York City. Many of the white ethnics on Long Island had only recently become "white" in the U.S. racial order, a structure that over time had gradually embraced as fully "white" a variety of immigrants, including those from Ireland and the nations of southern and eastern Europe (Roediger 2005). Many of these recently whitened immigrants of Long Island fit squarely into the working or nonprofessional classes, thus they were not part of the elites of the "universal" city. Despite all of its perceived relative inferiority to the city desk, the suburban desk was staffed by highly experienced journalists, some of whom traced their history to another day and age in New York City journalism.

"What could he be thinking?" I wondered again about the city editor. The story I had pitched was about civil rights conflict and justice. These problems were global to me; my very life depended on reasonable resolutions of these issues. However, from my editors' perspective of white privilege, these were marginal concerns. Dutifully, I followed instructions and pitched the story to the suburban desk editor.

The main suburban desk editor was seated in the rectangular-shaped pod of desks housing his team. These people had a variety of pull-outs to create, and each suburban editor had a deep pile of stories he or she had to review and edit over the course of each day. More than at any other desk I remember, these editors' eyes were always trained on their computer screens, and they rarely got up for breaks. I stood next to the editor, talking into his ear to pitch my story. He listened without taking his eyes off the screen. When I finished, he looked up at me quizzically.

"Natalie, that's not a suburban story. Take that to the city desk," he said.

"I know," I replied emphatically. "But they told me to give it to you." I could feel frustration mounting within me. The suburban editor made a face and a disparaging remark about the judgment of the city desk editor. One of the palpable splits in the newsroom was age or experience. Many of the people staffing the city desk and the news desk were members of the new symbolic elite—they were yuppies. They were not the old-timers from the 1950s, who remembered working during the heyday of journalism in New York City, when there were about ten daily newspapers competing against each other. Reporters and photographers at the *Daily News* from that era mythologized that period in newspaper history.

Rare was the day that went by when someone did not recount experiences from the *Journal American* or the *Herald Tribune*. During that earlier time, the requirements for being a journalist did not include a degree from a journalism school or even a college education. Most of the journalists from that era learned on the job. And many had a fly-by-the-seat-of-your-pants approach that made for some tall tales. I loved those stories; they were quintessential New York stories told from the point of view of the sons of European immigrants. Many in this group had become "white" based on tangible immediate sacrifices they watched their parents make (Roediger 2005). In the newsroom, these sons of European immigrants could be defined racially by way of their perception of the job. To them, journalism was not a profession; it was a craft—skills you acquired as an apprentice on a job that paid enough to raise a family in a middle-class— read that "white"—lifestyle. But the current generation that was in charge of the city desk—the grandsons and granddaughters of immigrants—understood the symbolic importance of whiteness from a different perspective (Roediger 2005). So normalized in their psyche was their white privilege that they had no awareness of the proximity they shared with those outside the "universal" city.

The suburban editor turned me down with a suggestion: "Why don't you take the story to the Sunday editor?" I loved the idea. The Sunday paper was big; it had the largest circulation of all the days of the week—1.1 million at the time.[7] The Sunday paper even had its own editor, who oversaw or planned the stories that would fit around the ad bonanza that existed on Sundays. The major stories that ran on that day were typically not breaking news; they were planned, overview pieces about a particular subject related to significant events or breaking news pieces that had run during the previous week or weeks.

Reporters were given space and time to develop their articles for the Sunday paper—more than the space and time devoted to the stories that ran on other days. It was not unusual to see Sunday pieces bylined by the more established or more tenured reporters. The main Sunday stories were usually considered major news, so they would typically have some kind of art accompanying them, either a photo or some other type of image. The Sunday paper was typically put to bed on Fridays, with the expectation that some space—a little— would be left to accommodate breaking news. Maybe the front page photo would change, or the headline on the front page would be redone to make room for a big breaking news story such as a fire or a cop being shot, but once put to bed, the main stories in the Sunday paper rarely changed.

The Sunday editor's office was against the wall, in a row of offices with large windows looking outside and with glass walls facing into the newsroom. I looked across from the suburban desk and saw the Sunday editor in his lair. I did not know him except by sight. My pitch may well have been our first extended conversation, so I did not anticipate a particular outcome.

"Hi," I said, beginning my pitch, "I went to a press conference today called by young people at an organization in Harlem named Youth Action Program." I went on. Mentally I knew I had to wrap up the story in a pitch line, preferably one sentence, that captured the essence of the story. I did not want to come across as lame and inexperienced. "They actually called the press conference to complain about the jogger coverage," I continued, "but while there I discovered that the Central Park precinct now has a policy requiring the cops patrolling the park to card black and Latino kids and demand that they produce identification if they want to stay in the park."

He looked at me with no noticeable reaction. "He must need more information," I thought. I continued, "If they can't produce ID, they're threatened with eviction from the park or incarceration. They can hold people for up to 72 hours without a charge."

"Are you really surprised that's happening?" he asked me. He was standing behind his desk. The look on his face said, "She can't be serious."

"They can't do that," I said, "that's like the South African law requiring blacks to carry passbooks." "This is America," I added. "This is a clear violation of their civil rights."

"Are you angry?" he asked. This question caught me off guard. I paused, unsure of how to respond. "Is he asking me if I'm angry at him?" I wondered, because I was surely annoyed at being jerked around about this story. "Or is he asking me if I'm angry at what's happening to the kids in Central Park?" I did not understand where he was coming from and I wanted to give the right answer. He stood behind his desk watching me, watching my face, and I realized that how I composed myself, everything about my demeanor, would be weighed as part of the answer to this question. His eyes stayed on me and I could feel everything about me being judged.

"I'm not angry," I said quietly.

"This will blow over," he countered just as quietly. Then it dawned on me; he thought I was angry because "black" children were being mistreated. It was the same old thing—the objectivity of black reporters becomes suspect when covering issues related to race or other black people. Whites cover whites all the time without anyone being concerned about their ability to make professional judgments (van Dijk 1993b: 245). However, "black journalists must often settle for the tentative embrace of editors who lavish them with praise when they write critically of African American people, since their ability to write harshly about blacks is seen as a barometer of their objectivity" (Newkirk 2000: 138). Whites in journalism (as in other industries) often subject their black colleagues to litmus tests in an effort to identify where the black colleagues place their allegiance (Nelson 1993: 53–54). Since the beginning of my participation in the jogger coverage, this standoff with the Sunday editor represented the most serious litmus test of my adherence to the dominant perspective.

I made myself very still and looked backed at him. We both had our poker faces on. I grew intensely aware of all my responses, as well as his. I looked across the desk at him, composed my thoughts, and decided on an approach. I continued, "I'm making a professional assessment here. This story merits major coverage for journalistic reasons." I listed the reasons: "We have been intensely covering the jogger. We have covered reactions to what happened to the jogger from all corners of the city. This is a reaction story, highlighting changing police department policy. In addition, this new policy violates the civil rights of blacks and Latinos."

"I think it's a major story," I said, wrapping up my case.

"If you think that's a story, I seriously question your judgment as a journalist," he said. He had dropped the hammer. Not only was I being dismissed;

I was being sent away classified as an unqualified journalist. This was too much. Now I was furious. And, in one unthinking move, I committed political suicide in the newsroom—I went over the Sunday editor's head to the editor-in-chief, Gil Spencer.

At the back of the newsroom, ensconced behind the large office of his secretary, was the cloistered domain of the editor-in-chief. His office was part of a suite that also housed the offices of the editorial page.[8] Spencer was a tall, lanky man with salt-and-pepper hair—one of those in the newsroom who reportedly was not college educated. When I entered his office, he came out from behind the desk. We stood talking in the center of the room. I laid out the situation: the press conference, the story, the ping-pong ball routine I had just experienced in the newsroom, and finally the details of my encounter with the Sunday editor. Spencer listened. His manner was always one that suggested a joke lay just beneath the surface. With a wave of his hand, he seemed to bat away the tension and the discord from the earlier situation—at least for me.

"The Sunday editor doesn't know what he's talking about," he said, "that's a great story." He seemed to be excited about it. "Do it up," he said, "get comments from the precinct cops, from Ben Ward [the police commissioner], and civil rights attorneys. We'll run it on a Sunday. Plan on 24, 25 inches." While at the *New York Times* a 25-inch Sunday story is not much, at the *Daily News* it is a very big deal.

## Legitimizing the Story

I exited the editorial suite and walked into the newsroom. It was the first time since joining the city desk that I had done that. I saw the newsroom from a different perspective at that moment. It appeared to be a space I could navigate, a space with room for me. Thrilled as I was to be able to really do this story, I knew it would not be easy. I had a civil rights attorney in mind for comments. It did not even occur to me to turn to Mason or Maddox.[9] I instinctively thought it best to go to a white attorney—someone whose objectivity or legal reasoning would not be questioned by my editors. I knew getting police comments would be difficult, both from the precinct and from Ben Ward. I knew what I needed to do. I started making calls right away.

Reporting the story took much longer than I had anticipated. One of my first calls was to the Central Park precinct. The officer who answered the phone identified himself, then I identified myself.

"I'm Natalie Byfield from the *Daily News*," I said.

"I've seen your byline; you use a middle initial," he noted.

"Yes, I'm Natalie P. Byfield," I said.

"What does the 'P.' stand for?"

"Patricia."

He slipped into an Irish brogue and repeated "Patricia" a couple of times. I played along. He chatted me up a bit, asking me questions about the *News,* how long I had been there, things like that. Most of the time when a reporter calls a precinct and speaks to a police officer he or she does not know, the reporter is told to call DCPI, the office of the Deputy Commissioner for Public Information, which is the press office for the NYPD. Distribution of information to the public or the press is supposed to be centralized and managed. Officers in precincts only speak to reporters they know and trust. This man was a complete stranger to me. He tried to bond with me based on a false presumption about our common heritage. I interrupted his banter and started talking about the reason for my call. I made my voice light, innocent almost.

"I heard black and Latino kids are being stopped, while in Central Park, by cops from your precinct and being asked to produce identification," I said.

"Yeah," he replied, sounding noncommittal. "Is he being evasive or is his tone matter of fact?" I wondered. I pressed on.

"Is this something new?"

"Yes, since the jogger was raped in the park."

"It's policy?" I asked.

"At the start of shift, when the officers meet, these are the instructions the officers on patrol are given," he said. "They are told to card black and Latino youth in groups larger than three; the kids are to be removed from Central Park if they can't produce identification." His tone is still matter of fact. I had what I needed. "Don't use my name," he said. I wondered if he was getting nervous about all he had said to me. He did not seem to be. It did not appear that he thought he had divulged sensitive or off-limits information to me. But I was not ready to celebrate just yet; I still had to get an interview with Ben Ward. He was the city's first African American police commissioner. He had been appointed by Mayor Koch, under whose administration the relationship between African American communities and the police department had headed south.

I called DCPI to reach a police spokesperson. The routine was to call with a question, and a spokesperson would provide an answer. But, when I made this call, I requested an interview with the police commissioner. I gave my purpose as covering a story about the Central Park jogger case. I said I wanted comments about the Central Park precinct procedure of stopping black and Latino kids in the park for identification in the wake of the jogger's rape. I was told someone would get back to me. No one returned the call. After a few days and a few more requests, I was told to fax my questions for the commissioner. I called back and said I would prefer an interview. We were at an impasse. Spencer had said to get Ward, and Ward would not make himself available.

Shortly after arriving for my shift one Sunday, I was asked to cover a parade. "What," I wondered, "no jogger update?" I was caught off guard. I had not had to cover a parade since my earliest days on the city desk. "Okay, I'm game," I thought, "There doesn't have to be a connection between the recent happenings in the office and the parade assignment." Still, I left for the parade wondering what the assignment might represent. When I arrived at the parade, as luck would have it, I discovered that Ben Ward was the grand marshal. It was too good an opportunity to lose. I got my parade story and turned toward Ward.

I approached him, the press pass around my neck identifying me. Perhaps he thought I wanted comments about his participation in the parade. Then I asked my question: "There are reports that in the wake of the jogger's rape, the Central Park precinct instituted a policy that called for black and Latino youth in groups larger than three to be removed from Central Park if they cannot produce identification. Is this accurate?" He seemed surprised, not sure how to respond.

"I'm not saying it's not so," Ward said, "But I have not received anything confirming that." Out of nowhere came a few of his press people; one said very firmly, "Natalie, that's enough." The nondenial would have to serve as confirmation. I now had all the necessary pieces. I could not wait to get back to the office and write it up.

## The News That's Fit to Print

The next day I was in Gil Spencer's office with a printout of my story. We stood in the middle of the room again as he read it. The story I submitted highlighted the civil rights violations that such policing practice represents. I had tried to anticipate all the possible questions Spencer could raise, but I was caught off guard once again.

"The cop from the precinct: what's his race?" Spencer asked. I was taken aback. From my first days on the city desk, I had been told including the race of a subject is not necessary unless the story is about a racial incident.

"You've got to be kidding me," I thought. "I think he's white," I said nonchalantly, adding, "I spoke to him over the phone." Spencer's question sounded to me like just another version of the old racial objectivity/reliability correlation test.

"Okay," he said, "we'll run it on Sunday." We turned away from each other, him toward his desk, me toward the exit. The race test had left a sour taste in my mouth and I never stopped to check his demeanor, measure his excitement about the story, or even look for his barely buried sense of humor.

The week went by and I eagerly anticipated the appearance of my story. There had been no questions for me on Friday as the Sunday paper was put to bed. The next day, Saturday, I was home when the phone rang. It was Spencer. Why was Spencer calling my house? He was not this closely involved in the day-to-day management of the newspaper; that is, he did not do line editing. What was he saying about my story? Problems? What problems? Finally, I was starting to make sense of some of his words.

"Natalie, we won't be able to run the story tomorrow," he said.

"Why?"

"There are some problems with it," he said.

He wrapped up the call saying, "We'll talk about it Monday."

I wondered what kind of internal upset the story had caused. Had it come from the city desk, the copy desk, the news desk? In the newsroom, there are other important pods of desks that exist above the one a reporter immediately answers to: for example, the copy desk and the news desk. Desk editors and any number of assistant editors staff the copy and news desks; no reporters work directly for them. The copy desk is made up of copy editors, who in some operations write headlines and in general read and assess each story for readability and potential libel. The news desk assesses stories based on their news value and may make a judgment about the size of type for a headline or how contextually well constructed a story is based on its perceived news value. This is a very powerful desk. It assesses the paper's overall position regarding what is presented to the world as news. The responsibility for framing stories and maintaining the integrity of the narrative in use rests with the news desk. This was where the narrative of the jogger story was shaped over time. The job of coordinating all of these desk editors and the stories they help bring to fruition belongs to the managing editor, who oversees the daily operation of the enterprise. Above the managing editor sits "*the* Editor," Spencer. He answers to the publisher, who can dictate policy on both the editorial and business sides of the paper. But, as I sat participating in that wooden conversation in which Spencer pulled my story, I thought, "If he didn't have the power to get a story in the paper, who did?"

I wondered about the paper's relationship with the police. Maybe this was an issue of not biting the hand that feeds you, especially given the subject. My story remained in limbo for weeks. Close to a month after I had submitted it, Spencer finally said, "We better get this story in the paper before it gets a longer beard." The article appeared on the obituary page of a Saturday paper, which typically had a circulation of about 200,000. The guts had been cut out of it. It had gone from 24–25 inches to about 10 inches. The most egregious injustice with the version that ran was the headline. It read, "Cops Targeted Youths?" The question mark that followed those words said it all: "We're doing our job as journalists to run this story. But, readers, you have all the reason in the world to question this allegation."

## The Frame That Mattered

The story that was printed did three things. It highlighted as a possible misinterpretation the charge made by some blacks and Latinos that they were the targets of illegal police action. It referenced a possible civil rights violation. And it showed conflicting police accounts of departmental practices. The following is an excerpt of the story:

## Cops Targeted Youths?

In the weeks after a white jogger was raped in Central Park, some young blacks and Latinos in the park were randomly stopped by cops and ordered to produce identification, two community groups charge.

A top police official denied the allegations, but officials of the Youth Action Program and the New York City Outward Bound Center said cops asked youths to identify themselves and in at least one instance told them to leave the park.

Another police official, who spoke on condition of anonymity, confirmed that for three weeks after the attack, people in the northern end of the park were stopped randomly and sometimes asked to produce identification.

He said that blacks and Latinos were not being singled out, but were found in greater concentration in that area of the park.

"They [black and Latino youths] were being harassed," said Sonia Bu, director of Youth Action Program, an East Harlem community center.

Capt. Charles Gunther Jr., of the Central Park Precinct, denied the allegations. "We don't arbitrarily stop people," he said.

But Police Commissioner Benjamin Ward said, "I'm not saying it's not so. But I have not received anything confirming that."

The police official who requested anonymity insisted that after the attack on the jogger more cops were diverted to the park and people were being stopped in an effort to make the police presence there more pronounced.

The extra police are still there, but cops are no longer stopping people, the official said yesterday.

Civil liberties attorney Richard Emery said it's illegal for the youths to be stopped unless there is "probable cause to believe that they are committing an offense." (Byfield 1989b: 11)[10]

Whether my editors could articulate it or not, I should have known that for them the story of the oppression of blacks had no place within the context of the coverage of a white woman allegedly raped or victimized by blacks. One frame practically canceled out the other. The message coded into their jogger narrative reiterated the reasons some whites have given since the end of the Civil War for their fear and distrust of blacks. That is, without structures like slavery to keep blacks in check, society would be subject to their "'brute' propensities" (Fredrickson 1971a: 259). The jogger coverage provides evidence of the survival of this frame, which in part made it salient to so many in the audience, particularly whites, when viewed through the lens of gender.

But coded into the narrative of the Outward Bound story was a very different message: It was the story of institutionalized oppression that many blacks could and would likely connect with on a personal level.[11] Here, repressive police tactics were a tool of oppression used for the exploitation and oppression of blacks—not for the protection of "white womanhood." For some blacks and Latinos, the message in the Outward Bound story would cast the jogger narrative in stark graphic relief, exposing its racist roots. Joe Klein, a writer at the time for the popular *New York Magazine,* tried to capture the status of race relations in the city in the wake of the jogger incident, and in so doing also exposed his own limited understanding of the racial frames used in this society to interpret everyday life. Klein's (1989) article about post-jogger race relations read, in part:

> There is also a new outbreak of the half-crazed paranoia and conspiracy-theorizing that have become quite popular in the black media in recent years. *The City Sun,* considered a "respectable" black weekly, published a truly vomitous account of the incident, including a fantasy description of the victim's body as "the American Ideal . . . a tiny body with round hips and pert buttocks, soft white thighs, slender calves, firm and high breasts." The author of this trash went on to opine that—if you omit the question of whether the rape actually occurred—the children who committed the Central Park abomination were being subjected to the same sort of treatment as the Scottsboro boys, the blacks falsely convicted of raping a white woman in Alabama 50 years ago. This sort of nonsense is of a piece with the increasing numbers of blacks nationally who, according to one pollster, believe that the drug crisis is a conspiracy on the part of white society to "commit genocide" against blacks. "The really disturbing thing is that the more solid the black middle class becomes," this pollster said, "the more its fundamental views of the issues seems [*sic*] to diverge from middle-class America."

The best I should have hoped for with the Outward Bound story—framed as it would be in the context of the jogger coverage—was that new police actions could and should have been expected. In fact, the *Daily News* had run such a story. Eight days after the first jogger story appeared and about a month before the Outward Bound story saw the light of day, an article about stepped-up police patrols in the northern section of Central Park ran on page three. An excerpt from that story follows:

### More Patrols Set for Park

Authorities announced steps yesterday to bolster security in Central Park as officials, clergymen and activists met to discuss ways to ease racial tensions caused by the rape and beating of a jogger.

The group met with Manhattan Borough President David Dinkins and announced a "unity march" to be held next week in Central Park, near the spot where the attack took place.

Many at the meeting said they fear the incident is being used to worsen racial tensions in the city—because the victim was white and the youths allegedly involved were black and Hispanic.

As to the attack, "We are obliged to do all we can to prevent this kind of thing from ever happening again," Dinkins said.

Seeking to prevent similar attacks, Parks Commissioner Henry Stern said there would be increased use of police decoys, mounted cops and patrols of volunteer runners equipped with walkie-talkies.

**May 8th Target**

The added patrols will target the northern end of the park and the 102d St. transverse—the east-to-west pathway where the woman was set upon by marauding teens April 19.

Stern said at a news conference that he hoped the added crimefighters would be in place by May 8. (Harris 1989: 3)

This earlier story seems to suggest that the police action was relatively innocuous. It does not hint at the types of reports I would get just a few weeks later. The reaction of the Sunday editor to my questioning the need for police patrols that would violate individual civil rights suggests the normalized expectation among those producing media content—and thus in the dominant culture—that blacks and Latinos have fewer rights under the law.

## Race Matters

The fallout from such perspectives continued across the city. Meanwhile, in the newsroom, a separate battle over race was being waged. Two notable things occurred during the summer after the debate about how to report the East Harlem kids' story. In Brooklyn, a black teen was killed by a group of white kids after venturing into a white ethnic enclave to look at a car he wanted to purchase. And, at the *Daily News,* the editor who hired me and who had supported me in the Outward Bound story, Gil Spencer, resigned from the paper after a fight with the publisher that had racial implications.

In August 1989, an African American teen from Bedford-Stuyvesant—a predominantly black section of Brooklyn—traveled with three friends to Bensonhurst—a predominantly white section of Brooklyn—to look at a used car. The black teens encountered a group of reportedly as many as thirty white teens who believed one of the blacks was there to see a local white girl. Some in the white group carried baseball bats, and at least one had a gun. They attacked the group of black kids, and Yusuf Hawkins was fatally shot (Blumenthal 1989).

I covered young Hawkins's funeral. The church could not hold the crowd that turned out, so I was not able to get in. I listened to the service over a speaker system with the throng in the streets. Most were black people, young and old, and they came from all over. I tried to image how this incident must resonate with older blacks who had been experiencing things like this all their lives. Politicians of all stripes, elected and otherwise, also attended. I remember particularly Governor Mario Cuomo and Reverend Al Sharpton, who were inside the church. There were also many reporters there. They stood out, but not just because of their press tags. Other than politicians, they were the only whites in attendance. After the service, many reporters followed the family to the cemetery for the burial.

I do not remember now if it was after the funeral or if it was another day when I attended an event organized by Reverend Sharpton about the Hawkins incident. It exposed me to some of the unmasked anger blacks in the margins felt about these interminable and lethal racial boundaries. The white journalists from major mass media outlets were gone. There I was, sitting down in the orchestra area, in the middle of a very hostile crowd that was angry and frustrated about the fatal shooting of Hawkins. I sat there with my press pass visibly hanging from a chain around my neck as Sharpton preached to the crowd and denounced the racism of the white mainstream media.[12] And he did not stop there: Sharpton continued his exhortation, painting the black journalists who worked for the white press as nothing but traitors. I sat there wishing I had tucked my press pass away and feeling a little bit like a race traitor. Other than recent history—meaning the lawsuit against the *Daily News* filed by the four black journalists—I was not aware of the specific racial history of mainstream newspapers. What I really wanted to do was scream out, "You don't know what it's like working in there. You get steamrolled. Everybody gets steamrolled."

The steamrolling continued—at a much higher level—the following month. Within the editorial board of the *Daily News,* principal board members and the publisher knocked heads over who to endorse in the city's ongoing mayoral campaign. They were divided between Manhattan Borough President David Dinkins, who was the city's first strong African American candidate for mayor, and incumbent Mayor Edward Koch (Jones 1989a). Gil Spencer, the editor-in-chief, and Michael Pakenham, the editorial page editor, wanted to back Dinkins. The publisher, James Hoge, wanted to support Koch for another term. Spencer lost that battle; shortly afterward, he resigned from the paper. The *New York Times* reported on the split (excerpted here):

## Mayoral Pick Creates Fight within Paper

The Daily News has endorsed Richard Ravitch for the Democratic mayoral nomination after a weeklong dispute in which the publisher was dissuaded from his first choice, Mayor Edward I. Koch, by strong opposition from top editorial staff members. They wanted the newspaper to endorse Borough President David N. Dinkins of Manhattan. . . .

The News has an editorial board of about six writers, presided over by Mr. Pakenham, that debates editorial policy. Mr. Pakenham makes a decision based on that discussion, and he can be overruled by Mr. Spencer, who can be overruled by Mr. Hoge.

### Used Power Before

Mr. Hoge has not demurred from using that power in political endorsements, the executive said. Mr. Hoge insisted that the paper endorse Ronald Reagan in 1984 and George Bush in 1988 over the objections of Mr. Spencer and many on the editorial board, the executive said.

The News endorsed Mr. Koch in both the Democratic primary and the general election in each of his three previous mayoral campaigns.

But in the last two years, The News has become one of the Mayor's most outspoken critics, especially for what the paper says is his insensitivity in racial matters. (Jones 1989a: B1)

## The Need for an Accounting

Long after I left the *Daily News* and began to study media as a sociologist, I continued to reflect on the significance of the events surrounding publication of the Outward Bound story. Was the civil rights attorney I had turned to not important enough? I had deliberately *not* chosen Mason or Maddox, black attorneys commonly involved in such matters. At the beginning of my time on the city desk, I likely would have pointed to the lack of racial diversity on the paper as the main reason for the reception my story received within the newsroom. After the Outward Bound story, I was not so sure; a black female reporter and a white male editor-in-chief could not get the paper to run a story contextualized as an issue of civil rights violation. It seemed almost like Dred Scott all over again—trying to get some whites to acknowledge that blacks do in fact have rights in the system.

This chapter has focused on the news media's internal organizational structure and its impact on newspaper content. Was there something particular about the structure of the newsroom that led to the Outward Bound story or the overall Central Park jogger coverage developing in the ways they did? The question must be raised, because the impression could be gotten that some "natural" process had allowed this to happen or that it was "common sense" that the jogger story would become a major news media event.[13] This is an issue that is at the heart of this study. Clearly, the historical background and the media's relationship to the police contributed to making this an important story. But what structures in the media made this story *so* major—one that, as one journalist put it, "thundered across the airwaves and into newsstands" (Hancock 2003)?

Some of the most notable aspects of how the *Daily News* handled the Outward Bound incident are the different layers of personnel and the various roles they played in the story selection process, the relative ability of outsiders to influence the process, and the relative significance of external stakeholders in the story—in this case the police versus black and Latino youths from Harlem. The newsroom discussions described in this chapter highlight the importance of the desk system in developing the type of perspective and meaning assigned to a story. I have also illustrated the process media organizations use to develop hegemonic representations of things like race, even when in the case of the Outward Bound story no obviously pejorative racial terms were used.

## The City Desk as the Hub of Coverage

The desk in a newsroom functions as a privileged space[14] inside the newsroom for all relationships with external individuals and institutions. Desks cover a combination of subjects and geographic areas. Within this privileged space, legitimation of institutions and legitimation of discourse from the external environment take place. The desk is the venue within the newsroom that selects what constitutes the news and ascribes meaning based on the myriad pieces of possible information from the external arena. In the fourteen years of coverage of the Central Park jogger story that I examined for this study, 92 percent of the 251 stories in the entire sample were generated from the city or metro desk: 88 percent of 103 articles from the *New York Times* and 95 percent of 148 articles from the *Daily News*. The selection of the reporters who covered the story was not based simply on skill level, or reporters' interests, or managers' discretion. The reporters who were a part of the coverage—myself included—were in a position to get the assignment largely because they worked for the city desk.[15]

Inside the *Daily News,* it appears as if the choice of the city desk as the main hub of coverage for the jogger case was "common sense." But, upon examination, the city desk was organized to include external institutions such as the local courts, the police, and the medical system—all institutions that were germane to the resolution of the incident that occurred in Central Park on the night of April 19, 1989. The city desk at the *News* also assumes the perspective of the "universal" city. What seems like "common sense" was a routinized process for using language to negotiate power between the internal and the external arenas. That is, a story will likely be placed with the city desk if media insiders determine that the main elements of the story represent external institutions that are part of the purview of that desk and significant to the "universal" city.

The jogger story was quite important to the main subject or topic desks at both the *Daily News* and the *New York Times*. The newsroom's internal administrative structure includes divisions that further separate external events by how they are arranged within the newspaper, which also affects how readers determine meaning. Gans (1979: 19) notes that newsmakers' decisions on media content are, in part, based on prominent geographic, economic, political, social, and governmental divisions or institutions in society at large, and this is evidenced by the structure of news products. For example, a newspaper or magazine may have sections on government, or business, or religion, or the law, or geographic regions. In the case of the *Times,* during this period, the metro section was a regional demarcation; in the *News,* the various suburban sections represented regional zones.

These sectional or regional placements are related to prominence. If news managers decide a story is big enough, it escapes placement in a regional or topical section of the paper and is placed in the main section—the "A" section of the *Times* or "up-front" in the *News.* While it could appear to readers that the Central Park jogger stories just ended up serendipitously with the placement they received, my content analysis indicates otherwise. The placement of stories is decided in the planning meetings I described earlier. So, it is no accident that some stories remain high in the public consciousness. Thus, the decision to place my Outward Bound story on the obituary page in a Saturday paper can be viewed as a type of censoring.

When viewing the Central Park jogger coverage in total, it is clear from the placement of the stories that news managers intended to put a great deal of emphasis on the case. My content analysis shows that the *New York Times* and the *Daily News* placed similar amounts of emphasis on the coverage. The findings for the entire sample ($N = 251$) show that about six out of ten of the stories (64 percent) received prominent placement over the fourteen years of coverage I assessed.[16] Over the full period, 65 percent of the stories in the *Times* and 63 percent of the stories in the *News* were prominently placed. During the stage of the coverage that I define as the first time period (roughly the first six weeks),[17] 72 percent of the *News* stories and 63 percent of the *Times* stories received prominent placement. While this study does not include comparative data on coverage of other types of stories over time, space is at a premium in the media, and the decision to devote this amount of important space to the coverage of the jogger case cannot be taken lightly. In sum, frequent prominent placement indicates the level of importance media content makers assign to a particular story. Although the amount of emphasis placed on the story changed somewhat during different periods of the coverage, the jogger story consistently got prominent placement, indicating to readers that it should be interpreted as a very important story. While the internal organization of the desk system—in which the purview of a desk can sometimes determine prominence—is one of the ways to determine the assigned level of prominence for a story, it is not the only way in which news media representations reproduce hegemonic order.

# The Media's Imprimatur

Previous studies (Herman and Chomsky 1988; van Dijk 1993b) have indicated that media managers use their power to veto sources; the ability to eliminate from stories the input from a particular source gives media enormous power in representation of a topic or a particular story. Media systems regularly work to control sources. At the *Daily News,* there was a centralized list of sources that reporters, particularly the new ones, were directed toward. The failure of the media to incorporate a multiplicity of perspectives in their content is often and rightly blamed for undermining demands for social justice in the larger society. But these critiques often do not spell out the social processes that enable the media to replicate hegemonic relationships through content production.

Surprisingly, my content analysis of the jogger coverage shows that the defense attorneys were the most heavily relied upon source in the overall coverage. As such, the featured narrative of the story could have been "White woman raped in Central Park; black and Latino youths railroaded by police." The question is, why was that not how it unfolded? How did the selection of the desk through which the jogger coverage was managed and delivered lead to the narrative we got? Could this selection have influenced the outcome of the trial? The purview of the desk will determine the closeness of the relationships that desk has with institutional sources outside of the media. Thus, it is important to look at the frequency of reliance on different sources of information. The answers to the questions raised, in general terms, ultimately address how the media produce knowledge, ideas, and culture and more specifically provide some explanations for how race is an integral part of the news producers' enterprise of reproducing culture and ideology.

The exclusion of some external institutional sources from the umbrella of a desk is not necessarily a self-conscious or conspiratorial attempt by internal media forces to exclude or delegitimate aspects of the external arena (S. Hall et al. 1978: 57–58). The disparity in the treatment of sources by newsroom managers is what Stuart Hall and colleagues describe as an articulation of "primary and secondary definers." Hall et al. posit the following:

> These two aspects of news production—the practical pressures of constantly working against the clock and the professional demands of impartiality and objectivity—combine to produce a systematically structured *over-accessing* to the media of those in powerful and privileged institutional positions. The media thus tend, faithfully and impartially, to reproduce symbolically the existing structure of power in society's institutional order. . . . The result of this structured preference given in the media to the opinions of the powerful is that these "spokesmen" become what we call the *primary definers* of topics. . . . The important

point about the structured relationship between the media and the primary institutional definers is that it permits the institutional definers to establish the initial definition or *primary interpretation* of the topic in question. This interpretation then "commands the field" in all subsequent treatment and sets the terms of reference within which all further coverage or debate takes place. (1978: 58)

Hall et al. (1978: 58) identify the media exercise of objectivity—which they loosely define as the media's gathering of "'objective' and 'authoritative' statements from 'accredited' sources"—as one of the reasons sources are stratified in media content. Hall et al. contend that those external institutional sources that are readily accessible to the media are likely to become primary definers, thus the media end up reproducing in their content the power structure in the external arena. But what of situations where two external institutional sources are powerful? In 2002, during the time when the office of the District Attorney petitioned the court to vacate the convictions of the original suspects in the jogger case after another man—Matias Reyes—confessed to being the lone rapist, the police opposed the DA's actions. However, the DA's point of view dominated coverage during that period, leaving the police in the unfamiliar role of secondary definers.

The point here is that given the power of the media in U.S. society, anyone or any institutional source can become a secondary definer relegated to having its perspective inserted into the primary definer's interpretation of "'what is at issue'" (S. Hall et al. 1978: 58). Cardinal O'Connor, the Archbishop of the Roman Catholic Archdiocese of New York from 1984 until his death in 2000, visited the suspects twice when they were incarcerated at Spofford Juvenile Center, a juvenile detention facility, and Rikers Island, the city's jail (Santangelo 1989). By the second visit, the *Daily News* reported on the attention the suspects and their families received from the Cardinal in a negative context. Mike Santangelo began his *Daily News* story with the following: "In spite of hundreds of critical letters and phone calls, Cardinal O'Connor met for a second time with six youths who were arrested in the rape and beating of a jogger in Central Park, he said yesterday" (1989: 18).

Another religious leader in the city reached out to one of the suspects, and he too received negative reports in the press. In this case, the priest was related to a reputed mob boss, and the *Daily News* pointed that out early in the story (Gearty 1989). And, in an unusual move, reporters showed up at the priest's church after mass to interview him. A prelate such as Cardinal O'Connor is regularly covered by the media, but a relatively minor priest normally does not get this type of media attention. A portion of the Gearty article about this priest's support of one of the suspects reads:

> A Bronx priest said yesterday that he posted $25,000 bail for one of the teens accused of raping the Central Park jogger "to give a boy one chance."
>
> The Rev. Louis Gigante, a former city councilman and the brother of reputed Genovese crime boss Vincent (The Chin) Gigante, called on his parishioners at St. Athanasius Church, Hunts Point, not to be guided by the environment in this city and nation that is bloodthirsty and vengeful.
>
> Gigante was addressing the controversy surrounding his decision last week to post the bail for Kevin Richardson, 14, of Manhattan. He said: "I only have to answer to God and to you, my parishioners."
>
> After the 9:30 A.M. Mass, Gigante met with reporters outside the Tiffany St. church and blamed the media for blowing the matter out of proportion. (1989: 7)

Placing religious leaders as secondary definers of these situations suggests that, in these instances, the media wanted to subordinate the role of the church to the role of the state. The media were not concerned with whatever rights the suspects had; they also sought to chastise others who stood up in support of those rights regardless of their position in the social structure.

Not surprisingly, the stratification of sources oftentimes reflects larger societal stratification along the lines of race, class, and gender. While my study did find that the media's reliance on institutional sources in the larger society is, in part, based on each source's inclusion within the desk's domain, external institutional sources—like anything else in the external arena—are subject to stratification for a number of reasons, including race, class, gender, or relative amount of power. For example, the media would rely heavily on the police as a source. Likewise, in this case it would be extremely unlikely that family members or other non-attorney advocates of the suspects would be in a position to be primary definers of issues. The newsroom administrative structure does not include a desk that specifically covers civil or human rights or the institution of the family in the same way that the international desk at a newspaper would cover the United Nations or a foreign head of state through an overseas bureau. I evaluated the reliance placed on institutional sources in the external arena that may or may not have corresponded with the internal desk system and found that inclusion within the purview of a desk is related to position in the social structure, which is dependent on race and class. Thus, being relied upon as a source is not just a consequence of inclusion within the purview of a desk but also a reflection of one's position in the social structure.

Notably, the defense attorneys were the most relied-upon source in the jogger case, but they are not within the purview of the city desk, nor are they—for the most part—in hegemonic positions over issues of race or class. The myriad defense attorneys for the suspects were a combination of public defenders and private attorneys, some of the latter with reputations for political radicalism (Chancer 2005: 50–59; T. Sullivan 1992: 57). Although newspapers in New York City may have reporters who cover the work of attorneys who serve as public defenders, the papers do not have bureaus at the Legal Aid Society nor do they cover public defenders or private attorneys as a beat. But these particular lawyers knew how to access the media and were covered regularly. Despite their prominence as sources, they remained as secondary definers in the mass media's process for incorporation of sources from the external arena. Timothy Sullivan's (1992) book that chronicled the jogger trials referred to one particular lawyer—who represented one of the teens charged in the attack on the jogger, but who remained peripheral to the main case—as follows:

> Joe Mack, an activist lawyer who wore his hair in long dreadlocks, had been retained for the [Michael] Briscoe family by the United Africa Movement. The UAM was a civil rights organization controlled by [Alton] Maddox, the Reverend Al Sharpton and attorney C. Vernon Mason, the trio that had, for a while, skillfully exploited Tawana Brawley, the black teenager whose explosive allegation of rape by a group of white men was later exposed as a fraud. (p. 57)

Language such as "skillfully exploited," the description of the Tawana Brawley case as "a fraud," as well as the reference to "long dreadlocks" indicate that these lawyers could not pass through mainstream boundaries. The lawyers representing the six main defendants in the Central Park jogger case included Michael "Mickey" Joseph, Robert "Bobby" Burns, William Kunstler, Peter Rivera, Howard Diller, C. Vernon Mason, Colin Moore, and Jesse Berman. Mason and Moore were locally famous civil rights attorneys, and Kunstler had an international reputation as a civil rights and constitutional lawyer.[18] The credibility of these lawyers seemed to have been in question because they aligned themselves politically with those at the bottom of society's hierarchy. My study's findings that indicated the inability of the defense attorney to impact the coverage in the jogger case supports the notion that stratification based on race, class, or relative amount of power in the external arena—combined with exclusion from the domain of the privileged space of the desk—relegates one to the status of secondary definer. Such status would no doubt affect the language or representations being used in the coverage.

# 6

# The "Facts" Emerge to Convict the Innocent

## The Narrative Is Set in Stone

**BY THE TIME** the story of the East Harlem kids being ejected from Central Park by the police had run, the jogger had been released from Metropolitan Hospital in Manhattan. Her departure had occurred two weeks earlier with a great deal of fanfare, all of which had been media generated (Byfield 1989d). My experiences at the *Daily News* had made me a more politicized journalist. I had not turned jaded or cynical; I had simply become more aware of how institutions, such as the media, shaped the world. I continued to follow developments about the jogger's health, but I had become less inclined to generate enterprise stories about other aspects of the case. Then a tip fell in my lap: An anonymous source informed me that a prosecutor had conducted an unsuccessful interview with the jogger about the attack. In other words, she had no recollection of what happened to her. In the competitive journalistic environment that shaped our media world, I did not anticipate that the *News* would want to risk getting beaten on this story regardless of which side could potentially benefit from the information being publicized. My expectations for a positive response from the city desk proved to be a mistake. The main narrative of the coverage had crystallized; stories that did not support it would not fly. That should have been the lesson I took away from the outcome of the Outward Bound story.

After that experience, I had no inclination to push for stories my editors did not want. But, I could not resist giving it a try in this case and went to them with the story of the jogger's lost memory.

"Oh, I don't know," said one of the city desk editors without commitment when I pitched the piece. The reluctance to run the story made me suspicious. Newspapers typically use the management of assignments as an administrative tool for keeping reporters in line (Sigelman 1973: 144–146; Wilson and Gutierrez

1995: 164). Was this response a message to me? If not, was it indicative of my editor's belief in the strength of the case against the teens? Did he really think of the case as such a "slam dunk" that the jogger's lack of memory would be irrelevant? Or was there something else going on of which I was unaware? My diminished confidence led me to ask supportive colleagues for advice.

"People tend to lose their memories with severe head injuries," one offered. "It may be a non-story."

"The DA's office is usually covered by court reporters. Maybe the editor is protecting their beat," another suggested.

As plausible as these rationales sounded, I did not buy them. I thought the story important enough to trump such considerations because it would concretely narrow down the kind of evidence the court case against the boys could and would eventually rely on. But self-doubt crept in nonetheless. Since my contribution to the coverage had centered primarily on the hospital and the jogger's physical condition, my normative state was to focus on those aspects of the case. However, the editors on the city desk, the copy desk, and the news desk—particularly the news desk—had a more global appreciation of the overall coverage, particularly in relation to other existing stories. Maybe some aspect of the coverage, of which I had been unaware, needed greater consideration.

The whole narrative of the coverage[1]—with its internal logic and external boundaries—was the purview of these editors. All of the up-front stories and many of the other articles in the paper went through the news desk. I understood the role of these editors even then. Upper echelon editors, such as the news desk's main editor, sometimes reminded me of the captains on an old-fashioned galleon, having to manage a huge internal staff while simultaneously maintaining awareness of the slightest shifting wind from the outside. An upper-level editor on the news desk would often stand by his or her desk in the newsroom and survey the sea of reporters hunched over computer terminals in the various topic/geographic divisions of the newsroom. I would sometimes wonder about the level of contemplation these editors put into the impact of the stories they produced. And I also speculated about their relationships with some of the individuals whose lives could be touched by these stories.[2]

Years later, as a sociologist, I would think about all of these news workers and their institutional relationships with each other and with other people outside media as they fulfilled their roles—just as I fulfilled my role, the reporter meeting with sources to gather information for my desk, the city desk. These editors would line edit our stories, then send them on to the reviewers above, the copy and news desk editors, who would assess all of the details—some of them invisible details to which the reader barely gave a second thought. But, in the context of evaluating what happened in the coverage of the Central Park jogger case, these unseen aspects seemed to carry the most weight, such as the source of the information, how the information became "fact," the structure of the story, and the logic of its narrative.

The up-front stories that the news desk appraised typically were hard news stories, the ones considered the most important, the ones filled with "factual" details (Tuchman 1978: 47).[3] The structure of hard news stories is oftentimes an inverted pyramid, with the lead containing the most newsworthy information. Below the lead, the subsequent information includes a wide array of relevant types of "facts": key quotes, supporting evidence, "the-other-side-of-the story" or alternative information in the form of quotes or supporting evidence, less important information, and background (Campbell, Martin, and Fabos 2005; Fairclough 1995; Tuchman 1978; van Dijk 1993b).

The "facts" of a hard news story represent information gathered following professionally accepted routines and organized in a particular order so that the information and the sources validate each other *and* tell the story—a system of internal self-validation that Tuchman (1978: 82–103) referred to as a "web of facticity." For example, had the prosecutor's office denied that the jogger had been interviewed, that information would not have been considered factual despite it having been generated from a source in a position to know. The presumption in journalism is that some sources are infinitely more credible than others, particularly those from some segments of officialdom. Thus, the use of certain sources in stories validates other types of required information as "facts." All of the pieces of information constructed as "facts" are held together by a logical relationship, which is known as "the narrative." In news stories, the narrative in and of itself plays a significant role in creating meaning (Tuchman 1978).

I think of the news desk as the site that maintains the paper's institutional memory,[4] that is, it closely manages the most important elements of the hard news stories—the lead, the "facts," and the narrative.[5] The news desk ensures that the "facts" reported in past papers are not contradicted in current editions unless acceptable new "facts" are allowed to supplant them. It also makes sure that the relationship among the "facts"—the narrative—is consistent, except when new, up-to-standard "facts" become a part of the story and change the direction of the narrative. This layering of the roles of the various desks in the editorial process ensures that changes in the direction of a story's narrative occur only with the approval of management.

To maintain the consistency of the jogger narrative, the editors circumscribed the meaning of the Outward Bound story for reasons that appear, in part, to be related to its lack of relevance to the narrative under construction. Had the initial refusal of my pitch to do a story about the jogger's loss of memory about the incident been another attempt to maintain narrative coherence? Some of my colleagues did not seem to think so. At the time I remained unsure; I had been, in part, trapped within the narrow focus of my part of the coverage. I had pitched the story to a city desk editor. I do not know if any discussion of the story pitch went beyond our conversation. Had that individual mentioned it to the news desk editor or the managing editor, those with an even more global purview in the case, those possibly more aware of the shifting winds in the outside world? I do not know, nor will I ever know.

But I am sure of one thing. Years later, as I studied the coverage academically, I came across a *Daily News* story I do not remember seeing at the time. I was not the first *News* reporter to raise the issue of the significance of the jogger's memory of the incident. A month before I took my story to the editors, the *News* ran a speculative article discussing the relevance of the jogger's memory:

### Jogger Case Looks Strong but Likely to Drag

The case against the teens charged in the rape of a Central Park Jogger appears strong, but legal procedures could drag out the trial process for more than a year and keep jurors from hearing some of the most damning confessions, law-enforcement experts say. . . .

The weaknesses in the case, they said, are that the victim probably will not be able to testify and there are no witnesses who are not suspected accomplices. (McCoy and Marques 1989: 5)

There it was. The *News* had already posited the possible lack of memory as a potential weakness in the case. But, when I went to a city desk editor a month later, providing a source for the information that the jogger did not really have any recollection of events, I had turned this speculative piece of information into a "fact" in the coverage, a "fact" that would not help the narrative. At the time, my editor's disinterest in that "fact" highlighted for me the amount of exploitation taking place in the coverage. It reflected an unrelenting desire to dismiss anything that would not support the police narrative and to exploit anything that would. Therefore, every "fact" about the jogger's healing could and would be subject to exploitation. Every denigrating "fact" about the personas and lifestyles of the accused teens could and would be subject to exploitation. And my very involvement as a black female serving at once as cover for possible accusations of racism and also as the person to cull this information about a woman violated in one of the worst ways a woman can be violated represented my own personal exploitation.

## Who Was behind the Narrative Used by the Press?

Over the years, as time has put distance between the incident and those of us who felt a sense of close connection to what transpired, I have asked myself why the guilt of these teenagers came across with such certitude in so many corners. Why were so many willing to buy the narrative? The media's repetition or coverage of particular "facts" over an extended period of time signals to an audience the importance or the veracity of those "facts." Even with the benefit of some hindsight long after the convictions had been handed down, I had half-assumed that the drumbeat of repetition of the same version of the original incident in a vast number of stories *combined* with repetition of the alleged confessions had created this certainty regarding the guilt of the boys within many sectors of the media and the audience.

Only when I conducted a content analysis of the coverage—that is, applied a scientific approach to study the articles presented to the public—did it become clear to me that the assuredness in the "facts" of the narrative could *not* have been based also on the alleged confessions. In my study of a sample of 251 articles from the *New York Daily News* and the *New York Times,* I found some discrepancies in the elemental "facts" used to construct the narrative. For the narrative to be accurate, in the mainstream media's journalistic terms, it needed to be based on properly sourced pieces of information that had been elevated to the status of "fact."

Much of the work in creating the narrative took place during the first phase of coverage, the period when I spent most of my time at the hospital. Fifty-five of the articles in the sample were published during this period. Of those stories, 84 percent included references to the original incident—it was a story subject in 60 percent of the articles and the lead in 24 percent. While the original incident was an oft-repeated theme, the alleged confessions were not echoed nearly as often. Only *one in four* (25 percent) of these stories included as a type of "fact" information about the alleged confessions as story subjects and in the lead. The relative paucity of use of the confessions as "fact" indicates their relative lack of significance to the construction of the narrative. This suggests that the narrative came from some other place. What was its genesis? It appears the narrative was so because the editors said it was so. And they said it was so because the police and the district attorney's office said it was so.

Not only was the building of the narrative problematic, but the journalistic construction of the "facts" was also questionable. It would seem that, based on standard journalistic principles, the original incident, sourced by the police, and the confessions, properly sourced (i.e., from information provided by defense attorneys), together should have provided the "facts" for constructing the narrative. Instead, the police were the main source for information on both the original incident and the alleged confessions.[6]

My content analysis showed that the police were paraphrased in 27 percent of the articles in the sample during this time period, while the defense attorneys for the teens were paraphrased in only 11 percent of the stories, when the facts and narrative were under construction. Journalists are often inclined to rely on a single source from officialdom to develop "facts" when they have no other choice. But it is not the professional preference to opt for this route over extended periods of coverage. It stands to reason that other sources would emerge. Compounding this reliance on the police as the main source in the jogger case was—as Rosenthal (1989) has argued—the paltry use of the term "alleged." In my sample of 251 stories, the term "alleged" showed up in only four of the fifty-five stories from the first phase of coverage. When the lead paragraphs of the fifty-five articles in the sample during the first time period were examined, the problem of the construction of the narrative became more glaring. As noted earlier, 24 percent of those articles mentioned the original incident in the lead. But only two of the articles mentioned the confessions—something so central to the legal case as well as the narrative—in the lead. None mentioned in the lead that the confessions were questionable. In short, the narrative came from the police and the district attorney.

The question remains: Why did the narrative resonate as factual? On the most basic level, the jogger narrative—"White woman jogging in black section of park raped and beaten nearly to death by black and Latino boys on a rampage"—echoes an old cultural narrative with two messages. That is, white women crossing racial boundaries are in grave danger, and blacks have a propensity to rape white women. The "facts" generated from the reporting in the first phase of the coverage unfolded to tell a modern-day cautionary tale based on an old cultural narrative from the days of traditional racism.

## Trying to Put on the Brakes

The one-sidedness of the coverage was not lost on everyone. In a column that would later prove to be prescient, Abe Rosenthal, the legendary former executive editor at the *New York Times* who worked as a columnist during this period, expressed his dismay at the tone of the coverage. In one of his pieces, which ran two weeks after the story broke, Rosenthal took his journalist colleagues across the city to task for ignoring the basic tenets of journalism. He wrote:

### The Guilty Verdict

Please, wait—just a few questions about that gang of thugs arrested for beating and raping the jogger in the park. Who ruled they are guilty? What judge listened to the argument of their defense lawyers? When did he make the crucial decision about admissibility of their confessions? What did he then say to the jury before they filed out to consider a verdict? What jury?

The city—public, press, officialdom, politicians—has convicted the arrested gang members before trial, face it. Now all that is left is to lock them up for the rest of their lives.

As a newspaperman, I have been watching and reading, astonished, as journalistic rules about not assuming or implying guilt before a trial went into the garbage can.

The people in jail are wolves—no, worse than animals, some kind of hideous mutants. That was what some of the tabloid columnists and headlines screamed. Most of the rest of the press, print and electronic, also has decided those people in jail are guilty and hardly bothers to hide it. Sprinkling an "alleged" here and there does not change the tone. (1989: 35)

Rosenthal based his criticism of the coverage on one of the foundations of the American justice system, a feature inherited through English common law: the right to a trial by jury—a jury of one's peers which, through established legal procedures, applies rules that determine the legal "facts" of a case. He found the prejudgment in the press a threat to American society just as dangerous as those who "beat and rape" (Rosenthal 1989). Rosenthal could challenge the coverage in this way because he wrote a column, and such freedom is within the nature of this particular type of newspaper content. Columns are based, in part, on the writer's opinion. In mainstream newspapers, columns are often placed in the editorial section, which is the province of management's official positions (Tuchman 1978; van Dijk 1993b). The structure of an editorial is different from that of a news article; editorials have a "persuasive function" and they are intended to be "argumentative" (van Dijk 1993b: 265–266). Rosenthal's column resided on the page opposite the editorial page—the op-ed page— and like editorials, columns are intended to be argumentative and persuasive; however, they are based on the writer's opinions, not management's. (Other papers may place their op-eds differently.) Rosenthal saw a narrative solidifying and warned that prejudging guilt with the then-indeterminate journalistic and legal "facts" in the case would place the U.S. Constitution in peril. At the time, very few in power listened.

## Hidden Narratives in the Text

The failure of the media community to hear the alarm Rosenthal sounded about the dangerous level of prejudgment in this case and the significance of ignoring the rules of journalistic and legal "facts" suggests that something else was going on here. This contemporary version of the old narrative also contained hidden messages. In the era of color-blind racism, where expressions of race are often hidden or coded, the existence of coded message should not be a surprise. Race and racial meanings have been transformed in the post–civil rights era, in which it is considered inappropriate to voice anti-black sentiment (Bonilla-Silva 2006; Entman 1992; Entman and Rojecki 2001).

I look back again at myself in that moment trying to navigate my managers at the *Daily News* and the sources to which I had access in order to gather and create "facts." My assignment to cover Metropolitan Hospital generated quotidian "facts" about the jogger's health which, in the context of the narrative, articulated the threat to her life that had resulted from her border crossing and produced a positive skew in the number of stories about micro-level changes in her medical condition. Forty-two percent of the stories in the 251 articles in my sample included information about the jogger's physical well-being (an element in establishing her iconic status for women; Bumiller 2008: 22–23). Surprising levels of detail about issues related to her health and recuperation became germane to the story. At the outset of the coverage, I naïvely thought that my assignment to report on the jogger's survival and recovery at the hospital kept me out of the swirling vortex of racial conflict at the center of the case. I could not have been more wrong. Instead, my work helped identify the rape as a "worthy" rape, which further articulated the jogger's position as an upper-class white woman. My role simply reinforced one of the foundations for the narrative.

## Learning to Read between the Lines

My early analysis of the events transpiring in the newsroom during the coverage of the Central Park jogger case represented my interpretation based on my position as a reporter. At the time, I lacked the language necessary to provide a more in-depth analysis of all that had been unfolding during that period. But my experience reporting on the case stayed with me, shaping my future. It made me intensely aware of two things: first, how little media audiences understood the system producing the information they used to make decisions in their lives, and, second, the role of language in shaping our world. I remained at the *Daily News* until 1993, when I was let go amid a massive downsizing that took place when Canadian-born real estate developer Mortimer Zuckerman bought the paper. I was largely ambivalent about returning to daily reporting and so I moved on.

I taught journalism for a while and then worked in the nonprofit world, where I consulted with administrators and teachers for kindergarten through grade twelve. My job was to help them incorporate media literacy into their curricula. I remember trying to convince these educators of the importance of getting young people to create their own media: "Kids will organically develop an awareness of the production behind the media they consume. Even more important, they will be able to articulate a perspective about it." The purpose of media literacy is to prevent audiences from become passive receivers of media messages.

While doing this, I became more interested in developing the necessary language to articulate my perspective of how the multifaceted system of media communication worked and how it impacted our lives. Thus, I studied sociology and became a cultural sociologist specializing in media. In the process, I came to see the text and images used in media products as a particular type of discourse or language, which I referred to as "media language," and this became the focus of my investigations. Other scholars who do related work include Alan Bell and Peter Garrett (1998), Norman Fairclough (1995), Roger Fowler (1991), and Tuen A. van Dijk (1988, 1991, 1993b). They are sometimes described as sociolinguists, and their work includes analyzing language to ferret out meaning or structures of power—sometimes hidden meaning. Such meanings are hidden not from the perspective of meanings concealed as a result of a conspiracy but as meanings encoded by the history and culture the language represents, the social milieu in question, and the types of communicative events taking place. I used this approach to critique the narrative employed in the coverage of the Central Park Jogger incident: "White woman jogging in black section of park raped and beaten nearly to death by black and Latino boys on a rampage." Foremost in my mind as I assessed this narrative was the fact that it emerged early in the coverage—long before all the components of the legal system had any time to assess the guilt or innocence of the alleged perpetrators.

After my work reporting on the jogger case had ended, I realized that even more messages had been encoded in the stories than I had originally recognized. But I was unable to articulate all of the elements and levels of the media language, their relationship to each other, and how they shaped even the hidden meanings. The narrative, as I discussed earlier, was a compilation of constructed "facts" in some sort of logical relationship—it represented one element of the text and only one level in which meaning was being created. As such, the narrative may be a manifest or apparent element of text in general (Barthes 1977) and of media language in particular (Fairclough 1995: 90–94). Implied or connotative meaning also exists in other units of media language or discourse. It resides in the "non-event-line-element" of the narrative (Fairclough 1995: 92). Such elements include words or phrases that frame or focus the narrative or that situate it in a particular place or time (Fairclough 1995: 92).

Part of what troubled me at the time I was working on the story—but that I was able to express only years later—were the connotative messages about citizenship and disenfranchisement also encoded in the development of "facts" and language used in the coverage. These other messages, which required teasing out, said, "The criminal justice system is fair. If blacks did not receive equal treatment, it was because they weren't deserving of it." The first message is an application of the color-blind ideology. It uses the frames of that ideology described as "minimalization" and "abstract liberalism" (Bonilla-Silva 2006: 28–29). In the former, mainstream social actors suggest that "discrimination is no longer a central factor affecting minorities' life chances"; the latter suggests that disparity in racial outcomes results from individual choices (Bonilla-Silva 2006: 29). The second hidden message hearkens to the days of the Penny Press, when a consistent narrative disputed the rights of blacks to be included in the union as citizens (Saxton 1984).

The evidence of these implied messages in other elements of the media language from the jogger reportage can be found in the failure of the media producers to adequately interrogate the criminal justice system—the police and the district attorneys—about their approach to the case. This failure represents the near-universal belief or ideological notion within the world of the mainstream media that the criminal justice system—like other institutions—operates with racial neutrality, and the instances when it does not are simply exceptions to the rule. That message exists as such an ideological totem in the media milieu that it is virtually invisible—or, at least, is only rarely directly articulated in media content. In the jogger coverage, I found the message hidden in the structure of the narrative, evidenced by the homological relationship between the sentences supplying important "facts" in the case and other elements of the media language or discourse[7] (Barthes 1977). I also found it in the monologic nature of press reports of what had transpired that night in Central Park (Fairclough 1995).[8] That is, in the presentation of events or a story, there is an institutional logic behind the sequence of sentences used to describe what happened. The media coverage of the Central Park jogger case represented the voice of the criminal justice system.

## Transition in the Coverage to the Legal Case against the Boys

In June, the jogger departed the city to undergo rehabilitation at Gaylord Hospital in Connecticut. After that, jogger stories from me were scarce relative to the sustained coverage of the first eight to ten weeks. I planned a trip to the rehabilitation hospital, but I did not expect much to come out of it; that is, I did not expect to see or interview the jogger. Summers always tended to be slower periods in the news. The buildup to the trials in the jogger incident was expected to start in earnest in the fall, when some important hearings would begin. I eagerly anticipated the defense cases.

The unfolding legal case had not looked good for the teens. In addition to the fairly direct messages about the dangers of racial boundary crossings for white women and the propensity of black men to rape white women, the hidden messages suggested a latent narrative. The longer I worked on the coverage, the more palpable those hidden messages had become. The latent narratives clearly communicated another meaning: these children who stood accused did not deserve justice. That certainly seemed to be the message coming out of the dismissal of the Outward Bound story.

The beginning of fall heralded the start of the pretrial hearings about admissible evidence. By this time, it was clear from my lack of assignments on the story that my involvement with the jogger coverage was a thing of the past. I spent the remainder of the fall drifting in and out of general assignment stories, hoping to get regular assignments and a regular byline. I floated the idea of me possibly getting a beat; that suggestion went unanswered. Then I heard there was a plan afoot to send me to Albany (New York's state capital)—in the winter. At some papers, a move to cover the statehouse, state legislature, and ancillary state agencies could be considered a promotion. At the *Daily News,* I was not so sure; the Albany bureau had been a one-person bureau for a while. So, I asked.

"Is this a promotion?" I directed my query to one of the editors in management.

"I dunno," he said, practically chuckling. That told me everything I needed to know. The phrase "cooling my heels in Albany" came up in the conversation. I do not remember now if I introduced it or if the editor had used it un-prompted by me. But I believed that the idea to send me to Albany did not reflect a plan for the development of my career at the *News*. It seemed more like an attempt to get me out of the thick of things in the city room. At the time, I interpreted it as payback for trying to insert an unwanted perspective into the jogger coverage.

## The Narrative Makes Everything Seem Pat

For me, the legal phase of the coverage began after the jogger left the city and continued until the charges against all the suspects were addressed. This inter-minably long period started about June 10, 1989, and extended into March 1991. When it began, the overall narrative of the coverage had already been set in stone. The prosecution's case, as presented in the media, characterized the events that had transpired in the park as a chronology, which suggested that the police had gathered all the necessary details to piece together what had happened in the park (Broussard et al. 1989). Press reports in this period covered several pretrial proceedings, including hearings about the judge who would preside over the trials as well as hearings about the admissibility of dif-ferent types of evidence. The media also reported that the defense planned to advance several motions, including the following: "A request to send the case back to Family Court for a closed trial. A challenge to the reliability of DNA genetic fingerprint testing. . . . A demand for separate trials for each defendant. A request for change of venue" (Clark 1989b: 31). Those hearings took place during the fall of 1989 and the winter and spring of 1990.

I read the stories figuratively and literally from a distance: I no longer cov-ered the story, and by the winter of 1990 I was in Albany. I had trouble keep-ing track of which lawyer represented which teen, and which teen was accused of doing what. I could not imagine that the general audience was any better able to sort through the complexities of the case. While all eyes had been kept on the jogger, readers were periodically reminded that other assaults had taken place in Central Park that night and that the boys also faced charges for attacks on four other joggers, a couple on a tandem bicycle, and a person described in the media and by the prosecutors as a "bum" (T. Sullivan 1992). I would come across those references, typically in the lower portions of stories about the jogger, and think, "Oh yeah, that's right. They're other things going on here."

During the earlier period, which I defined as the first phase of coverage, the media had relied heavily on the police and prosecutors as the "primary defin-ers"[9] of the narrative about what took place that night. This reliance gave the appearance that the press had abdicated its role as a platform for mediated communication. Compounding the problem of limited input from defense attorneys in the first time period of coverage, the press reports used a mono-logic reconstruction of the events. That logic supported the need of the police and prosecutors to build a case that would be tried in a court of law, a milieu that was supposed to have its own specific set of rules, particularly rules of evidence. In this situation, the story being promulgated involved a set of frenzied circumstances that included anywhere from thirty to fifty fairly young teen boys (press reports kept changing the number) who were running around in the dark in a wooded area of the park, some allegedly using weapons—which *may* have included parts of their bodies (fists and penis), a knife, a metal pipe, bricks, and rocks—against several people peacefully enjoying the park. The police and prosecutors needed to build a case that drew correlation and caus-ation between the kids who were allegedly a part of that group, the weapons used, and the injuries heaped on the people who were harassed and assaulted— as described by the injured parties or medical personnel. Accurately recon-structing events that drew these kinds of connections and that involved any-where from thirty to fifty kids going in separate directions in the dark in the woods would be a monumental task for anyone. The press readily bought the notion that the police could solve such a complex case in a mere twenty-four hours. No other voice with another type of reasoning was interjected into the narrative as presented in the mainstream press.

When I first read the early press reports, several important things jumped off the pages at me. First, it was several hours *after* the police began looking for and picking up teens who were possibly involved in the relatively more banal assaults in the park that the jogger's comatose, near-dead body was found at 1:30 A.M. Police and prosecutors, while trying to construct a logical sequence to explain what is often described vernacularly as "muggings," decided *then* that these alleged teen muggers, some of whom they had in custody, were now also rapists (Hornung 1990: 34). Thus, they sought evidence that would allow them to include the rape as part of the logical sequence of events that had transpired in the park. Early press reports also contained a quote from an NYPD spokes-person seemingly mocking the way in which the suspected kids were pointing fingers at each other: "Everyone's giving everyone else up here" (McKinley 1989). The point here is that what could only have been an extremely chaotic situation ended up being flattened into sentences neatly placed in a particular logical and chronological order that connected individual teen boys to various elements of a series of legally defined physical assaults and rape. The police and prosecutors were ready with the confessions and more stories representing evi-dence of how they drew the connections. In general, the press did not appear overly concerned with how the police got those confessions or the logic of the statements in them. The former was one of the criticisms Abe Rosenthal had heaped on his fellow journalists (Rosenthal 1989).

**TABLE 6.1**  Frequencies of Use of Sources in Coverage (in percent)

| Source | Time Periods 1–4: Apr 21, 1989– Dec 31, 2003 | Time Period 1: Apr 21, 1989– Jun 9, 1989 | Time Period 2: Jun 10, 1989– Mar 14, 1991 | Time Periods 3 and 4: Mar 15, 1991– Dec 31, 2003 |
|---|---|---|---|---|
| DA paraphrase | 30.0 | 20.4 | 29.2 | 38.2 |
| NYPD paraphrase | 26.7 | 27.3 | 25.0 | 28.9 |
| Defense attorney paraphrase | 36.3 | 10.9 | 50.0 | 32.9 |
| Suspects' families, etc. | 17.1 | 10.9 | 16.7 | 22.4 |
| Medical system | 11.6 | 36.4 | 4.2 | 5.3 |
| Mental health system | 1.2 | 0.0 | 0.8 | 2.6 |
| Religious institution | 2.8 | 9.1 | 1.7 | 0.0 |
| Academia | 0.4 | 0.0 | 0.0 | 1.3 |
| Legal system expert | 7.2 | 1.8 | 5.8 | 13.2 |
| Department of Corrections | 2.0 | 3.6 | 0.0 | 3.9 |
| Defendants | 8.8 | 1.8 | 9.2 | 13.2 |
| Jogger | 6.8 | 0.0 | 7.5 | 10.5 |
| Sample size | $N = 251$ | $N = 55$ | $N = 120$ | $N = 76$ |

During part of the legal phase, I watched the case intermittently from my post in Albany. With the opening available for the defense to present its side, would or could the narrative change? Giving some of those stories a close read as the volume of articles about the court proceedings picked up pace provided me with little evidence that the narrative would change. In journalistic terms, the introduction of new "facts," particularly by the defense attorneys, should have been able to chart a new course for the narrative. I had searched for those "facts" then, just as I searched for them while I studied the case in graduate school, and just as I search for them now. Always, I came away thinking, "There's nothing new there; no new narratives emerged." Why not?

In the content analysis I conducted many years later, I unearthed a surprising finding: During this phase of the coverage, the defense attorneys were paraphrased more than any other source, including the police and district attorneys. A defense attorney was paraphrased as a source in 50 percent of the legal-phase stories (the second time period in my analysis), as compared to a police representative in 25 percent of the stories and a district attorney in 29 percent (Table 6.1). The same process that constructed prosecution-sourced "facts" also created defense-sourced "facts." How could this be possible and yet no new narrative surface? Apparently the media's power does not stop at its ability to construct a narrative for the public; this power also plays a significant role in shaping meaning. The meaning came from several places: (1) the timing with which constructed "facts" became a part of the articles, (2) the invisible culturally and juridically based homological sequence used to order the sentences in the narrative, and (3) the source of those "facts." These factors all seem to be related.

## The Significance of Timing in the Construction of Meaning

When the media choose to construct an event as a "fact" in a story, the timing does not necessarily reflect the first emergence of the particular event. A "fact" or signifier of something in the world would not necessarily have the same impact or meaning if it had been introduced at a different point in time when a different set of events would contribute to shaping that meaning. Thus, the significance of the "facts" developed by the media is related to the moment at which those "facts" are presented as news. The dominant narrative may determine the appropriate time for presentation or sequencing of a "fact." I saw evidence of this first-hand when the *Daily News* city desk editor decided to temporarily withhold release of the "fact" that the Central Park jogger had no recollection of the attack. When later presented in the context of her release from Metropolitan Hospital, this piece of "breaking news" appeared to have little significance. The storyline that attracted the attention at that time was her release from acute care.

The media's power to shape meaning by controlling the timing of the creation of "facts" may have also played a role in the failure of an alternative narrative in the jogger case to come into view. Two stories that appeared in the *New York Times* in the summer of 1989 illustrate this power. At issue in this example is the diminished significance the media gave to the process used to appoint the judge who would preside over the case. The selection took place in early May, but readers of the *Times* did not find out until August that defense attorneys had opposed the procedure that had been applied. It took three months for the news managers at the *Times* to present the position of the defense on this matter in their publication. The dispute initially began during a May 10 arraignment to set bail for some of the accused. At the arraignment, defense attorneys had expected Justice Carol Berkman to follow the typical path and "spin the wheel" in the internal lottery system to select the trial judge. Instead, Berkman "announced that she had been ordered to bypass the standard procedure by which trial judges were randomly selected and . . . assign the case directly to Justice Thomas Galligan" (T. Sullivan 1992: 61).

In the following day's report about the arraignment, the *New York Times* did not mention this procedural anomaly or the defense attorneys' objections given Galligan's reputation for being prosecution-friendly. Instead, the paper's story the next day focused on the claim made by an anonymous source that the prosecution had an eyewitness to the attack (R. Sullivan 1989d). This report also included "facts"—which by the time of the trials had proved to be false— asserting that there was physical evidence linking the boys to the jogger. Thus, the *Times*'s next-day coverage of the May hearing essentially drew the focus of the audience toward the seemingly air-tight case of the district attorney and away from the defense attorneys' charges of bias in the selection process for the presiding judge—and away from the possibility that the deck was being stacked against the boys.

The appointed judge took the assignment, and *he* oversaw an August hearing to determine whether or not he should remain on the case. News managers at the *New York Times* used the story announcing this new hearing to inform their readers that defense attorneys had cried foul months earlier. This story, which finally revealed the bias charge, downplayed the accusation in three different ways (R. Sullivan 1989b).[10] First, with the headline "Critics Fault Selection of Judge in Jogger Case," the story after the August hearing did not make clear at the outset that it was the defense who was challenging the decision by the administrative judge to bypass the standard lottery system. Second, the number of mitigating circumstances used by the *Times* writer to justify the selection of Galligan obfuscated the explanation given by the administrative judge for Galligan's selection. Third, the article presented the reason for the change from the usual proceedings in the nineteenth paragraph of a twenty-six-paragraph story. Administrative Judge Milton Williams had picked Galligan because he doubted that most of the judges in the lottery pool could manage the style of defense that would likely be presented by the teens' attorneys: "Justice Williams ordered the wheel to be bypassed and the case assigned to Justice Galligan, whose name was not in the wheel, whose calendar was clear and who has a reputation for strict courtroom decorum and for being tough on flamboyant lawyers" (R. Sullivan 1989b: B4).

The article about the August hearing singled out Alton Maddox, who had been made infamous by the Tawana Brawley case. According to the *Times* report on that August hearing, Maddox had "promised protracted legal challenges" (R. Sullivan 1989b: B4). Maddox was an aggressive attorney who was a well-known and vigorous civil rights advocate. His willingness to manipulate the system to serve his ends—as evidenced in the Brawley case—had been cast in the press as a negative trait (McFadden et al. 1990). He would later be disbarred for his handling of the Brawley case.

The August story in the *New York Times* did not directly mention the existence of poor relationships between the court system and the defense attorneys, most of whom were black and Latino. The issue was simply not raised or addressed at all. Hidden from sight in the article was the fact that justices, defense attorneys, and prosecutors might have encountered each other multiple times in the courtroom or might have had interactions that could signify a relationship. Instead, these individuals were represented in the *Times* report and others as disconnected players assuming discrete roles in the upcoming drama. In fact, at least two of the defense attorneys had repeatedly challenged the power structures of the legal and political systems and decried them as racist. It would seem that the criteria for selecting a judge in the jogger case had extended beyond his ability to maintain "strict courtroom decorum" (R. Sullivan

1989b: B4) to include an ability to neutralize the defense attorneys' analyses of racial disparities in the criminal justice system. However, the timeline of the *New York Times* coverage of the selection process had essentially diverted attention from the issue until after it had been resolved in court.

## The Monologic Narrative Continues during the Trial

A few weeks before the pretrial hearings under Galligan began, a "breaking news" story in *Newsday* made it clear that the videotaped confessions had been leaked to the press (T. Sullivan 1992). *Newsday* reporter Timothy Clifford (1989) got a copy of about five hours of the videotaped confessions that had never before been made public. The article did not state it specifically, but it gave the impression that Clifford had heard or read the confessions of the six teens who were suspects at the time.[11] Although it would later be reported by Timothy Sullivan (1992) that publication of the story of the leaked tapes was explosive, that development does not stand out in my memory from that period.[12] The story focused on the confession of one of the teen suspects—Korey Wise—who would be a defendant in the first trial.

The article seemed to serve as a very public reminder to everyone—the public, the judge, the attorneys involved—of the horrific nature of the events of April 19 in Central Park. The story detailed Korey's confession, which included an argument the teens allegedly had in which they debated whether or not to kill the jogger after raping and beating her (Clifford 1989). In the piece, the teens come across more as cold-blooded, heartless killers, who could have been debating what movie to see, and less as frenzied young people who had lost control. The defense attorneys were not mentioned in the article; the story focused strictly on the content of the leaked tape(s). What was also mentioned in the story was that the teens' narratives about the attack were "conflicting." However, this aspect of the confessions was not interrogated by the reporter; Clifford (1989: 3) simply stated, "In their accounts of the rape, the suspects provide different lists of the people who participated and conflicting narrations of the attack."

The story based on the leaked tapes seemed to create more "facts" to support the denotative narrative promoted by the criminal justice system. The article also supported the connotative or hidden narrative. The writer's failure to question the contradictory confessional statements was related to that hidden narrative. That is, any possible questions that could be construed as supportive of the teens, creating even the appearance of justice, were not relevant to the media discourse in this case. This hidden meaning had been a feature of the coverage from the beginning, as evidenced by the criticism leveled at Cardinal O'Connor for visiting the teens at Rikers Island soon after their arrests. This *Newsday* story is an example of the use of a monologic discourse in the coverage for making meaning.

On October 10, 1989, the *New York Times* ran an article in which it established as a "fact" the failure of DNA tests to draw a connection between the six boys and the seminal fluid found on the jogger (R. Sullivan 1989c). This revelation had the potential to be a blow to the prosecution's case. But the *Times* used a variety of semantic and argumentation devices that undercut the significance of the findings. In a sleight of hand, semantically speaking, the author or the *Times* news managers used the technique of nominalization to introduce vagueness into the DNA findings. Nominalization removes the acting subjects from the sentence structure and gives the impression that no social actors are involved in particular outcomes (van Dijk 1993b: 257–258).

Thus, the *Times* article stated that FBI laboratory tests "appear inconclusive." The term "inconclusive" was not defined in the story. It was only during the trial that this issue would be articulated more clearly to state that the DNA samples from the boys did not match DNA found on the jogger. However, in this pretrial stage, in the public eye, obfuscation of the evidence served the prosecutors' interests. The piece also said, "If the Federal Bureau of Investigation tests fail to show a DNA match between the semen and the blood of any of the defendants, prosecutors said they would lose a critical piece of evidence" (R. Sullivan 1989c: B1). Again, use of the semantic technique of nominalization created meaning that hurt the defendants' cases. The crucial sentence construction is "the Federal Bureau of Investigation tests fail." This suggests that there was something wrong with the tests, not that the evidence was not there to support the allegation that the boys had raped the jogger.

Such reporting begs the question of whether the mainstream media were blindly unaware that they had ceded symbolic control to the prosecutors' office or were knowingly working in the interest of the criminal justice system. There is no way of knowing the answer without direct statements from journalists indicating that they had indeed operated with such goals. Van Dijk (1993b) would argue that the mainstream media share the same cognitive approach as the ruling elite; thus, the ruling elites' attitudes toward blacks and Latinos are reflected in media discourse. In this case, the mainstream press coverage continued through the fall of 1989 to be so favorable to the prosecution that when *Daily News* columnist Earl Caldwell, who is African American, wrote a column in January 1990 arguing that the prosecution's case was falling apart, the column seemed to have come out of nowhere. Caldwell's piece, titled "Jogger Rape Case Coming Unglued," made clear that the only "evidence" the prosecutors really had were the confessions, which were questionable. He also pointed out that white and black communities had divergent perceptions about the case because, in part, the FBI findings had been widely circulated within black communities.

In February 1990, Judge Galligan ruled that the confessions were admissible. Both the *Times* and the *Daily News* covered the pretrial hearings, and in their coverage, they noted complaints from the defense attorneys about the process used to acquire the confessions. But there were no in-depth investigations of the complaints made by the defense attorneys and other advocates for the suspects. In the mainstream press, the defense protests were typically reported in a very succinct manner, with the premise that the criminal justice system had worked appropriately. In a story about Judge Galligan's ruling to allow the confessions, *Times* reporter Ronald Sullivan noted:

> Defense lawyers argued for suppression on the grounds that some of the arrests had been unlawful, that the statements had been coerced and that the juvenile rights of five defendants had been repeatedly violated by the police and an assistant district attorney, Elizabeth Lederer, who took charge of the case soon after the first youths had been arrested. (1990b: B3)

Audiences did not get the opportunity to learn the details of *how* these alleged violations took place.

It was only in the popular alternative newspaper the *Village Voice,* with a much smaller circulation, that audiences could learn about possible problems with how the district attorney's office and the police had constructed their case. An investigative report published shortly before Judge Galligan's ruling about the admissibility of the confessions dissected the police department's early investigations in the case and noted several ways in which the rights of the young defendants had possibly been violated. The *Village Voice* story, titled "The Central Park Rape: The Case against the Prosecution," argued that police investigative methods had basically jeopardized the case against the boys (Hornung 1990). The writer, Rick Hornung, cited a number of alleged legal violations, including a detective's extended interview with fifteen-year-old Kevin Richardson without legal representation or a parent present in which Richardson implicated himself in an assault on "a 40-year-old male jogger with a pipe" and in "a murder" (1990: 30). It was only after these purported admissions that the detective read Richardson his rights (Hornung 1990: 30). The press reported that, in his ruling, Judge Galligan had essentially concluded that the teens had waived their rights to legal representation before they spoke to the police and that Miranda laws were not violated when police began questioning the teens without a lawyer present (Ingrassia 2002; R. Sullivan 1990a).

Hornung (1990) also alleged violation of the teens' rights with the police decision to take Steve Lopez and Raymond Santana into custody after they had received reports of joggers being assaulted in the park. Cops spotted Lopez and Santana with a large group of kids outside the park near 100th Street and Central Park West (on the opposite side of the park from where the attack on the jogger took place). As the police approached the group, all ran, with the exception of Lopez and Santana. Defense attorneys argued that probable cause did not exist for the police stop. Hornung stated:

> Adds Jesse Berman, who represents Lopez: "[Police Officer] Reynolds testified [in the pretrial hearing] that the group was not doing anything disorderly and were not carrying any weapons. He had *never* seen any of those youths in the park, nor had he seen any of them exit the park."
>
> When pressed about the probable cause to arrest Lopez and Santana, [Assistant District Attorney Elizabeth] Lederer concedes that it "is at very least a close issue," but claims in legal papers that "the police can hardly be faulted if the court with the benefit of calm reflection finds that they erred. . . . The police acted in good faith. In short, even if Raymond [Santana]'s arrest had been illegal, his statements were clearly not thereby tainted." (1990: 33)

In the interview with Hornung (1990), Ms. Lederer gave the impression an improper arrest did not have to matter. Her comments fit in with another connotative meaning or hidden narrative in the coverage—a message that questioned the legitimacy of any rights that blacks might attempt to exercise. For me, one of the most striking statements about the confessions in the mainstream press was the open acknowledgment that had the suspects been more affluent, their legal representation would have been handled differently and the confessions would have been a moot point. The *Times'* Ronald Sullivan wrote an article on the eve of the first trial that featured a section titled "Legal Pitfalls for the Poor," in which he stated:

> Along with resolving the case against the defendants, legal experts say the trial will delineate the legal pitfalls that often confront poor people accused of crime and the legal protections readily available to better-off suspects who know their rights and can afford a lawyer to protect them. (1990c: B3)

This issue of race and class bias in the criminal justice system was presented in the article as a matter of fact. It is not treated as a serious societal concern whose implications ought to be factored into how the public thought about the information coming from the district attorney's office in the jogger case or any other.

In March 1990, the court decided the defendants should be broken into three groups for trial; therefore there would be three separate trials. The prosecutors wanted to coordinate the trials based on the sequence in which evidence could best be revealed to help them present their cases. Yusef Salaam, Antron McCray, and Raymond Santana would be prosecuted in the first trial, which was scheduled for June 1990. Kevin Richardson and Korey Wise would be tried in October 1990. Steve Lopez, the sole defendant who never admitted to anything, would be tried last. (The charges against him would eventually be resolved in a plea bargain agreement a year later.) Throughout some of these decisions coming out of the pretrial hearings, I was based in Albany. Like the rest of the newspaper audience, I was being primed[13] for guilty verdicts through the framing of the coverage, which employed a particular narrative and incorporated a monologic discourse that represented elite interests.

The original trial date had been set for April 1990, but shortly before the appointed day, the prosecution found more evidence: Semen was discovered on a sock that had been collected from the crime scene. Initially, this revelation postponed the trial indefinitely. The sock had to be subjected to DNA tests, and it was determined that the DNA there matched previously unidentified semen found inside the jogger. (Years later, this semen would prove to belong to Matias Reyes, the person who had actually raped the jogger.) At the time, the prosecution concluded that the DNA simply matched a person the police had not caught who was present at the scene of the rape with the other boys. An alternative narrative was offered by the defense and supporters of the boys: "Someone else committed the rape of the jogger." But, during this period before the first trial, the mainstream media coverage made all evidence fit the prosecution's narrative.

## The Multidimensional Significance of Sourcing

The legal phase of coverage (the second time period in my content analysis) made clear that having a source—not even necessarily a source from officialdom— was enough to "factualize" information. Also important to constructing facts and meaning is who the source represents and the source's position relative to other sources who could serve the narrative. It is very important to keep in mind that there were few challenges to the prosecution's argument in the articles that appeared during the first phase of coverage. The defense attorneys were paraphrased in 11 percent of those stories, which were published as the narrative was being constructed. This stands in contrast to the police, who were paraphrased in 27 percent of the articles during that time period. (See Table 6.1.) In the description of events, as individuals we all use a monologic approach to construct narratives (Fairclough 1995). That is, in the presentation of events or a story, there is only one type of logic behind the sequence of sentences used to describe the event. But, the press, a zone for mediated communication among a variety of parties, often presents reports that are dialogic, that is, featuring more than one voice in the narrative (Fairclough 1998).

During the legal phase of coverage, when it would clearly have been easier to construct dialogic stories incorporating the position of the defense attorneys, the media failed in this regard. It was not that reporters ignored the defense attorneys; at least one was cited in half of the stories in my sample during this time period. But simple inclusion in the reportage was not enough to ensure significance as a meaning-making element of the narrative. Thus, even with the inclusion of defense positions, the narrative remained monologic.

## No Way Out

The first trial started in earnest on June 26, 1990, and it seemed to be over before it even began. With the defense losing key decisions in the pretrial hearings—regarding admissibility of the DNA "evidence" and the confessions—from where I sat it was hard to imagine anything but guilty verdicts. The case began with the presentation of the prosecution's witnesses for the muggings and assaults on other joggers, the police, the DNA analysis from the FBI, and the jogger herself.

There were several other important moments during the prosecution's presentation of the case, when the defense attorneys tried to unravel the prosecution's logic or shift the narrative. The defense attorney for Yusef Salaam argued during a cross-examination of Dr. Robert Kurtz, the head of Metropolitan Hospital's Surgical Intensive Care Unit, that the jogger did not show signs of rape. Peter Rivera, who represented Raymond Santana, also seemed to argue that there was no proof of a gang rape. It seemed that they hoped to introduce into evidence the "fact" that the jogger did not exhibit signs of a rape or gang rape (Alvarez 1990e). The *Daily News* presented the testimony in a story headlined, "No Evidence of Rape, Says Lawyer in Cross-Exam: Jogger Defense Curve." Such assertions had been part of the discourse among supporters of the boys from the very beginning (claims of this nature have historical origins that I discuss in Chapter 3). But, in the context of the mainstream media discourse, such claims came across as the province of kooks and charlatans. When this language came from courtroom spectators who were there to support the boys or from groups who picketed in front of the court, the purveyors of these words were described in the press as "ignorant," "racist," and "race-baiters."

On another day of testimony, the FBI's DNA analyst made it clear that the "genetic fingerprint test" indicated that the tests were not "inconclusive," but rather that the DNA found on the jogger "did not belong to any of the suspects in the case or to the jogger's boyfriend" (Alvarez 1990b: 3). There were no follow-up stories in the media that questioned the veracity of the earlier reports about hair and blood samples found on the jogger that matched those of the young suspects.

Another major moment in the presentation of the prosecution's case was the day the jogger testified, July 16, 1990. Coverage in the *Daily News* the next

**TABLE 6.2**  Frequencies of Articles that Included the Listed Indicators for Victimhood (in percent)

| Victimhood Indicators | Time Periods 1–4: Apr 21, 1989– Dec 31, 2003 | Time Period 1: Apr 21, 1989– Jun 9, 1989 | Time Period 2: Jun 10, 1989– Mar 14, 1991 | Time Periods 3 and 4: Mar 15, 1991– Dec 31, 2003 |
|---|---|---|---|---|
| Random | 5.6 | 12.7 | 4.2 | 2.6 |
| [Left] Unconscious | 9.2 | 18.2 | 5.8 | 7.9 |
| Victim | 38.2 | 58.2 | 33.3 | 31.6 |
| Sample size | $N = 251$ | $N = 55$ | $N = 120$ | $N = 76$ |

day included several stories led by a front page that declared "Jogger Takes the Stand: She Didn't Weep, She Didn't Shudder. . . ." The reports inside presented her appearance at the trial as heroic. In the content analysis, I tallied words and terms that indicated the jogger's status as a victim (see Table 6.2). During the first period of coverage, 64 percent of the articles included *at least* one indicator for the concept of victimhood; but during the second time period that percentage fell to 37, representing a 27 percent drop in the rate of inclusion of victimhood indicators. (See Table 8.1, where the data are summarized.) It was as if once the legal phase of the case began and the jogger had her day in court, her status as a victim diminished. A *Daily News* editorial that appeared shortly after her testimony said:

## A Profile in Courage
When the Central Park jogger took the stand the only thing unsteady about her was her walk. Her voice, her words, her testimony were sure and certain. She conducted herself with an indomitable dignity. It put her detractors to shame. . . .

   This trial is about more than the rape and brutalization of a single woman. It is about the rape and the brutalization of a city. The jogger is a symbol of all that's wrong here. And all that's right, because she is nothing less than an inspiration.[14]

Shortly before the prosecution rested its case, a fairly balanced piece was published in the *New York Times*. It was one of the stories in my content analysis sample—a "Reporter's Notebook" item written by William Glaberson (1990)—and it made the point that the presentation of all the evidence thus far could support either side. Glaberson was not the usual *Times* reporter for the trial, and he argued that, given the evidence, the well-covered prosecution argument that the teens' evening of "wilding" culminated in the rape of the jogger was equally as plausible as the defense's counterargument that these black and Latino boys were being railroaded. A "Reporter's Notebook" piece in the *Times* falls somewhere between a column and a news story. Items classified as such share with the reader "color" from stories in the news or a reporter's take on transpiring events. These articles are not as driven as some columns are by the writer's opinion. And they offer a less formal presentation of news than the strait-jacketed inverted pyramid structure of hard news articles (discussed earlier).

In his "Reporter's Notebook" piece, Glaberson (1990) referenced the testimony of a New York City detective who read into evidence a statement he supposedly took from one of the accused teens, Raymond Santana. The point of the article was clear: The statement did not ring true as the words of an average fifteen-year-old. Glaberson's piece included portions of the confession Santana allegedly gave to the police, which was read into evidence by the police witness:

> "On April 19, 1989, at approximately 20:30 hours," Mr. Santana's statement began according to the detective, "I was at the Taft Projects in the vicinity of 113th Street."
>
> The statement referred to "male whites" and "male blacks" and it detailed a group of 33 people who went to Central Park "with the intent to rob cyclists and joggers."
>
> "We all walked southbound in the park in the vicinity of 105th Street," the statement continued, "when we all surrounded a male Hispanic who we were going to assault."
>
> The night ended, when the "police came and apprehended me and others," the statement read. (Glaberson 1990: B1)

The last part of the prosecution's case focused on the confessions. During the legal phase of coverage (Time Period 2), fewer published reports noted that the defense considered the confessions questionable, 37 percent, as compared to the number of stories that treated the confessions as unchallengeable "facts," 58 percent. More significant than the smaller number of stories that mentioned the questionable nature of the confessions was the way in which the mainstream media had failed to elaborate on the problems the defense had with how the confessions had been obtained by the district attorney and the police. Published reports in the mainstream, black, and alternative presses made it clear that the defense attorneys thought that the judge's admission of the confessions into evidence made it next to impossible for the teen suspects to be acquitted.

The defense took about a week to present their side of the case, as compared to the month used by the prosecution. The focus of much of the defense attorneys' rebuttal was that the confessions were both ill-gotten and false. Several moments in the brief defense stood out for me. The lawyers appeared to working at cross purposes. Against the wishes of the other defense attorneys, the attorney for Yusef Salaam allowed him to take the stand. He was the only one of the boys who testified. Press reports indicate that, in his testimony, he seemed to place himself in the park that night.

On August 18, after ten days of deliberation, the jury returned a guilty verdict. In one of the stories covering the verdict, which did not receive prominent placement, the *New York Times* reported that one juror had initially held out on convicting Antron McCray of rape due to "the conflicts between Mr. McCray's testimony and the police version of the attack" (Barron 1990). Eventually the juror acceded to the majority position of the panel. The three defendants were found guilty of rape and assault; they were acquitted of the attempted murder charge. The following month, they were sentenced as juveniles to five to ten years of imprisonment.

The second jogger trial, in which Kevin Richardson and Korey Wise were defendants, began in November 1990. The second case did not receive as much press attention as the first. By this time, the *Daily News* strike was under way, and one less competing paper can reduce the amount of coverage a story receives— that is the nature of media competition. A little more than a month after the trial began, the two defendants were found guilty. Richardson was found guilty of attempted murder, the only one of the boys convicted on that charge. He too would receive a five- to ten-year juvenile sentence (Cantwell 1991a). Steve Lopez pled guilty to reduced charges in January 1991; he was sentenced in March 1991. The case would remain a symbol of what some in the media termed "wanton urban violence" (Cantwell 1991b: 7).

Between the spring of 1991 and late 2001, when the district attorney's office quietly reopened the investigation into the attack on Trisha Meili, the Central Park jogger case was used in the media as an occasional reference in the coverage of other stories. It showed up as background information in some articles, particularly those involving black and Latino males and sexual assault. The term "wilding" became synonymous with black and Latino youth, and researchers found it was almost exclusively used to describe violent behavior allegedly committed by minority youth (Welch, Price, and Yankey 2002, 2004). There were relatively few articles during this period in which the jogger incident was the specific subject of focus. In setting up my content analysis, I referred to this phase of coverage as Time Period 3. However, due to the relatively small numbers of articles in the sample during this phase, in reporting the data I have combined this time period with the final one, which began when the district attorney's office reopened the case.

# 7

# The Case Falls Apart
## *Media's Brief Mea Culpa*

### The Fog of War Burned Away

**AS IS OBVIOUS** by now, I left journalism for other pastures. My desire to teach and write about what I had experienced in that field prompted me to return to graduate school. I chose sociology this time and plunged into my classes with gusto. I planned to study the media coverage of the Central Park jogger case. Eleven years had passed, and I had never really put it behind me.

Between my time at the *Daily News* and beginning graduate school, I taught journalism. In those classes, I talked about a lot of the stories I had worked on—the ones management had privileged and the ones they had dismissed. But the jogger case stood out. To me the story was then, as it is now, a classical case study in how news—and consequently reality—is constructed by media. It is also a great example of how language operates: how, as a system of knowledge, language reflects as well as reproduces the stratifications and disparities in any society. In 2002, purely by chance, I heard that the Manhattan district attorney's office had quietly reopened their investigation into the case. New evidence—the confession of convicted serial rapist and murderer Matias Reyes—led to the renewed inquiries. The more advanced DNA tests available at the time connected the unidentified semen found on the jogger to Reyes. A review of the old controversial confessions only then highlighted some inconsistencies in the teens' "statements." Some members of the press got wind of this and started covering the new developments. As it became clearer to those involved what was going on, it was hard to keep it out of the news.

The story that had made sense to police and prosecutors in 1989 that a group of thirty to fifty black and Latino boys were in the park looking for people to attack in any way possible, including rape, suddenly fell apart. It also seemed that on more than one occasion in the past, a possible solution to the case had been in the hands of the authorities. As the new "facts" developed, a *New York Times* article noted that two days before the jogger's rape, Reyes had raped someone else in the park (McFadden and Saulny 2002). That rape occurred close to the site of the attack on the jogger; the police had information about this rape but did not release it to the defense attorneys (Dwyer 2002). One of the *Daily News* articles about the latest turn of events noted that the DA's office had two sets of DNA markers from Reyes (Ross, McQuillan, and Lombardi 2002). One, a previously unidentified marker from the jogger case, did not match any of the suspects or the victim's boyfriend. The other marker was from one of Reyes' known rapes. The same assistant district attorney handled both sets of DNA markers. They were, of course, identical, but that went unnoticed by the ADA because Reyes was not a likely candidate for the Central Park rape because he typically acted alone (Ross, McQuillan, and Lombardi 2002).

The police and the district attorneys had gathered? found? created? evidence to support what they considered the most plausible story—a gang rape of a white woman by a group of black and Latino teens. The news media had been so stuck on this narrative that information that ran counter to it did not register with them or was ignored. Now they had to reconsider everything and figure out how such a travesty could have occurred. As the reinvestigation unfolded in 2002, I wondered why it had been so impossible for the press to see some of the inconsistencies that were being revealed in the new examination of the case.

In his analysis of the structure of narratives, Barthes (1977) makes the point that messages can be hidden in plain sight. When we ascertain meaning only by following the horizontal sequence of words, we miss a lot. To derive meaning we must also incorporate all other aspects of the structure of the narrative, such as the plot line or story and the background and history of the narrative's creator. In the context of media, the last two from that list could be equated with what is referred to as the "social dimensions of newsmaking" (van Dijk 1993b: 246–248). Without moving from one plane to the next, messages remain invisible. Barthes gives as an example Edgar Allan Poe's story "The Purloined Letter." Hiding in plain sight, the letter remained unseen by the police inspector searching for it due to his failure to consider the perspective of the one who concealed the letter. For mainstream journalists covering the jogger case, the prosecution's narrative made perfect sense. Only twelve articles out of my sample of 251 followed journalistic practices and used the term "alleged." Many authors never stopped to consider the history of the relationship of the criminal justice system to blacks and Latinos. They seemed frighteningly unaware of the old familiar ring to the jogger narrative—the connection of the discourse articulating the "savagery-of-nonwhites" narrative to the nation's racialized roots.[1]

The coverage was not contextualized as a story about the rape culture in our society. The context in which the information was presented was that of a white woman brutalized by "savage" black and Latino boys. The old cultural narrative about black men's propensity to rape white women is so normative in mainstream discourse that most white journalists appear to be woefully unaware when it is being put into play. Had they paid closer attention to the discourse, it would also have been possible for them to see the other narrative that remained hidden—"The criminal justice system is fair. If blacks did not receive equal treatment it is because they weren't deserving of it." But the inability of the producers of mainstream media to connect the dots of these narratives rendered all of this history invisible at the time of the coverage. Then, suddenly, in 2002, with the new information introduced and legitimized by the DA's office, there was a reconsideration of the original "facts" of the case. Black-run organizations and black individuals could have said the same thing until the end of time, but the narrative would not have changed without acceptance by important elements of the white power structure.

## A Brief Public Airing

Some reporters who had worked on the initial coverage—some still practicing at the time the case fell apart—publicly commented on their reactions to the new "facts" that absolved the teens of the rape. A group of them, which began meeting in 1989 in the wake of the incident and continued meeting "sporadically" for a decade after that, met again in November 2002 as Reyes's confession was under investigation (Hancock 2003: 39). They discussed the new "facts" and their thoughts about them. A former *Daily News* reporter, LynNell Hancock, wrote an article published in the *Columbia Journalism Review* about the reporters' reactions. Like me, some of these journalists talked about the "top-down narrative" that management would not allow anyone to challenge (Hancock 2003). But, if we use the long lens of history, this narrative is not exceedingly different from others used by media when people of color, particularly black men, are involved—it articulates blacks' position as a "marginalized other" in the dominant culture. Hancock's report does not mention whether concerns about repeating the old cultural narratives were expressed by any of the journalists involved.

Within the current era of color-blind racism in the media, we get language that uses fewer obviously racial terms, such as "savage," and a prevalence of other kinds of terms, such as words that are indicators for class or gender. These class and gender terms become stand-ins for race or latent racial indicators. While "rape" is an indicator of gender, it is also a latent or hidden racial term in this society. (See Table 3.4.) Race is there and not there simultaneously. When manifestly racial terms are used within the color-blind ideology, they are treated in the mainstream as if they are unconnected to historical or material realities of race.

The jogger coverage did distinguish itself by the willingness of the main-stream media to use pejorative language intended to diminish, degrade, and animalize. However, my content analysis showed that aside from the obvious racial references, the more frequently used terms referred to class, gender, and age. Those indicators served as stand-ins for race. Unique in this case was the way age took over the role of race and was used as a vehicle to elide race.

The coverage began with words like "wilding," "wolfpack," and "savage" and progressed to even "mutant."[2] Establishment of the boys as "other" continued throughout the reporting of the case. An example of this "otherization" without the use of animalistic terms can be seen in a column written by Bob Herbert, an African American former columnist and city desk editor for the *Daily News*. It is a report of one of the early days of the first trial and ran more than a year after the incident:

> This is not a pretty trio. Yesterday they sat together at the left-hand corner of the defense table. Some grown-ups had tried to dress them like divinity students or something, but it didn't work.
>
> McCray, 16, is little, a tiny headed, frightened, wimpish pipsqueak who looked for all the world like a black Joey Fama.[3]
>
> Salaam, also 16, was tall and awkward. He wore a gray suit and a red tie but the resemblance to a divinity student fell apart as soon as you looked at his ankles. His socks were the color of pistachio ice cream. (Herbert 1990: 4)

The important issue here is not the willingness to otherize with hidden or coded language but how, in the era of color-blind racism, other intersecting forms of domination such as class, gender, and age can mask racial oppression. When race, class, gender, *and* age intersect, they form a unique social location. A young middle-class or lower-income black person exists within the bounds of life experiences created by these intersecting race/class/gender/age structures of domination and oppression. The issue is how age works to transform the other structures.

The media did such a good job of racially otherizing the young suspects that some of the journalists with mainstream newspapers covering the case at the time it unfolded seemed to be unaware of how young they really were (Hancock 2003). Within the social locations of low- *and* middle-income black and Latino males, "young age" more or less equates with being devoid of childhood and any rights or privileges that bestows. The level of threat these children are perceived as presenting to society—*because* of their race and *regardless* of their class—forces upon them adult-type consequences for which they are unprepared developmentally to handle. The things they must consider to survive in the larger society from their social locations are vastly different from the normative experiences of young low- and middle-class white males. In the era of color-blindness, the role race plays here is almost imperceptible because the rationale for giving these young people adult consequences is to say they are doing adult things. Despite their young ages, the accused in this case were not seen as children and thus lost many of the rights and privileges of children. Black newspapers such as the *Amsterdam News* and the *City Sun* did not lose sight of their ages, however—the issue was one of the pillars of their demand for fair treatment of the teens. The *Amsterdam News* published the jogger's name—to much criticism from the mainstream press—precisely because of the disregard of the mainstream press for its traditional tenet of protecting youth by not identifying by name underage suspects or defendants. Journalist Timothy Sullivan (1992), who covered the case for Court TV, noted in his book the actions taken by Wilbert Tatum, who was then publisher of the *Amsterdam News,* to protect or defend the young suspects. Sullivan wrote:

> Back in April [1989] the *Amsterdam News* had been one of the first news organizations to report [the jogger's] name. Since then the vast majority of media had continued to withhold her identity, with occasional exceptions among black newspapers and radio stations. To justify that decision black editors pointed to two factors: The defendants had a constitutional right to publicly confront their accuser, and the white media had unfairly abandoned another traditional policy when they publicized the names and photos of the juvenile suspects, even before they were indicted. (1992: 91)

When the case fell apart years later, some of the mainstream journalists articulated their lack of awareness of this important component of the case and expressed surprise at the ages of the accused teens:

> Others conceded that they had never regarded the suspects as teenagers. (The boys' ages, in fact, had rarely been a focus in press reports.) "I was really surprised in reading recent accounts, to learn that the defendants were only fourteen, fifteen, and sixteen at the time," says *Newsday*'s Sheryl McCarthy, one of the few African-American journalists who covered the case for the mainstream press. (Hancock 2003: 39)

While Hancock (2003) supports Sheryl McCarthy's position and argues that the media "rarely" focused on the young suspects' ages, my content analysis found otherwise. My analysis indicated that the age of the young suspects was in fact a very important part of the coverage (see Table 7.1) and at times was even a statistically significant factor.[4] The prominent placement of articles that used a high number of words and terms that referenced age did not happen by

**TABLE 7.1**   Frequencies of Articles That Included the Listed Indicators for Age (in percent)

| Age Indicators | Time Periods 1–4: Apr 21, 1989– Dec 31, 2003 | Time Period 1: Apr 21, 1989– Jun 9, 1989 | Time Period 2: Jun 10, 1989– Mar 14, 1991 | Time Periods 3 and 4: Mar 15, 1991– Dec 31, 2003 |
|---|---|---|---|---|
| Youth | 50.2 | 54.5 | 54.2 | 40.8 |
| Teen, teenager | 46.2 | 61.8 | 34.2 | 53.9 |
| Young man | 17.9 | 5.5 | 5.0 | 47.4 |
| Children | 8.4 | 14.5 | 2.5 | 13.2 |
| Juvenile | 13.1 | 18.5 | 15.8 | 5.3 |
| Adult | 11.6 | 12.7 | 11.7 | 10.5 |
| Sample size | $N = 251$ | $N = 55$ | $N = 120$ | $N = 76$ |

chance. During the first time period, when the narrative was being constructed, at least one reference to the suspects' ages was used in 89 percent of the stories. (See Table 8.1, where the data are summarized.)

As the journalists who worked on the jogger case explored their own consciences to explain the coverage, they also raised the possibility that the climate in the city was partially responsible for the media decision-making at the time (Hancock 2003). The term "climate" was an often-used euphemism for the "seething racial tensions" and the "rising rate of youth violence" in the city. Blaming the climate is a curious point for defense of the media's actions. If anything, the climate of increasing racial antagonism against blacks should have made the journalists more sympathetic to the teen suspects. At the time, these two components of the climate—racial tensions and increasing youth violence— were often articulated in mainstream media language as being unrelated.[5] In the discourse, the term "racial tensions" was often synonymous with the Howard Beach and Bensonhurst incidents (Chancer 2005). This aspect of the climate should have emphasized black vulnerability, but it did not seem to at the time.

It was striking to me then that the discourse about the rising rate of youth violence in the city did *not* appear to include those incidents of fatal border crossings for blacks. (There had been no prominent fatal border crossings for whites. The jogger incident, even with the more accurate narrative that included the sexual attack by Matias Reyes, was not a racial border crossing. It has not been established that the jogger was targeted by Reyes because she was in the wrong racial space; she was likely targeted because of her gender.) Had the Howard Beach and Bensonhurst incidents of white-on-black attack been included in the framework used to view youth violence, then it would have been less easy to make black youth the symbol for youth violence. In his 2001 report, U.S. Surgeon General Dr. David Satcher attributed nationwide increases in youth violence in poor black and Latino communities—and more generally, regardless of regional, racial, or socioeconomic features—largely to the availability of guns.[6] There were instances when the media discourse in 1989 and 1990 equated the attack on the jogger with racially motivated attacks on blacks in the city. Rick Hornung, a *Village Voice* journalist, created a moral equivalence argument that compared—because of similar legal considerations involved—the rape of the Central Park jogger with the murder of Yusuf Hawkins in Bensonhurst (Hornung 1990). He presented the two crimes as cases that could be viewed as "black against white" and "white against black" violence (Hornung 1990: 32). But the terror and injuries of the victims in Bensonhurst (and in Howard Beach) did not become a part of the mainstream public memory in the way the jogger's many injuries did. The racial violence experienced by Yusuf Hawkins and Michael Griffin did not have the appearance in the media discourse, relatively speaking, of being nearly as brutal as the violence experienced by the jogger.

Bumiller (2008) discusses the importance to the women's movement of itemizing the violence experienced by sexual assault victims as part of a process of turning these assaults into symbols to marshal support. The Howard Beach and Bensonhurst incidents did receive classification in mainstream media discourse as ignorant and racist behavior (Chancer 2005), and indeed they were. But New York City in 1989 was a long way from type of environment that spawned the lynching of Emmett Till in the Mississippi of 1955. One of the reasons Emmett Till had become a symbol for racial violence was his mother's decision to keep his casket open so the world could see what had been done to her son. In New York City in 1989, racism was something blacks complained about when they felt they were not being treated fairly, not something connected to hundreds of years of searing physical violence heaped on blacks. Thus, the media classification of the Bensonhurst and Howard Beach cases as racist—without meaningful attempts to make the important historical associations—served to minimize the sheer terror that the men in Howard Beach or the kids in Bensonhurst must have experienced at the hands of the two white mobs that attacked them.

Even in 2002, as this gathering of journalists looked back on their participation in the coverage of the jogger case and blamed the climate in the city at the time, the significance they gave to the elements that constituted the climate and the connection between those components remained unclear (Hancock 2003: 39). The expression of these phenomena—"racial tensions" and "rising youth violence"—as separate streams of thought in 1989 suggests that the media discourse on the white-on-black attacks not only failed to incorporate the general and specific vulnerabilities of blacks in U.S. society but possibly also reinforced notions of black savagery. Without promoting a more expansive understanding of youth violence, there is the risk that such discourse serves to convey a subtle underlying suggestion that whites have real reason to react violently to blacks crossing racial boundaries and entering white spaces.

While some of the jogger coverage sought to draw connections between the rising crime rate in the black areas of the "margins" and the social and economic disadvantages experienced by blacks, there were mixed messages in the reports that also seemed to strengthen ideas about black savagery. Shortly after the jogger incident, the *New York Times* ran a story in which it painted the suspected teens as having come from homes where they had been imbued with middle-class values. However, the story, "Park Suspects: Children of Discipline," suggests the futility of such efforts:

> Some were the children of broken homes, and certainly all bore daily witness to the abounding pathology of drugs, drink and poverty. But four lived in a building with a doorman, and one went to parochial school. One received an allowance of $4 a day from his father, while another had just received a[n] A on a report he had written about John Steinbeck's "Of Mice and Men." One played tuba in a school band, and another was described by teachers and classmates alike as a talented sketch artist. (Kaufman 1989: A1)

This article seemed to suggest that even the inclusion of blacks in the middle class would not quell their "savage" tendencies. Therefore, there was no point in addressing racial or class disparities. As if in response to the *Times* piece, the *Village Voice* ran a more investigative article in which it challenged the premise that the teen suspects were ever viewed in the community as "good" kids. Over the course of the fourteen years of coverage I reviewed, the *Daily News* published articles that tied some of the suspects to other crimes committed before the jogger case, but none of the five teens who were convicted of raping the jogger had a criminal record before the incident.

At the end of the day, the public rehashing from some of the journalists who had covered the case concluded that the unrelenting narrative from news managers, the willingness of the media to follow the police version of events, and the climate in the city had contributed significantly to the tenor of the coverage (Hancock 2003). As I have pointed out in numerous contexts, it is clear all of these factors have a strong racial component. Yet, based on Hancock's reporting of events, race was one factor, and not a foundational one, in the discussion among these journalists. While Hancock's article does acknowledge "persistent stereotypes," the journalists apparently offered very little in the way of a racial analysis of life in New York City at the time, of the press, or of American history. The journalists all—the black ones included—strapped on a color-blind lens to view the case and its aftermath. This suggests ultimately that even as the criminal justice system had been unfair to the blacks and Latinos in this case, it had also been equally unfair to whites.

# The Old Inconsistencies Are Re-viewed in the Press

From the discussion among the journalists who met in 2002 to go over their role in the coverage and their feelings about the reversal of the convictions in the jogger case, it was clear that the old inconsistencies in the prosecutor's case took on a different meaning in light of the new revelations. Before the first trial, some people outside the mainstream media had raised the issue of the problematic DNA evidence and the prosecution's supposed physical evidence that could place the boys at the scene. The *Amsterdam News* and the *City Sun* had raised questions about the physical evidence. It appears as if those standing outside of the mainstream discourse were better equipped to detect the problematic messages coming from the legal authorities. But, at the time, the interpretations of these outside voices were dismissed. Foucault (1972: 216–217) points out that discourses operate with "rules of exclusion" that reduce to "folly" and "falsehood" any discourse deemed inappropriate relative to the one in use.

The mainstream media had been all too willing to mime the district attorney's language and stance in important elements of the case—elements that proved in 2002 to have been completely false. Various mainstream press reports before the trial, sometimes from confidential sources, indicated that there were several types of physical evidence—semen, blood, and hair—that could link the boys to the jogger. But even the reportage on the legal process during the trial failed to bring clarity to exactly what physical evidence actually existed. In the original coverage, the mainstream press either did not see this confusion or did not attempt to straighten it out.

One such incident of less than stellar reporting occurred in October 1989, on the eve of a series of pretrial hearings. The *New York Times* ran an article, based on information from an anonymous source, that focused on FBI reports about "genetic tests" they had performed. According to this story, the FBI found the tests "inconclusive": "Although prosecutors would not say definitely that the tests were negative, one law-enforcement official, remarking that he was not encouraged by the results, said an F.B.I. report termed them 'inconclusive'" (R. Sullivan 1989c: B1). The only physical evidence mentioned in that article was "semen"; no mention was made of other types of physical evidence that might have been tested or what any of those findings might have been (R. Sullivan 1989c).

In their 2002 review of the jogger case, Robert McFadden and Susan Saulny pointed out that, *during* the trial, the district attorney had labeled strands of hair found on one of the teens as "consistent with" or matching the jogger's hair. How could the hair have matched? Matched in what respect?

At the time of the trial, press reports did not raise this type of inconsistency as a concern despite the FBI findings that DNA tests performed on some of the physical evidence—again, with the exception of the semen, it is unclear *which* other evidence—did not match any of the boys' DNA. Members of the press adopted the language and posture of the prosecutors: They accepted that the hair found on one of the boys was "consistent with" the jogger's hair. In their stories, they treated the problem in finding a DNA match as a weakness in the *test* and not as a reflection of a lack of evidence. They had no choice, because the discourse in play would not let them see it in any other way. Because of the denotative narrative about the black male propensity to rape white women and the connotative narrative about the criminal justice system being inherently fair, the media had no real questions for the prosecutors. It was only after the confession of Matias Reyes and the new DNA analysis that the degree to which the evidence had been initially misrepresented became clear. Reporting on the DA's reinvestigation, McFadden and Saulny (2002) said:

> Strands of hair found on Mr. [Kevin] Richardson and on another youth who was charged but never prosecuted in the rape had been shown in recent DNA tests not to have come from the jogger, though prosecutors had exploited them in the trials as matching or "consistent with" hers. (p. A1)

During the legal phase of the coverage, press reports about the blood evidence were equally confusing. Citing an anonymous source, a *Village Voice* article mentioned blood found on the four suspects that might have come from the jogger. But references to this so-called blood evidence waxed and waned in press reports over the course of the coverage until they finally disappeared. In Rick Hornung's (1990) *Village Voice* article about the DA's poor management of the evidence, the reporter raised the issue of the existence of blood evidence connecting the teens to the jogger after mentioning that forensic tests could not link the semen found on the jogger to the suspects. The article said:

> Now, as it winds its way through the courts, difficulties in the prosecution's case are emerging. The forensic evidence is weak: no weapon was found, no fingerprints tie the defendants to the victim, and the only semen found was on the victim's underwear and a DNA "fingerprint" test matched it to the jogger's boyfriend,[7] whose identity has yet to be disclosed—it does *not* match any of the defendants. . . .
>
> Bloodstains on at least four defendants' clothes match the victim's blood type and will help the prosecution prove the various assault and attempted murder charges. But the absence of a semen match will damage Assistant D.A. Elizabeth Lederer's efforts to win a first-degree rape conviction. (Hornung 1990: 32)

What match? What blood on the suspects?

By the time of the trial, connecting blood evidence to the suspects was a moot point. At trial, the blood became a signifier of how badly the jogger had been beaten. Segments of the mainstream media reports on the first trial, when the prosecution presented its case, focused on the injuries the jogger had suffered, as well as the defense rebuttal about the actual lack of physical evidence tying her to the suspects. Examples of such reports include three *Daily News* articles by Lizette Alvarez headlined "Cop Describes Jogger: Bloody and Thrashing," "Jogger's Trail of Blood Recalled by Detective," and "DNA Prints Fail to ID Jogger's Attackers." The first of the three articles, "Cop Describes Jogger," focused on the testimony of a police officer who found the jogger at the scene of the attack. He described her as likely having put up a significant physical fight during her attack:

> He told how he found the woman jogger at 1:30 A.M., April 20, 1989. Two passersby saw him in the park drinking coffee when they told him they had seen a body and heard moans from near the trees.
> He drove to the spot the two men described and turned on his high beams. The lights fell on a bloody body kicking in the mud, he said.
> The woman, he said was still struggling for her life four hours after the attack in a desolate section of the park. . . .
> "She was moving her hands up and down; her feet were still kicking. She seemed to be in some kind of shock," [Officer Joseph] Walsh said. (Alvarez 1990a)

The second article in the *Daily News* series, "Jogger's Trail of Blood," reported on the extensive trail of the jogger's blood found in the park. The article read, in part:

> The Central Park jogger left a 225-foot trail of blood leading from the spot where she was first attacked and ending where she collapsed in her own blood, a detective testified yesterday. . . .
> Detective Robert Honeyman told jurors he saw two 2-inch wide splotches of blood on the 102d St. transverse, where prosecutors say the jogger first was attacked. . . .
> The trail of blood continued for more than 100 feet, deep into the wooded ravine, Honeyman said.
>
> **'Large Area of Blood'**
> Honeyman said he found a "large area of blood" under a tree, and next to it a dirty sock and the insole of a pink, gray and blue jogging shoe.
> "The blood trail went down through the roots to the mud puddle where the victim was found," Honeyman said, circling key areas in the

photos with a marker. "The roots were covered with blood." (Alvarez 1990c)

The third article in the series, "DNA Prints Fail" (Alvarez 1990b), reported on the lack of a DNA match between the jogger and any of the suspects.

Several problems immediately stand out in these articles: Although they focused on the prosecutor's presentation of the case, the reports did not raise questions about any possible weaknesses in the case. For example, only one of the defendants was said to have had any kind of injury on his body, and it was minor, just a scratch. Yet the description of the jogger fighting off her attacker(s) did not raise any reportorial questions about the lack of injuries found on the suspects. The story's emphasis on the amount of blood at the scene could or should have raised reportorial questions about significant amounts of blood being part of the physical evidence. Questions about the probability of the suspects being bloodied given the amount of blood at the attack site were not raised in that article. In fact, in the article about the lack of a DNA match (Alvarez 1990b), semen was the only physical evidence discussed; the issue of blood did not come up.

During the reporters' brief 2002 mea culpa, carried out as the reinvestigation ensued, questions about the lack of physical evidence seemed to have come up. In an article about the reporters' meeting and the coverage, LynNell Hancock (2003), a former *Daily News* reporter, noted that Steven Drizin, a researcher on false confessions, commented on the lack of bloody evidence. In her piece, Hancock described Drizin's reaction as follows:

> None [of the boys] was linked by DNA to semen or to any other evidence found at the bloody scene, a fact that raised eyebrows. "It is often said that teenage boys can't make a peanut butter and jelly sandwich without leaving evidence," Drizin says. "The victim lost three-quarters of her blood, and there was not a drop on these boys. Not a drop. It's difficult to fathom." (2003: 40)

The reports of physical evidence can be termed troubling, at best, because they were confusing for the audience. At worst, the media's failure to directly address the conflicting information from the prosecution and the ease with which they relied on unidentified prosecutorial or law enforcement sources could be labeled a type of bias. As an audience member receiving the story, I found the conflicting information about the type and extent of physical evidence from prosecutorial sources puzzling. And not even the press reports during the trial cleared up the confusion. Instead, the mainstream media poked fun at the defense attorneys and all but called them stupid for not doing a better job of defending their clients. The sad truth was that the defense attorneys' words clearly could never transform the narrative or the discourse that had spawned it. In my content analysis, during the second time period or the legal phase of the coverage, the defense attorneys were the most often cited sources, even more than the police and district attorneys. A defense attorney was named as a source in at least 50 percent of these legal-phase stories, as compared to sourcing by a police representative in 25 percent of the stories and a district attorney in 29 percent. (See Table 6.1.) However, as described in Chapter 6, even the heavy inclusion of the defense attorneys in this segment of the coverage did not generate enough "facts" to transform the narrative.

The defense attorneys were essentially shouting into the airless vacuum of space, because without power their words had no significance. Such is the impact of discourse and such is its relationship to power. This disparity in the significance of sources from the arenas external to the media is what Stuart Hall and colleagues (1978) refer to as situations involving primary and secondary definers. They posit the following:

> These two aspects of news production—the practical pressures of constantly working against the clock and the professional demands of impartiality and objectivity—combine to produce a systematically structured *over-accessing* to the media of those in powerful and privileged institutional positions. The media thus tend, faithfully and impartially, to reproduce symbolically the existing structure of power in society's institutional order. . . . The result of this structured preference given in the media to the opinions of the powerful is that these "spokesmen" become what we call the *primary definers* of topics. . . . The important point about the structured relationship between the media and the primary institutional definers is that it permits the institutional definers to establish the initial definition or *primary interpretation* of the topic in question. This interpretation then "commands the field" in all subsequent treatment and sets the terms of reference within which all further coverage or debate takes place. (S. Hall et al. 1978: 58)

Based on the notions developed by S. Hall et al. (1978), nothing contributed to the coverage by the defense attorneys could have changed the discourse, because they were powerless to change the narrative. Thus, the defense attorneys were there, but not there.

## Unshakeable Stereotypes

What is still quite striking is the lasting power of the old cultural narratives upon which the Central Park jogger narratives were built. The media appeared to have been unwittingly held captive by these old narratives. They were also conditioned by their own value system, which views the world through the same lens as the criminal justice system. With such a narrow view, there was no way for them to see the discrepancies in the prosecution's case. The inconsistencies that turned up thirteen years later did not end with the DNA. The new investigation also highlighted an implausible timeline for the crime and disparities in the confessions that had been explained away or ignored the first time around. In the coverage during the reopening of the case, *New York Times* reporters Jim Dwyer and Kevin Flynn (2002) reviewed all of the trial transcripts and discovered the following:

> If [these suspects were present at the attack], the crimes took place at a high velocity, given that the tandem bike attack took place at 9:15, and that the earliest of the reservoir muggings was put at 9:25 by that victim. If those times are reliable, the boys had 10 minutes to abandon their trek southward, double back to the north end of the North Meadow, intercept the jogger as she ran along the cross drive, drag or chase her nearly 300 feet from the road, subdue her during multiple rapes, cave in her head, and then race seven or eight blocks south, climb down a wall on one side of the transverse and up the wall on the other side in time to catch the first of the reservoir victims. (p. A1)

All along, the defense attorneys had argued that the confessions had been "coerced" and thus were problematic. After the convictions had been vacated, one of the journalism students I had mentored, and who then worked on a prominent East Coast newspaper, visited me. We talked about old times, and I asked if she had heard about the case being reopened.

"It's like a modern-day Scottsboro," I said, "I deeply regret playing any role in it." It was not so much that the jogger case resembled the Scottsboro case in the details.[8] What I meant was simply that the jogger case was the latest or most contemporary story that advanced the narrative about the dangers of black men. And this time, the narrative and discourse were unfolding as the U.S. media system had begun its consolidation into a handful of conglomerates (Bagdikian 1983, 1997, 2004; McChesney 1999, 2008). In the contemporary world, only one voice was dominant.

## The Long Lull in Coverage

For a little more than a decade after the sixth suspect, Steve Lopez, was sentenced, there was a long lull in the coverage of the jogger case. This period stretches from March 15, 1991, until December 31, 2001. With the seeming resolution of the criminal cases, coverage of the Central Park jogger story subsided. The subject would come up periodically, mentioned as a reference in articles covering other topics that might have been related to one of the many facets of the case. During this juncture, the jogger case became background information in other stories. The conviction of the six original suspects became the context used to interpret violent acts committed by black and Latino youths. The use of the case as background in new press reports on other stories also became a contemporary way to spread the denotative narrative of the jogger story—that is, the black male propensity to rape white women. This background "fact" in new press reports also continued to disperse the connotative narrative that blacks do not deserve the rights of full citizens.

The expectation that blacks should have fewer rights became such a part of the discourse in the jogger coverage that seven years after the convictions, when one of the young men petitioned the court to avoid being listed as a sex offender under the state's Sex Registry Act due to his rehabilitation, a *Daily News* columnist challenged his right to do so by questioning his entitlement to rights in this society. Columnist Mark Kriegel wrote, in part:

### Park Rapist Still Insults Our Senses

While incarcerated, [Yusef] Salaam earned a high school equivalency diploma and completed a course for sex offenders. The teenage truant is now a regular worshiper at a mosque. He's been working on a construction site since his release in March and plans to enter college.

"The system worked," says [Ron] Kuby [Salaam's lawyer]. "But people don't want to believe that Yusef Salaam has been rehabilitated. They want more punishment."

Is it any wonder why? He didn't go to a man's prison like Attica or Greenhaven. He didn't get a man's sentence [of] 12½ to 25 years or 17 to 50 years, depending on who's doing the math. Instead, he did seven years at Manhattan Valley, a facility for youthful offenders. Given his offense, the penal system was downright beneficent in its treatment of Yusef Salaam.

So, good, let him check in with the cops. Let him live with that stigma. The jogger lives with hers. Salaam has earned the right to have fewer rights. (1997: 8)

Even after the convictions were vacated and the press questioned how it could have missed so much in the first go-round, media coverage of the Matias Reyes confession and the reversal of fortune of the initial suspects continued to raise doubts about their innocence. Everyone has not been on board with this turn of events. The police challenged the new developments and conducted their own reinvestigation of the case. Some of the initial prosecutors on the case continue to doubt that the original suspects had nothing to do with the attack on the jogger. There have also been few discussions in the press about how, in fulfilling their role, the media likely contributed to this miscarriage of justice.

# 8

# Selling Savage Portrayals

## *Young Black and Latino Males in the Carceral State*

## Fanning the Flames

**AS THE** Central Park jogger story unfolded, policy makers, academics, and other researchers from across the city and the nation weighed in on the significance of the attack and offered explanations and potential remedies for violence in the streets. Their solutions often leaned in the direction of more punitive law enforcement methods, as opposed to increasing social programs, banning weapons, or instituting other preventative measures. Nearly a month after the jogger was raped, on May 15, 1989, President George H. W. Bush announced a $1.2 billion anticrime spending package. In his statement announcing the plan, the president mentioned the rape of the jogger in Central Park, along with the murder of Michael Griffith in Howard Beach.[1] His plan called for the bulk of the allocation, $1 billion, to be spent on building new federal prisons (Weinraub 1989).

The focus on punitive as opposed to preventative measures could hardly have been a shock for New Yorkers. Their state was one of the first to rely on the adult criminal justice system to address the problem of juvenile crime. In 1978, New York state strengthened its juvenile offender law to incorporate violent juveniles into the adult court system. And across the nation a few states followed suit. But in the wake of the attack on the jogger, policy makers renewed their efforts to incorporate juveniles into the adult criminal justice system. Included in the public policy response to the rape was a sea change in the ways in which the majority of U.S. states addressed juveniles who committed violent crimes. Forty-four states across the nation began to embrace juveniles within the jurisdiction of the adult criminal courts. The new juvenile justice laws had their greatest impact on the lives of black and Latino youths. In the wake of the jogger incident the discourse from elected leadership, officials in the criminal justice system, and the media stoked fears around the issue of crime and the associations among race, crime, and youth. As a result of the ensuing moral panic, communities across the nation reshaped themselves.

## Moral Panic, Wilding, and the War on Drugs

With the jogger case, the media introduced "wilding" into the public discourse as a new, depraved phenomenon in the ever-growing and increasingly heinous inventory of violent acts committed by young people. The New York City media appeared to be creating an association between acts of wilding and black and Latino youths. Moving forward after the rape of the Central Park jogger, the term "wilding" was reserved particularly for references to crimes committed by young blacks and Latinos (Welch, Price, and Yankey 2002, 2004).

The media construction of the wilding phenomenon as a part of the jogger incident allowed the case to have a greater significance for society than the traditional earlier associations of race and crime (Welch, Price, and Yankey 2002, 2004). "The term wilding made a greater impact on the culture by becoming another synonym for youth violence, contributing to fear of crime and moral panic" (Welch, Price, and Yankey 2002: 7). In this particular case, these researchers argue, the wilding incident caused a moral panic. But, as described in Chapter 4, juvenile crime and violence had been viewed in some sectors of the mainstream through a less hysterical lens up until the 1970s (Chang 2005). The circumstances surrounding the rape of the Central Park jogger were positioned far differently. While Welch and colleagues (2002) contend that the jogger incident facilitated a moral panic, I believe that the panic was already under way in U.S. society. While largely ignoring illegal drug use in white and affluent communities, law enforcement centered its attention instead on illegal drug use and the associated violence in minority urban communities; black and Latino youths became the focus of the panic. In Chapter 4, I outlined a number of New York City newspaper stories that conveyed mainstream concern that the drug problem in the United States arose from black and Latino communities and posed a societywide threat as it reached into the "silk-stocking" districts. The occurrence of the attack on the jogger during this period of heightened societal antagonism against young black and Latino males may have contributed to the level of sensationalism in the coverage of the case and the ease with which prosecutors drew the delusional conclusions they did. The jogger case is just another example of how a phenomenon exaggerated during a moral panic not only distorts the immediate reality but has the potential to transform future society in ways that suit the interests of the ruling groups that instigated the panic.

The notion of a moral panic is based on the work of Stanley Cohen (2002), who argues that individuals, groups, or events can sometimes be defined as a momentous threat to society and singled out for action. Through a commingling of interests, the media, clergy, elected officials, and criminal justice officials exaggerate the threat and use their resources to come up with self-serving solutions. Cohen's concept of moral panic (as expressed in his *Folk Devils and Moral Panics,* first published in 1972) was the basis of work by Stuart Hall et al. (1978) that examined the so-called problem of muggings in England in the 1970s. Hall et al. (1978) found that reports in the British press about the crisis related to this "new" phenomenon called "muggings" were really just exaggerated claims "factualized" in the media with the help of elected officials and the criminal justice system. Hall et al. (1978) concluded that these groups together set off the moral panic around the muggings. The moral panic represented a crisis in hegemony within the British state. They found that this crisis was, in part, created by changing attitudes among young immigrants, primarily black Caribbeans, who unlike their parents were not political accommodationists and were growing increasingly disenfranchised as an economic recession took hold and they became the targets of racist policies (Hall et al. 1978: 348–355).

In the United States in the 1980s, the moral panic around illegal drug use and the concomitant violence that goes along with the drug trade had already begun to single out young black and Latino males among the group targeted for extraordinary punishment by the state. This moral panic had the earmarks of a contemporary racial project for its potential to reorganize the society's relationship to blacks and Latinos. The type of marginalization experienced by young black and Latino males is tantamount to permanently kicking them out of or keeping them out of the "system," that is, denying them any type of access to mainstream life. Researchers have found a relationship among the nation's transition to a service economy from a manufacturing economy, high rates of unemployment for members of racially marginalized urban groups, and participation in the drug trade by members of these groups (Alexander 2010: 50; Bourgois 1995). While the economy was undergoing this structural transformation, federal, state, and local governments were also changing their criminal justice policies and policing practices to fight crime, specifically launching the so-called War on Drugs. Once they have been incarcerated, these young men have slim chance of finding regular gainful employment upon release.

Michelle Alexander (2010) argues that the War on Drugs was born out of a political response forged by conservative ruling elites threatened by African American demands for equality. This response began in the 1960s civil rights era as a backlash against the seeming social, economic, and political gains being made by African Americans (Alexander 2010). Crime became the rallying cry of right-wing and conservative politicians on their long march back from Barry Goldwater's 1964 Republican Party, as they sought to regain power and control over the social and political agendas of the United States (Pager 2007). The conjoining of the civil rights, black power, and middle-class (largely white) anti-war movements in the mid- to late 1960s so concerned those in power, primarily the political conservatives, that federal and state systems responded with a moral crusade implemented through stricter anticrime measures (Murch 2010;

see also Pager 2007).[2] The Nixon administration, which came to power in 1969, gave birth to the Omnibus Crime Control Act in the early 1970s and initiated the War on Crime. Anticrime measures were so much a feature of the identity of the Republican Party that members of even the liberal wing of the party joined the anticrime crusade (Pager 2010). Governor Nelson Rockefeller of New York instituted the Rockefeller drug laws in the early 1970s, which imposed mandatory sentencing for even low-level drug dealers and drug addicts at the street level. These draconian measures disproportionately punished blacks and Latinos.

The conservative movement of the 1960s and 1970s blossomed into the Reagan administration, whose drug war policies instituted in the early 1980s became the most important piece of a "moral crusade" against the upheavals of the 1960s. The law-and-order, anticrime agenda at the federal level was supposed to return moral order to the nation (Alexander 2010; Pager 2007). This new conservative political movement interpreted the social and political agenda associated with liberal programs like the War on Poverty as "permissive" and sought to frame society's conflicts over the appropriate socioeconomic and political path forward as a "problem of moral order" (Pager 2007: 17). The War on Crime, which began in the Nixon administration, would continue through subsequent administrations, each with its own focus and each incorporating more punitive means to address what was defined as the nation's crime problem. Reagan brought the crime-fighting focus to drugs, and in the mid-1980s, with the introduction of crack cocaine into the cornucopia of illegal drugs already used in the United States, the nation experienced dramatic changes in patterns of incarceration. Crack cocaine's marketability—given its relatively low cost—to poor urban kids, and the participation of the unemployed urban poor in the sale of crack through low-level street hustling, allowed for an association among drug use, drug-related crimes, and race. This association was seen as particularly strong in a relatively insulated arena of illegal drug activities in the United States—the segregated, isolated black and Latino "margins" in urban areas. But, due to the ongoing moral panic over crime and drug abuse, an association among youth, drug crimes, and race became defined as a societywide problem, with black and Latino youths demonized as the new folk devils (Reinarman and Levine 2006). This allowed the mainstream media to more fully participate in a racial project that began with the political right's attempt to reimpose the moral order.

## Symbols in Defense of the New Political Economy

After the introduction of crack cocaine into the illegal drug markets of the United States, the media became an important site for the government's advance campaigns in the War on Drugs (Alexander 2010: 50–51; Reinarman and Levine 2006). Alexander noted:

The Reagan administration leaped at the opportunity to publicize crack cocaine in inner-city communities in order to build support for its new war.

In October 1985, the DEA sent Robert Stutman[3] to serve as director of its New York City office and charged him with the responsibility of shoring up public support for the administration's new war. Stutman developed a strategy for improving relations with the news media and sought to draw journalists' attention to the spread of crack cocaine. (2010: 51)

The administration of George H. W. Bush launched the first campaign in its War on Drugs in the press. President Bush appointed William Bennett as his "drug czar," the media title for the head of the newly formed Office of National Drug Control Policy. Bennett had held a cabinet post from 1985 to 1988 as President Ronald Reagan's secretary of education, and he developed Bush's contribution to the drug war in a plan called "The National Drug Control Strategy." The plan, which would increase federal antidrug spending, cited crack as the cause of "the intensifying drug-related chaos" in U.S. society (Bennett 1989: 3). In selling this plan to the public, the Bush administration deliberately misrepresented the drug problem in the Washington, D.C., area. The first salvo came in a speech from the Oval Office:

On September 5, 1989, President Bush, speaking from the presidential desk in the Oval Office, announced his plan for achieving "victory over drugs" in his first major prime-time address to the nation, broadcast on all three national television networks. . . . During the address, Bush held up to the cameras a clear plastic bag of crack labeled "EVIDENCE." (Reinarman and Levine (2006: 48)

Bush announced that the evidence had come from Lafayette Park, across the street from the White House, in an attempt to illustrate how overrun the whole society had become by drugs (Bush 1989). However, the drug bust had been set up by Bush officials. The press would later expose the lengths the Bush administration officials had gone through to construct the scenario. Citing the September 22, 1989, *Washington Post* story written by Michael Isikoff, Reinarman and Levine wrote:

White House Communications Director David Demar[e]st asked Cabinet Affairs Secretary David Bates to instruct the Justice Department "to find some crack that fit the description in the speech." Bates called Richard Weatherbee, special assistant to Attorney General Dick Thornburgh, who then called James Mil[l]ford, executive assistant to the DEA chief. Finally, Mil[l]ford phoned William McMull[a]n, special agent in charge of the DEA's Washington office, and told him to arrange an undercover crack buy near the White House because "evidently, the President wants to show it could be bought anywhere" (Isikoff, 1989).

Despite their best efforts, the top federal drug agents were not able to find anyone selling crack (or any other drug) in Lafayette Park, or anywhere else in the vicinity of the White House. Therefore, in order to carry out their assignment, DEA agents had to entice someone to come to the park to make the sale. Apparently, the only person the DEA could convince was Keith Jackson, an eighteen-year-old African-American high school senior . . . (Isikoff, 1989). (Reinarman and Levine 2006: 49)

Revelations about these obvious attempts at public deception did not deter the Bush administration from its course in the drug war. Bennett planned to solve the nation's drug problems by pumping disproportionately larger amount of funds into law enforcement as opposed to treatment (Berke 1989). According to a 2007 report analyzing twenty-five years of the War on Drugs produced by the Sentencing Project, a nonprofit advocacy group focused on criminal justice policy issues, "Drug arrests have more than tripled in the last 25 years, totaling a record 1.8 million arrests in 2005" (Mauer and King 2007: 2). Law enforcement methods targeted street level dealers and the users of crack cocaine rather than users of powder cocaine (Alexander 2010; Reinarman and Levine 2006). "Drug offenders in prisons and jails have increased 1100% since 1980. Nearly a half-million (493,800) persons are in state or federal prison or local jail for a drug offense, compared to an estimated 41,100 in 1980" (Mauer and King 2007: 2).

This strategy incarcerated disproportionately large numbers of blacks and Latinos, who filled the ranks of street level dealers and who were predominantly users of crack cocaine, as compared to whites, who typically abused power cocaine (Reinarman and Levine 2006). While African Americans made up 14 percent of regular drug users, non-Hispanic whites 69.2 percent, and Hispanics 12.4 percent, "African Americans are 37% of those arrested for drug offenses and 56% of persons in state prison for drug offenses," according to the Sentencing Project report (Mauer and King 2007: 19–20). Media coverage of these law enforcement practices often ignored the racial disparities in the treatment of black and white offenders within the criminal justice system, reinforcing in the public discourse the association between black race and crime, particularly violent crime, and further advancing this association as some type of race-based biological imperative for crime and violence (Reinarman and Levine 2006).[4]

The news media were an important site for reconstructing the definition of black and Latino male youth as the War on Drugs got under way. The rape of the Central Park jogger in the midst of all this only amplified the existing state of moral panic. As it was represented in the media, the case heightened in the public's mind the type of threat that young black and Latino males represented in society. In my content analysis of the Central Park jogger press reports, I examined the features of an individual's social location that played a major role in the coverage—features of race, class, victimhood, gender, and age.[5] Here I highlight how the press reports of the jogger incident defined the suspects and the jogger in relation to each other.

While indicators for race were dominant in the press reports, indicators for class were the features of individual identities most often used to mark membership within categorical groupings. This made class the concept that appeared most frequently to readers.[6] Ninety-eight percent of the articles had at least one indicator for class (see Figure 1.1). In my study, three class indicators represented identity: runner, jogger, and avid runner. Nine class indicators represented institutions: jogger's universities, jogger's family and friends' universities, jogger's family and friends' jobs, jogger's non-Salomon job, Salomon Brothers, investment banker, schools suspects attended, suspects' family and friends' schools, and suspects' family and friends' jobs. Three class indicators represented social structure: jogger middle class, suspects' moderate income, and suspects' middle-class lifestyles. (See Table 3.2.)

From a sociological point of view, most of the indicators of class used in the jogger coverage were based on institutions. Thus, the meaning that the concept of class took on in the coverage was largely as an important societal institution. Given this link in the press reports, it is possible that the coverage left audiences with the impression that the attack on the jogger represented an attack on important institutions. The jogger worked for the now-defunct investment bank Salomon Brothers, one of the powerhouses of the Wall Street community at the time, which was central to the new symbolic economic order discussed in Chapter 4. This new economic system had shrugged off the manufacturing jobs that had at one time sustained the people in the margins. In their content analysis of the jogger coverage, which was organized differently from mine, Welch, Price, and Yankey came to a similar conclusion: "The rape of the 'young Manhattan investment banker' seems to represent a symbolic attack on the political economy by the so-called dangerous class" (2002: 21).

In the context of the press reports on the jogger's rape, the concept of gender was largely based on issues of identity. Seven of the ten indicators for gender were words related to gender identity: female, woman, pretty, attractive, bubbly, she/her, and breast. Three of the indicators for gender were based on violent social acts that subordinate: rape, sodomy, and gang-rape. The two most frequently used indicators for gender were "rape," which appeared in 84 percent of the articles, and "woman," which was included in 53 percent of the articles. (See Table 3.4.) Like race, gender is an aspect of identity. And, as in the case of racial identity, gender identity is constructed, in part, through interactions in the social world. As a subordinating act, rape gives gender its meaning.

In the context of the jogger coverage, the suspects' race is privileged over gender oppression/subordination as a feature of the coverage. In the analysis, the "black and Latino" race of the suspects cannot be separated from the act of rape.[7] Thus, the term "rape" also becomes associated with race, either the jogger's or the suspects'.

However, the concept of gender did not appear to dominate the coverage in a story purportedly about a rape incident. The jogger was a raped woman and as such her identity was marked by this vulnerability, which the media treated as something that warranted protection. Media organizations, in general, including those incorporated in my study, withheld publication of the jogger's name to protect her privacy. This is common practice when reporting cases of rape. However, the *Amsterdam News,* a Harlem-based black-owned and -run newspaper, published the jogger's name, to much criticism from the mainstream press. Journalist Timothy Sullivan (1992) noted in his book about the case that the *Amsterdam News* named the jogger because mainstream papers had identified the black and Latino underage suspects by name and address, a deviation from common practice concerning young people accused of committing crimes.

The significant point here is that the media appeared to use some type of hierarchy to determine who in the jogger case warranted protection. While it initially appeared that the issue of protection revolved around the identity category "raped woman," there may have been other factors operating. The person who was raped did not become known to the public as a "raped woman"; she became known as the "jogger." Additionally, other women who were raped around that time were not brought significantly into the coverage of the Central Park incident. In the context of my study, the term "jogger" is one of the indicators of class. In the coverage, it was the most frequently used indicator of class, appearing in 95 percent of all the articles in the sample and in 99 percent of all the stories in Time Periods 3 and 4 (the post-trial coverage). (See Table 3.2.)

Kristin Bumiller (2008) argues that the jogger became an iconic symbol within the movement against sexual violence, but she was a different type of symbol for the mainstream press. My content analysis suggests that, within the media, the jogger was not an iconic representation of crimes against women, because the rape culture in U.S. society was not an element of the coverage. Although the media had the opportunity to associate the attack with the agenda of the women's movement, they chose to use the jogger to deliver a different message.

The jogger was the iconic representation of an attack against an important societal and economic institution. Male-dominated corporate America, the physical representation of capitalism, was being symbolically projected in the mainstream media as vulnerable to disruption, and low-income, young black males were presented as the biggest threat to the behemoth system undergirding corporate America. While class and gender references constituted the most frequently used language in the jogger coverage, in the era of color blindness class and gender as concepts were used to mask a racist attack against young black males. Black male sexuality has historically been a symbol of danger in U.S. society, and it has typically been presented as a danger specifically to white women. Near the end of the twentieth century, as the mainstream grew more inclusive, however, those managing the mainstream boundaries appeared to be ensuring that black masculinity would be limited in mainstream spaces.

## "Science" Reshapes the Society

This would not be the first time black males were represented as a threat to society. There is a long history in U.S. culture, from the days of early America, of constructing associations between the black or nonwhite "race" and savagery (Fredrickson 1971a) and doing so with the help of "science" (Banton 2009; Jordan 1968). This new moral crusade also received its imprimatur from academia.[8] Theories about a black subculture of violence had developed from the late 1960s, when the moral crusade began (Wolfgang 1983; Wolfgang and Ferracuti 1967), and this work was used by others to develop newer theories about the propensity for violence among low-income urban black males.

The message in the media coverage of the jogger case, coming amidst the trend of rising youth violence, seemed to take hold of the imaginations of important members of the academic and governmental elites. Some in academic circles returned to "scientific analysis" to further develop the 1960s conceptualizations of black and Latino youths as innately violent. In the late 1980s, the research of political scientist John J. DiIulio Jr. (1989: 35) blamed the dismal life conditions of poor people of color in urban areas on "the large numbers of chronic and predatory street criminals." By 1995, he had constructed his notion of the "super-predator," a category of juvenile criminals who supposedly would be more deadly than anything witnessed before in the United States (DiIulio 1995).[9] DiIulio (1995) based his conclusions on (1) old birth-cohort studies of 10,000 Philadelphia boys born in 1945 (Wolfgang 1983)[10] and (2) research by contemporary criminologists that extrapolated from the birth-cohort studies to predict the number of juvenile offenders in the future (J. Q. Wilson 1995). DiIulio stated that of the boys between ten and eighteen years old in the birth-cohort studies, "more than one-third had at least one recorded arrest by the time they were 18" (1995: 31). He also noted that "two-thirds of all the violent crimes committed by the cohort" were committed by about 6 percent of the boys (DiIulio 1995: 31). The findings of the birth-cohort study, along with projections of an unchanging rate of delinquency led DiIulio to concur with predictions by James Q. Wilson and other criminologists that, given the birth rates of the time, an "additional 500,000 boys who will be 14 to 17 years old in the year 2000 will mean at least 30,000 more murderers, rapists and muggers on the streets than we have today" (DiIulio 1995: 31).

DiIulio (1995) predicted that this newly expanded group of "super-predators" would be much more dangerous than earlier groups because they were being raised in a state of moral poverty, which he defined as follows:

> [It] is the poverty of being without loving, capable, responsible adults who teach you right from wrong. It is the poverty of being without parents and other authorities who habituate you to feel joy at others' joy, pain at others' pain, happiness when you do right, remorse when you do wrong. It is the poverty of growing up in the virtual absence of people who teach morality by their own everyday example and who insist that you follow suit.
>
> In the extreme, moral poverty is the poverty of growing up surrounded by deviant, delinquent, and criminal adults in abusive, violence-ridden, fatherless, Godless and jobless settings. In sum, whatever their material circumstances, kids of whatever race, creed or color are most likely to become criminally depraved when they are morally deprived. . . .
>
> The abject moral poverty that creates superpredators begins very early in life in homes where unconditional love is nowhere but unmerciful abuse is common. (DiIulio 1995: 31)

The message here was clear: The rising rate of youth violence was unavoidable and our society had better be prepared for it. The youth who were primarily targeted in DiIulio's (1995) declaration were black and Latino young males living in urban areas.

At the nexus of research and public policy, DiIulio's work was quite influential. He wrote, along with William Bennett and John P. Walters, *Body Count: Moral Poverty . . . And How to Win America's War against Crime and Drugs,* about the centrality of drug abuse to crime (Bennett, DiIulio, and Walters 1996). Given his access to high-level policy makers (including testimony before Congress) and the national media attention his ideas received in *Time* and *Newsweek* (Annin 1996; Zoglin, Allis, and Kamlani 1996), it is no surprise that DiIulio's work also had a dramatic effect on policies affecting juveniles (Keenan 2005). This work shaped policy by way of contributing to state and federal authorities' reliance on incarceration as a means of addressing crime (Pager 2007). Years later, DiIulio would recant his theory of the rise of the "super-predator" (Becker 2001), but that came after it had already buttressed the transformation of juvenile justice laws, supporting the use of more extreme law enforcement methods—including imprisonment in adult facilities—for young offenders (Hancock 2003; Keenan 2005). In 2012, DiIulio went so far as to join in a friend of the court brief filed with the U.S. Supreme Court in two cases involving harsh sentencing of juveniles.[11] The brief argued, in part, that the "super-predator" theory had no validity.

Although DiIulio had been renouncing his own theory publicly since 2001 (Becker 2001), as recently as 2005, his colleague William Bennett continued to promulgate biological correlations between race and crime. While in conversation with a caller to his syndicated radio talk show, Bennett offered a "hypothetical proposition" for reducing crime—"Abort every black baby" in the country—then immediately countered that this solution to crime was "morally reprehensible" (CNN 2005). Underlying Bennett's comment, however, is the assertion that there is likely a biological association between race and crime.

Society's response to the growing drug problem in the United States was to construct associations between race and crime. These associations have become much more salient because research that draws connections among race, crime, and youth has been given a great deal of attention in the media. Media language has used such connections to essentially form a symbolic framework that allows for the reification of associations among race, crime, and youth.

## Reifying Racial Meaning in the Criminal Justice System

The moral panic in which the Central Park jogger's rape was enveloped had already embraced increased rates of incarceration as a solution to the problems of crime in general and drug crimes in particular. The sensationalized coverage of the rape exacerbated this approach; as some juvenile justice advocates noted (Ryan and Ziedenberg 2007), it intensified the panic, leading to a transformation in the juvenile justice system.[12] Of the six young suspects charged with the jogger's rape, five were tried in adult court (the sixth entered a plea bargain), but five were sentenced as juveniles. In my content analysis of the press reports during Time Period 2, the legal phase of the coverage, one of the most curious findings was the sharply diminished use of words or terms that served as racial indicators (see Figure 1.1). In Time Period 1, during the construction of the narrative, 67 percent of the articles included at least one indicator for race. This was a relatively low frequency of use for racial indicators, considering that so many perceived the case to be about race. Even more surprisingly, however, during the second time period (the legal phase), the proportion of articles with at least one racial indicator fell to 49 percent. This was a decrease of 18 percentage points in the use of indicators of racial categorical groupings. (See Table 8.1.) What could account for such a steep decline?

**TABLE 8.1** Percentages of Articles that Included at Least One Indicator for Each of the Major Concepts of Coverage, by Time Period

| Concept | Time Period 1: Apr 21, 1989– Jun 9, 1989 | Time Period 2: Jun 10, 1989– Mar 14, 1991 | Time Periods 3 and 4: Mar 15, 1991– Dec 31, 2003 |
|---|---|---|---|
| Race | 67.3 | 49.2 | 78.9 |
| Violence | 96.4 | 92.5 | 92.1 |
| Class | 96.4 | 96.7 | 100.0 |
| Gender | 98.2 | 93.2 | 94.7 |
| Age | 89.1 | 74.2 | 89.5 |
| Victimhood | 63.6 | 36.7 | 36.5 |
| Sample size | $N = 55$ | $N = 120$ | $N = 76$ |

It appears that, for media content producers, when the legal system was part of the subject of press reports, representations of black and Latino racial groupings[13] were less important as an explicit feature of the coverage. This may have been the case because race, particularly black racial identity, was becoming much more associated with the criminal justice system. New anticrime measures had vastly increased the rate of incarceration in the United States for all people (Mauer and King 2007: 2; Pager 2007), but incarceration of African Americans was disproportionately high relative to their rate of arrest (Mauer and King 2007: 2; Pager 2007; Wacquant 2002). This disparity suggests that the moral panic that drove the War on Drugs had transformed the criminal justice system into a system of mass incarceration for black males, and had so united perceptions of "criminal" and "black race" that the societal meaning assigned to members of this racial group had been transformed. Thus, the War on Drugs greatly exacerbated the marginalization of people in a social location that included black race, lower income, male gender, and conviction for a felony. Sociologists Devah Pager (2007) and Loïc Wacquant (2002) and critical race scholar Michelle Alexander (2010) have come to similar conclusions in recent studies. Wacquant (2002) argues that the increasing levels of incarceration of African Americans have come to represent one of four "peculiar institutions" (the others being slavery, Jim Crow, and the construction of the ghettos) that have confined blacks over the course of U.S. history. Given the way in which the War on Drugs criminalized blacks, and the attendant increase in rates of incarceration of blacks, the black racial grouping became closely associated with people ensnared by the criminal justice system. This close association between "black race" and "subjects in the criminal justice system," which was supported by the results of my content analysis, came shortly after the period in U.S. history when blacks for the first time began to outnumber whites in the national inmate population.[14]

## Incorporating Juveniles into the
## System of Mass Incarceration

By the time the Central Park jogger story broke, public discourse had been primed with these notions of an association—possibly biological but certainly cultural—between race and crime. One of the greatest ironies and injustices of the jogger case is that the six accused teens were in fact innocent. Media sensationalism in the coverage of the story has been blamed for heightening the atmosphere of fear in society. In the wake of the case, there was a ramping up of juvenile justice laws, beginning in the period 1992–1999, in which most states in the United States passed laws designed to try more juveniles as adults (Keenan 2005; Ryan and Ziedenberg 2007).[15] After spiking in the mid-1990s, rates of juvenile crime have declined "for a dozen years to a 30-year low" (Ryan and Ziedenberg 2007: 4).

Following the attack on the jogger and the trials of the defendants, states across the nation expanded the scope of their juvenile justice laws by changing the boundaries of jurisdiction for juvenile courts. Between 1992 and 1997, forty-four states put new laws on the books or expanded existing laws that allowed juveniles to be tried as adults in criminal court, according to a report published by the U.S. Department of Justice, Office of Juvenile Justice and Delinquency Prevention (Snyder and Sickmund 1999). Academics and policy makers at the highest levels of government provided a rationale for these changes through the construction of the now-defunct theory of the "super-predator" (DiIulio 1995; Krajicek 1999). The jogger case seemed to add to the empirical evidence needed to justify the racial project that right-wing policy makers began in the wake of the social movements of the 1960s. The problem, of course, is that the case against the suspects in the jogger attack itself was constructed; the boys were innocent.

The transformation of the juvenile justice system in the wake of the jogger case has had a disproportionate impact on black and Latino youths in the United States, forever ensnaring them in this nation's system of mass incarceration. According to juvenile justice advocates, approximately 200,000 youths are prosecuted in adult courts annually (Ryan and Ziedenberg 2007). Although many of these minors do not end up in adult prisons, thirty-one states now have laws that require that young people tried once in juvenile court must be tried for subsequent offenses in adult criminal court. These changes in juvenile justice laws suggests a possible impact of media coverage of youth on U.S. social structure. The disproportionate impact on black and Latino youths indicates how media associations of race, youth, and crime have become reified in the social structure.

While juvenile justice advocates are fighting for changes in the system, it is important to note the effectiveness of these laws. The changes have become institutionalized as crime prevention and reduction measures. However, researcher Jeffrey A. Butts (2012) found that there is no relationship between the placement of juveniles in the adult or criminal court system and a reduction in violent crime. He noted:

> At first glance, it may appear that the greater use of transfer lowered violent youth crime, but this argument is refuted by a simple analysis of crime trends. In the six states that allow fair comparisons (i.e., where all juveniles ages 16–19 are originally subject to juvenile court jurisdiction and sufficient data exist for the calculations), the use of criminal court transfer bears no relationship to changes in juvenile violence. (Butts 2012)

States have been increasing prosecutorial power or have created laws that enable them to bypass family court and transfer youthful offenders to criminal court. According to Butts (2012), "entire classes of young offenders are transferred without the involvement of the court."

The reification of associations of race, youth, and crime in the social structure is dialectically related to the mainstream media renditions that normalize the marginalization of black and Latino youths, particularly male youths, from the mainstream. They stand apart, distinct from categorical groupings of other youths, vulnerable but despised.

# 9

# They Didn't Do It!

## The Central Park Jogger Case as a Racial Project

**BY DEFINITION**, a racial project does "ideological 'work'" that creates or changes the nature of racial "dynamics" (Omi and Winant 1994: 56). The case of the Central Park jogger definitely changed forever the lives of the five teens put on trial. Prior to this case, none had ever been arrested. The Central Park Five, as they came to be known, were tried as adults under New York State law. Based on statute, four of the five received juvenile sentences. Those sentenced as juveniles served the early years of their sentences at a juvenile facility and were moved to adult prisons at age twenty-one. Antron McCray, fifteen, was convicted of rape, assault, robbery, and riot. He spent his adult time at Clinton Correctional Facility (also known as Dannemora) (Burns 2011). Yusef Salaam, fifteen, was convicted of rape, assault, robbery, and riot. At twenty-one, he also was moved to Clinton Correctional (Burns 2011). Raymond Santana, fourteen, was convicted of rape, assault, robbery, and riot. Upon becoming an adult, he served at Downstate Correctional Facility (Burns 2011). Kevin Richardson, fourteen, was convicted of attempted murder, rape, sodomy, assault, robbery, and riot. He served his adult time at Coxsackie Correctional Facility (Burns 2011). Korey Wise, sixteen, was the lone defendant in the group who was tried and sentenced as an adult. He was sentenced to five to fifteen years; he served thirteen years at Auburn Correctional Facility (Burns 2011).

The injuries the boys suffered as a result of their arrest, trial, conviction, and incarceration are immeasurable. That would be bad enough if the case had affected only the five young men and their families and loved ones. But the evidence suggests that the impact has been much greater. I argued earlier that the Central Park Five were ensnared in the growing association between young black and Latino males and criminality that developed with the War on Drugs. After the sexual assault on Trisha Meili, the "wilding"/"wolfpack" narrative built by police and prosecutors *also* provided support for spurious claims being made by the media and by a prominent political scientist whose research falls within the field of criminology. John J. DiIulio Jr. (1995), among others, promoted the idea of an impending youth crime wave that was purportedly indicative of a real relationship between young minority males and crime.[1] This hypothetical affinity young black and Latino males have for crime supposedly exists for those in their late teens *and* for those just entering their teens. In a 1995 article published in the *Chicago Tribune,* DiIulio appeared to reference the Central Park case in discussing criminal activity of fourteen- to seventeen-year-olds: "While it remains true the most violent youth crime is committed by juveniles against juveniles, of late young offenders have been committing more homicides, robberies, and other crimes against adults. There is even some evidence that juveniles are doing homicidal violence in 'wolf packs.'"[2]

The media coverage of the jogger case—with its lurid headlines of children committing interracial rape and violence—occurred almost a decade into the War on Drugs. The race-neutral frame used in the prosecution of the drug war, which focused on individual choice, would make it easier for minority male *minors* to be locked up in adult facilities as states changed their juvenile justice laws to incorporate the underaged into the adult court system. With these changes, more and more minority male youths would be saddled with criminal records, locking them out of the possibility of advancement into the mainstream and making it more difficult to achieve a just social order. Critical race theory scholar Michelle Alexander (2010) contends that the drug war was implemented with "race-based targeting" of cases by police and prosecutors; this made young black and Latino males primary targets for law enforcement agencies. "Imprisonment . . . now creates far more crime than it prevents, by ripping apart fragile social networks, destroying families, and creating a permanent class of unemployables" (Alexander 2010: 224). The increasing rates of incarceration of minority male youths set this group apart, marginalizing them into a "caste," Alexander (2010) argues.

But the contours of this caste system have taken on a particular character—the members are very young. And the numbers of those under eighteen years old included in this group are growing. Black youths (younger than eighteen years old) are even more overrepresented in the total population of juveniles arrested than are black adults in the total population of adults arrested (Free and Ruesink 2012: 12). In 2009, black juveniles were 31.3 percent of the juveniles arrested and black adults were 27.8 percent of the adults arrested (Free and Ruesink 2012: 12). An even more striking discord exists between the rate of arrest of black juveniles and their representation in the population of all youth under eighteen years of age. According to 2010 U.S. Census data, only

15.3 percent of all juveniles are black, meaning that they are arrested at roughly twice the rate of their occurrence in the population.[3] The Campaign for Youth Justice, an advocacy group for youthful offenders, blames the jogger case for changing the nation's approach to youthful offenders, though this claim cannot be scientifically established. Beginning in 1992, just three years after the assault on the Central Park jogger, "almost every state passed new laws to make it easier to try and sentence youth in the adult criminal justice system" (Ryan and Ziedenberg 2007: 3). The long-term effects of policies that promote the incarceration of minority male youths give a type of permanence to a particular life outcome for people in that social location, which could possibly transform racial meaning and arrangement far into the future. In this way, the Central Park jogger case evolved into a racial project.

## Framing the Jogger's Rape in the Contemporary Narrative of Color-Blindness

The charges and guilty verdicts against the teens seemed to represent a continuation of the old cultural narrative about the black male propensity to attack white women. Although the media used terms like "wilding" and "savage," the application of this narrative in the age of "inclusion" did not come with a biological interpretation. Instead, it likely fell within the cultural frame of color-blind racism—suggesting that blacks and Latinos are *culturally* inclined to rape and, in particular, to rape white women. Within this frame, rape, which is a society-wide problem, would not be discussed as a gender issue or as an aspect of gender oppression, as feminists in the 1970s argued it should be. Feminist scholars (Bumiller 2008; A. Davis 1981) have noted that analyzing the problem of rape in this society would require an intersectional approach. This acknowledges the differential power and privilege among social actors based on the society's divisions around race, gender, and class that (as discussed in Chapter 3) have been built into the social structure. Without a critique of how these divisions hinder solutions to a society-wide problem like rape, perceptions about rape victims and offenders would be based on the prevailing race/gender/class hierarchies.[4] White women would be perceived as the most vulnerable to rape. They would not only appear to face possible threats from white males but also would *also* face danger from black males. White men would be less likely to be perceived as sexually dangerous. Black women would be viewed as being the least susceptible to sexual assault. This would occur not necessarily because black women were genetically predisposed to sexual promiscuity, as earlier narratives claimed, but because there would be a perception of a lesser likelihood of them being raped.

However, the perceptions underlying the contemporary framing of rape and race defy reality. According to a U.S. Department of Justice study published in 1991, near the time of the attack on the jogger, "black women were significantly more likely to be raped than white women" or women of any other racial group (Harlow 1991: 8). The report also showed that intraracial rapes were more prevalent, particularly in instances of one offender and one victim. "Rapists and their victims were likely to be of the same race. In rapes with one offender, about 7 of every 10 white victims were raped by a white offender, and about 8 of every 10 black victims were raped by a black offender" (Harlow 1991: 10). In instances of gang rapes (i.e., those with more than one offender, which constituted 12 percent of all rapes), white victims were sexually assaulted 49 percent of the time by white offenders, 29 percent of the time by black offenders, and 13 percent of the time by a mixed-race group (Harlow 1991: 10). When black women were victims of multiple-offender rapes, 72 percent of the time the offenders were black (Harlow 1991: 10). Thus, these statistics indicate a *reduced* likelihood that the jogger would have been gang raped by a group of black and Latino teens.

Using the contemporary frame of color-blind racism to discuss the jogger's rape would also suggest that any woman attacked like the jogger had been would have received the same attention and calls for justice. But, in their coverage, the media applied the logic of the legal practices that define some rapes as "worthy" of prosecution. In other words, stranger-rapes, or sexual assaults in which the victim is badly hurt, or rapes in which the victim is white or affluent garner the most attention. Such an approach supports existing gender hierarchies that privilege some women and subordinate others. These attitudes make it difficult to discuss rape as a problem of the entire culture. In the case of the Central Park jogger, the suggestion was that the black male teens were more prone to attacking a white woman. Helen Benedict argued that while studies of gang rape indicate that these assaults are "overwhelmingly committed by teenage boys on a lone female . . . [t]he majority of rapes are committed within races: whites against whites, blacks against blacks, and most gang rapists are white, just as most people in this country are white" (1992: 211). There is a lesser likelihood that there was a coded racial message in this rape and a greater likelihood that it was yet another example of a crime against women.[5]

## They Were Children

The post-1990s emergence of young black and Latino males as a "caste" defined by criminality has also been associated with violent crimes, such as rape. What became striking during the 1990s and 2000s is the degree to which children were incorporated into that group. In some respects, this society's willingness to burden young people with pejorative definitions, particularly minority children such as those accused in the jogger case, suggests the impossibility for success of the racial project we know as the civil rights movement.

The teens from the jogger case are now men in their late thirties. They became known as the Central Park Five and they have filed a $250 million lawsuit against the city of New York, among others, charging that their civil rights were violated. Aside from the district attorney's office, other arms of the government and other leaders have been reluctant to acknowledge any wrongdoing (Burns 2011). In a *New York Post* editorial run on April 21, 2011,[6] the *Post* management argued against the city settling the lawsuit with the Central Park Five, using the logic that has been applied by police and some prosecutors since Matias Reyes stepped forward to admit to raping and beating the jogger by himself: Just because Reyes's DNA was present does not mean that the five teens did not happen on the jogger either before or after Reyes and also rape her.

As I studied the media coverage of the case, one of the things that occurred to me was how little the young suspects must have understood what was happening to them at the time, as well as its historical significance and its implications. When I hear the original suspects talking about a "nightmare" and feeling as if "I was in a dream," it really hits home how surreal the whole experience must have been for them. How could fourteen- or fifteen-year-olds fully grasp the impact on their lives of being told they faced ten years in a dangerous prison? Or how could they grasp the disparity in treatment they would receive because the victim they were accused of raping was white and not black? Or how could they grasp the winds of change around them vis-à-vis changing attitudes toward youthful misconduct and crimes. Not one of them had ever been arrested before.

One of the early press reports, which largely goes unnoticed now, presented the initial *moderated* response from one of the police brass. The day-one story from the *New York Times* included a striking quote from Chief of Detectives Robert Colangelo, in which he cast the suspects as children up to "mischief":

> Chief of Detectives Robert Colangelo said he believed that the spree did not foretell a chaotic spring or summer in the park. The Chief speculated that the youths, all believed to be between the ages of 13 and 15 and all from northern Manhattan, might have been out late because schools were closed yesterday for Passover. "They went into the park to do some mischief, and this mischief led to this tragedy," he said. "It's safe to jog in the park. Certainly, there are precautions that should be taken." (Wolff 1989)

The *Daily News* editorial the following day—April 22, 1989—took Colangelo to task for this comment, chiding him as follows:

> There was speculation that a day off from school and the unusually warm weather drew the youths to the park to do "mischief" and it escalated into

tragedy. Mischief? Mischief is scrawling graffiti on a wall. "Mischief" is overturning litter baskets. "Mischief" is not mugging. It is not gang rape. It is not beating someone's face to a pulp with fists and crushing someone's skull with a rock.

Summer's coming, with no school at all and lots of warm weather. Will more wolves be making "mischief" in Central Park? Or anywhere they damn well choose?[7]

On that first day of coverage, to describe *some* of what had happened in the park, Colangelo gave the media the word "mischief"—a word often used with children. Helen Benedict, in her 1992 analysis of the case, interpreted that quote as an acceptance of the "boys will be boys" mentality that enables rape. In their push-back, media leaders at the *Daily News* quarreled with the use of the term "mischief." They did not directly make the case for discussing the problem of rape in U.S. society but instead argued for a stronger description of the alleged perpetrators and their actions, which included an animalistic reference.

The naïveté of youth that shaped the young suspects' early responses to the police has been erased by their horrifying life experiences during the prosecution of the case and their period of incarceration. The boys who were picked up in 1989 believed the police when told, "Once you tell us what happened at the rape of this jogger you will get to go home." So they concocted stories to that end, only realizing later they were being tricked into implicating themselves.

They were not the first to be tricked in this way, and they would not be the last. In addition to becoming statistics among the growing ranks of youthful offenders, the Central Park Five fit into some troubling patterns found in a recent study of 343 wrongfully convicted African American men (Free and Ruesink 2012). The researchers, Marvin D. Free Jr. and Mitch Ruesink, discovered that "false confessions for rape and sexual assault are more likely to involve juveniles . . . [a]nd finally the data suggest the possibility that prolonged interrogations may have played a greater role in obtaining false confessions for rape and sexual assault than for murder" (2012: 146). Free and Ruesink also found that while most rapes are intraracial, "the ones that result in wrongful conviction apparently are more likely to be interracial" (2012: 137–146).[8]

Some of the men of the Central Park Five now make frequent public presentations to warn young people about the dangers of trusting the police—of believing that they naturally could serve a positive purpose in neighborhoods of communities on the margins. One mentioned that, after his release from prison, his most comfortable place at home was a small room, because it reminded him of his prison cell. It was as if his body had been released from prison but his mind and spirit remained incarcerated.

During their imprisonment, these individuals stopped being malleable children and became men of conviction. After their initial confessions, the teens denied participating in the rape. They continued to insist on their innocence even when facing parole boards during their incarceration. They refused to admit to the rape even if it meant not getting a shorter sentence. Despite the damage the period of imprisonment heaped on them, they steadfastly maintained their innocence.

## Stories I Heard

What is clear is that most of the Central Park Five missed the bulk of their teen years. After their exoneration, as I continued to follow the case in graduate school and beyond, I would periodically see notices that a member of the group would be speaking publicly about the ordeal. On two occasions, I went to hear them speak: once on a college campus and another time at an event organized by a community group. The first time I attended one of these presentations was somewhat surreal for me. I do not often meet the subjects of news media stories I have worked on years after the fact. And, I have never before participated in a story with such an outcome.

At one of the gatherings at a local college (one of the four-year colleges in the City University of New York system), I sat in the audience anticipating what would come. The professor who had organized the event was an African American woman, and most of the students in the classroom were African American and Latino. The amphitheater-shaped lecture hall was maybe two-thirds full. There was a buzz of excitement in the room. I wondered what the students knew about the story, how well they knew it, and what they thought of the Central Park Five. Had the members of the group become heroic in some way now? They seemed to have achieved the status of some type of folk legend, characters in a cautionary tale. It was our own cautionary tale, traveling discursively through black communities. It would be repeated time and again, becoming part of the knowledge in black communities regarding what to expect from the police and the criminal justice system. And it has the potential to shape racial interactions and interactions between black communities and the police for years to come.

Transcending the lasting effects of the past on their lives seems to be one of the most difficult things these men now face. They all have had trouble either finding or maintaining good jobs (Burns 2011), a situation common to most that have been incarcerated (Pager 2007). One of the things that makes it difficult for them to rise above their past is that many who hear about the convictions being overturned do not believe the charges were dropped because of their innocence. Instead, many people believe that some technicality—not the innocence of the accused—led to the convictions being vacated.

One of the stories that has stayed with me during interviews and presentations regarding the case serves as a chilling reminder of how easily mistakes can be made in police investigations of crimes. One of the Central Park Five tells an unsettling story of a claim made by Matias Reyes about the jogger's rape. Reyes told a television news reporter that he had been friendly with some of the police in the neighborhood. Reyes reportedly did odd jobs in the area to support himself and sometimes even slept in the back of a bodega. On the night of the attack, Reyes apparently ran into one of the police officers he knew and stopped to chat with him moments after leaving the battered jogger in the park. Reyes told the reporter that there was blood still on his pants, and had the officer looked down or had it been the light of day maybe he would have seen it.[9]

Another story that has stayed with me reflects the degree to which the arrests and convictions also transformed the lives of the Central Park Five's family members. One of the parents, unwilling to allow her son to become even more of a statistic, went to extraordinary lengths to maintain regular contact with him, a factor that helps the incarcerated to maintain a sense of themselves. Family visits are very difficult for New York City residents imprisoned in the correctional system. Most of the New York State prisons are very far upstate, some close to the Canadian border. The distance makes the maintenance of family bonds very challenging. One parent practically lived in her car for a while so that she could visit her son regularly so he would not feel abandoned by his family.

Another of the Central Park Five tells a story of being transferred with another group member to a new prison and seeing the windows of the building completely darkened, but not because shades were drawn or there were no lights on inside. The reason for the darkness was the masses of bodies pressed against the windows trying to witness the arrival of the young men at the facility. Their reputations had preceded them; they were infamous and reviled. The case was famous, and rapists are only one cut above child molesters in the prison system.

## Status of the War on Drugs

I noted earlier that the War on Drugs had arisen from a moral panic and served up young black and Latino males as the new folk devils (Reinarman and Levine 2006). The drug war's targeting of poor African Americans and Latinos and its concomitant role in disproportionately increasing the numbers of young blacks and Latinos in the criminal justice system will mark future generations. Compounding this damage is the drug war's failure to eliminate or significantly reduce illegal drug use or drug trafficking in the United States. Supporters of reforming drug laws have claimed that they have won the moral and intellectual debate, but the political debate is ongoing. While the issue is being hashed out, what cannot be understated is the role of the drug war in our construction of the definition of young blacks and Latinos, particularly males, as extremely deviant.

There has been a little relief. The administration of President Barack Obama has attempted to reform the approach to the drug war by defining a "new" mainstream. In August 2013, the Obama administration issued its latest National Drug Control Strategy, the annual report from the Office of National Drug Control Policy.[10] This report builds on the administration's new direction, which frames the nation's drug problem as a public health issue.[11] The 2013 Strategy claimed that more was being spent on prevention and treatment than on law enforcement. The previous year's Strategy noted that the administration had "pursued a mainstream approach to the drug problem—an approach that rejects the false choice between an enforcement-centric 'war on drugs' on the one hand and the notion of drug legalization on the other."[12] Despite Obama's continuing support of the drug wars, his was the first administration in forty years to address the racial disparity in drug sentencing laws. As part of the policy outlined in the 2010 Strategy, Obama achieved passage of the 2010 Fair Sentencing Act, which addressed the disparity in legal penalties for the more affluent whites who abuse powder cocaine, as compared to the lower income blacks and Latinos who abuse crack cocaine. However, this law only *reduced* the amount of the disparity. The legal system has yet to treat blacks and Latinos as equal to whites when it comes to drug laws. Prior to the 2010 legislation, there was an "unfair and unjustified 100 to 1 sentencing disparity between offenses for crack and powder cocaine."[13] The new act reduced the disparity to 18 to 1.[14] Even if President Obama were to "end" the drug war today by eliminating the $25.2 billion allocated for the various components of this policy, the change would not immediately transform society. The drug war has literally changed our culture.

I argue in this book that the drug war became a pernicious force in U.S. society because of the moral panic used to launch it. As a result of this drug war, race, youth, and crime were reified in the social and symbolic systems and institutions of U.S. culture, particularly in the media and sectors of law enforcement such as the police. In Chapter 8, I argue that due to the drug war, by the time of the jogger incident, black race had become a "naturalized" aspect of the criminal justice system. This made it unnecessary for the media to use indicators of racial categorical groupings when representing the criminal justice system in media products.

The role of the media in reinforcing racial meaning could be teased out from the results of my content analysis. As noted in Chapter 1, the content analysis provided results that indicated the existence of important associations between some of the variables or conceptual categories such as race, age, class, gender, and victimhood. Some of the most interesting associations involved the relationship between any one of the life category variables and prominent placement of articles. Prominent placement informs the reader about internal newsroom values, and prominent placement of any story indicates to the audience that newsmakers have prioritized its message. Sixty-four percent of the 251 articles in my sample were prominently placed.

I found a statistically significant association between prominent placement and high numbers of indicators of the categorical grouping "age" in articles.[15] In other words, the media content makers prioritized stories that had a high age component in their content. Most of the indicators for age referred to the young black and Latino suspects.[16] This statistically significant association between the young suspects' ages as a social category and prominent placement is an important finding because it likely represents a shift in society's attitudes about youngsters, specifically minority youth. Age is seen here as a social category that can be masked by or defined by black racial group membership. For the young suspects, their race defined how they would be perceived and treated as young people. In the context of this case, age likely served as a marker of criminality for these young black and Latino suspects.

Two other important relationships should be noted at this point. In my content analysis, I looked at the relationship between the occurrence in articles of high numbers of racial terms and high numbers of terms relating to violence. Stories with high counts of racial indicators also had high numbers of violence terms, an association that was statistically significant. It is unlikely that the stories with high counts of racial references accidentally ended up with high usage of violence terms. Through their presentation, media content makers—whether consciously or not—linked race and violence in the minds of their readers. I also found a statistically significant association between racial categorical indicators and references to the jogger's status as a victim. Stories with high usage of racial indicators also included high usage of terms regarding the jogger's status as a victim. This is an indication of the rather traditional fear, discussed in Chapter 3, that black males pose a danger to white women.

Historically in the United States, a relationship has been drawn between race and violence. Blacks and Latinos have long been portrayed as being more violent than other races. The news media in the United States have historically been involved in this kind of representation of blacks and other people of color, dating back to some of the earliest newspapers and their portrayals of Native Americans and African slaves (Saxton 1984). Lori Dorfman and Vincent Schiraldi (2001) found that the news media unfairly connect "minority" races and crime, especially violent crime. In their study, which is a meta-analysis of about seventy-seven content analyses that incorporated media content published or broadcast between 1910 to 2001, the researchers found that white Americans "overestimate their likelihood of being victimized by minorities by three to one" (Dorfman and Schiraldi 2001: 16). These symbolic representations of young black and Latino males serve to further marginalize them in U.S. society.

## The "Worst of the Worst"

While it would be impossible to draw direct connections between media content and the treatment received by the young suspects in the Central Park jogger case, the accounts of their experiences point to some of the themes that stand out about the significance of the case. While the men blame the press and the police, their comments should not be perceived simply as complaints. The comments provide evidence for Luhmann's (2000) theory about knowledge-producing institutions. Niklas Luhmann (2000) contends that it is impossible to make a distinction between the internal reality of the newsroom and the external reality of the world outside the newsroom. There is no way to know the actual genesis of the knowledge being generated in news products because one cannot determine which reality (internal or external) served as the primary source for the knowledge produced. Due to the close relationship between the press and the criminal justice system, particularly the police, it is impossible to delineate, in the case of the jogger coverage, the boundaries of the media—that is, to know where the world outside media began. At the time, whatever the police said became "real," despite the unlikelihood of such a result based on the statistical evidence. Establishing the "fact" of the innocence of the young men continues to be elusive because many law enforcement officials continue to support the idea of their guilt in the rape. And, although it was not the 1940s, 1950s, or 1960s, it would not be hyperbole to interpret the Donald Trump ads in the city's four major newspapers pushing for reinstatement of the death penalty in New York (discussed in Chapter 4) as something akin to a call for a lynching. While there was no lynching per se, there is no denying the realness of all the experiences of the Central Park Five—from their arrests and interrogations through their trials and long incarceration. The word that constantly comes to mind—and that I have heard them use themselves—is "surreal."

The surreal quality of the lives of these men has not ended. With all they have been through, they wonder about people's continued faith in the system and the way most people unquestioningly accept the relationship between the press and the police—a relationship they see in which the media serve as a mouthpiece for police interests. They also have a deep and abiding sense of insecurity that comes from understanding how their status as ex-convicts in the minds of some and their fame as the individuals who were accused and convicted of raping the Central Park jogger put them in a position where almost anyone else in society can exercise power over them. They have experienced the status of ex-convict, in which a person is not only at the mercy of those in positions of authority, like the police, but also at the mercy anyone who wants to tell or remind a boss or a landlord of exactly who the person is. Suddenly everything can change, and the ex-convict may have to start over one more time.

Obstacles constantly crop up to block success. The feeling is like being stripped of citizenship; one remains in prison even when not physically in that space.

The positionality of the young men who went through this ordeal is bifurcated. In many respects, it is both renown and infamy. They experienced notoriety for having been accused of this rape, and they experienced fame for not having done it. They are famous and infamous. The most sociologically interesting part of the fame/infamy dyad for me is the fame. The whole world saw the development of the coverage and the infamy it produced. The young suspects became the "worst of the worst." But their position as famous people is less contingent on that April 19, 1989, incident. Their fame is derived from their having survived the ordeal and being able to tell their stories. They now participate in public speaking engagements in which they describe the injustices they have experienced. They not only represent the people who were wrongly convicted in the Central Park case; they also represent other young African American men who were wrongly convicted, who were incarcerated, who had to learn to survive in a prison context, who struggle to maintain jobs in spite of their past. They represent a much larger group than the five boys who share the history of that April day in 1989. When they tell their stories, the latent message in their narratives is simple: "If you are a young black or Latino male, it could happen to you too. In fact, it's happening to lots of people just like us, in similar and in different ways." Most do not want to believe it could happen to them—not the police accusations, not the wrongful convictions, not the false confessions, and not the unjust incarceration.

## The Vulnerability of Young Black and Latino Males— Inside and Outside the Mainstream

The history inscribed on the bodies of young black and Latino males makes them one of the most feared and most vilified groups in U.S. society. Many aspects of their multiple intersecting identities of age, race, class, and gender contribute to their marginalization, but what stands out particularly is the normalization of "the concept of Black men as sexual predators" (P. H. Collins 2005: 162). Two situations come to mind that point to the vulnerability of the members of this group. On a national level, there is the case of Trayvon Martin. On a local level, there is the continuing struggle in New York City to end the New York Police Department's stop-and-frisk program, which is executed under the state's forty-nine-year-old stop and search law. Both of these situations are by-products of the moral panic that began in the 1960s, which spawned the drug war and the continuing association of minority youth of color and violent crime. These young men are regularly subjected to racial profiling "based on . . . [their] *'potential'* threat" (P. H. Collins 2005: 153).

Racial profiling often leads to situations that disproportionately ensnare young African American and Latino men in the criminal justice system or violate their civil and human rights. And sometimes racial profiling incidents are fatal. The Trayvon Martin case is the story of the fatal shooting of seventeen-year-old Martin in a gated community in Florida. This African American teenager walked unarmed in an outdoor space within the community where his father's fiancée lived. Martin's presence in this social location was considered questionable by twenty-eight-year-old George Zimmerman, founder and reportedly an overzealous member of the neighborhood watch group (Green 2012). Zimmerman, who has been described in the media as part Latino, seemed to believe he had the power to determine Martin's right to enter mainstream spaces—in this case, a space that was predominantly white. Press accounts have described the gated community, called The Retreat at Twin Lakes, which is in Sanford, Florida, as racially mixed—50 percent white, 20 percent black, and 20 percent Latino (Green 2012). It was an area that had also been experiencing a series of "petty crimes," which led in September 2011 to the formation of the neighborhood watch group (Green 2012).

On February 26, 2012, Zimmerman saw Martin walking in the rain, viewed him as suspicious, and called the police to voice the perceived threat he thought Martin represented. Zimmerman had a history of making repeated calls to the police about possible criminals in his community, some of whom he had identified as black. That night, Zimmerman—who was armed—decided to pursue Martin through the complex. In a confrontation that ensued, Zimmerman fatally shot Martin (Green 2012). Police arrived at the scene, decided not to arrest Zimmerman, and cited Florida's Stand-Your-Ground law as the basis of his self-defense.

A national public outcry arose, with people across the nation protesting the failure of the police to arrest Zimmerman and to conduct a full investigation. The protest period, which lasted about a month, culminated in Zimmerman being charged in early April with second-degree murder; a trial was scheduled for mid-2013.

The Florida Stand-Your-Ground law was widely debated in the press, primarily in the context of the appropriateness of Zimmerman and the police using it as justification for the fatal shooting. What rarely comes up in the context of the discussion of Stand-Your-Ground in this case are the rights of Trayvon Martin. About two months following Zimmerman's arrest, court-released tapes revealed his claim that he had ended his pursuit of Martin and that the teen had then sneaked up on him and attacked him (Alvarez and Williams 2012). Zimmerman claimed that he had fired the fatal shot as he tried to defend himself from Martin's attack. A press report of the more extended version of Zimmerman's story of the events (Alvarez and Williams 2012), which is based on police interviews with him on February 26, 27, and 29, shows that the police officer who conducted the interviews regarded portions of Zimmerman's account with skepticism. The account quotes the police officer interviewing Zimmerman as follows:

> "What if, in his mind's eye, which I can't get into because he has passed, he perceives you as a threat," Mr. Serino said, drawing no answer from Mr. Zimmerman. "He perceived you as a threat; he has every right to defend himself, especially if you reach into your pocket to grab your cellphone." (Alvarez and Williams 2012)

In seeking justice for the dead teenager, Martin's family members and supporters gave the press a variety of images of him that constructed him as a sweet innocent. These were desexualized pictures of Martin taken at a slightly younger age than his seventeen years. The press initially also presented Martin as the all-American student jock in a football uniform, a possible attempt to associate him with the mainstream and distance him from the image of a young black male who would automatically be perceived as dangerous. The constructions of Martin possibly point to the representation of a more acceptable black masculinity. A desexualized young black man—that is, someone less likely to prompt imaginings of the uncontrollable sexual predator—would be "safe" and thus able to garner support within the mainstream.

Managing the image of Trayvon Martin presented in the mainstream media was not an unnecessary strategy for securing justice in the case. Mainstream commentator and journalist Geraldo Rivera opined that maybe Martin had looked threatening because of the hoodie sweatshirt he was wearing that night (Jonsson 2012). Rivera cautioned black families to prevent their teen boys from wearing hoodies—in order to save their lives. Rivera's blame-the-victim logic revealed mainstream logic about the social location of low-income young black and Latino males, In this case, the hoodie sweatshirt could be a cultural indicator for the categorical life experiences of class. It seems that the hoodie acted as a class marker that intersected with Martin's racial categorical grouping. Since race was able to define/construct class as a categorical life experience, Zimmerman would or could be expected to imagine Martin as someone who did not belong in that gated community. Through this intersection, Zimmerman would have to assume that Martin belonged to a "lower class" and should be perceived as being that much more dangerous. This is the multiplicative effect of intersectional identities that Deborah King (1998) discussed.

On July 13, 2013, George Zimmerman was acquitted of second-degree murder and manslaughter by a jury of six women. In the wake of the acquittal, protests erupted around the country. Five days after the verdict, President Barack Obama held a poignant press conference in which he spoke from the point of view of another black man who has had to suffer racial profiling. He said, "I think it's important to recognize that the African-American community is looking at this issue through a set of experiences and a history that—that doesn't go away."[17] When I read President Obama's statement, it reminded me of conversations in my own home between my parents and my brothers about this very issue.

The New York Police Department's controversial stop-and-frisk program, in which police officers can stop and search people they deem suspicious, has been particularly contentious under the administration of Mayor Michael Bloomberg. However, the level of controversy about the program has been growing since 1997, when the occurrence of such stops soared.[18] The debate over the constitutionality of these practices likely contributed the decline in stop-and-frisk incidents in 2012. That year, the NYPD made 532,911 stop and frisks (New York Civil Liberties Union 2013: 2). The 2012 figure represents a substantial decrease from the nearly 700,000 stop and frisks in 2011; 87 percent of those incidents involved males of African American and Latino descent (New York Civil Liberties Union 2012: 2, 5). In addition, critics argue that the stop and frisks have led to numerous unlawful arrests. Opponents of this policy have framed it as a type of Jim Crow practice. A broad-based multicultural coalition of organizations that represent a variety of interests has been organizing to end the practice.

Police contend that the law is an important tool for reducing crime and violence. However, the stop-and-frisk practices have dramatically increased the numbers of marijuana arrests (New York Civil Liberties Union 2013). Under a New York state law in place since 1977, possession of a small amount (less than 25 grams) of *concealed* marijuana warrants only a violation—a ticket. However, if the subject of a stop and frisk search is ordered to empty his (or her) pockets or bag and marijuana comes into public view, that individual can be charged with a misdemeanor. In essence, a minor marijuana violation turns into a crime when the subject of the stop complies with the police officer's order (Koch 2012). In this way, stop and frisk has saddled many young black and Latino males with police records that stunt their educational and employment opportunities. New York Governor Andrew Cuomo, in coordination with New York City officials, attempted to enact compromise legislation that would make possession of small amounts of marijuana, regardless of concealment, a violation (thus avoiding criminal charges), but the effort failed in the state legislature (Koch 2012). That the governor would offer a softening of drug laws as a solution—as opposed to addressing the human rights violations inherent in the practice—points to how dramatically narratives from the War on Drugs have changed our society. It also indicates how willing people are to treat laws, rules, and practices as if they are blind to peoples' race, class, and gender. Ann Ferguson (2000), in her ethnographic study of the punishment system in a Los Angeles school district, found that society's "moral authority" creates laws, rules, and practices that are in fact *not* blind to people's race, class, and gender.

It is clear that the stop-and-frisk practices are not so blind, given the disproportionate numbers of black and Latino males affected. A 2012 *New York Times* short documentary film, *The Scars of Stop-and-Frisk*, addressed the impact of these practices on the lives of young men of color. In their article accompanying the film, Dressner and Martinez (2012) noted the following:

> The practice of stop-and-frisk has become increasingly controversial, but what is often absent from the debate are the voices of young people affected by such aggressive policing on a daily basis. To better understand the human impact of this practice, we made this film about Tyquan Brehon, a young man who lives in one of the most heavily policed neighborhoods in Brooklyn.
>
> By his count, before his 18th birthday, he had been unjustifiably stopped by the police more than 60 times. On several occasions, merely because he asked why he had been stopped, he was handcuffed, placed in a cell and detained for hours before being released without charges. These experiences were scarring; Mr. Brehon did whatever he could to avoid the police, often feeling as if he were a prisoner in his home.

The practice of stop and frisk suggests that mainstream boundary enforcers identify significant aspects of black masculinity as "suspicious," that is, possibly criminal. This would make black males, in general, unfit for mainstream participation. New York Civil Liberties Union reports have revealed some startling facts about the city's stop-and-frisk program. In 2012, "the number of stops of young black men neared the entire city population of young black men (133,119 as compared to 158,406)" (New York Civil Liberties Union 2013: 2). In the previous year, stops of young black men exceeded the number of young black men in New York City (New York Civil Liberties Union 2012: 2). On August 12, 2013, a federal judge ruled that the NYPD stop-and-frisk practices were unconstitutional. It remains to be seen how blacks and Latinos will fare as conflicts around these practices are resolved.

## Human Rights in the Age of Obama

The broadening swath of the right-wing political project to regain the moral authority that began in the 1960s has reorganized our culture at the same time the mainstream was being reconstructed to be more "inclusive." The dominant forces that control the mainstream have been able to appear all-encompassing while leaving more people out, due to the way in which the mainstream inflects and articulates all categorical groupings. The narratives about racial color blindness that came out of the post–civil rights era helped to frame the narratives about the drug war. Laws would be perceived as blind to people's race, class, and gender; and individual choices, cultural differences, and market forces would be put forth as explanations for racially disparate outcomes. In this era of color-blind racism, our approaches to organizing society—particularly around issues related to race, class, and gender—have saddled huge numbers of young black and Latino males with cultural artifacts and attributes that will prevent them from ever accessing mainstream opportunities and privileges—in some respects denying them the benefits of full participation as citizens in U.S. society. The irony of such a design in the age of Obama is that as more blacks reach lofty positions in U.S. society, the easier it is to keep large numbers of others out.

The high degree of marginalization taking place in the United States today is becoming so acceptable in the mainstream that when Trayvon Martin died because he had violated a mainstream boundary, President Obama could only issue a personal statement about the problem of marginalization of black males in America. He said, "If I had a son, he'd look like Trayvon." There was a backlash to even that mild statement (Coates 2012). One can only imagine the degree of backlash had he discussed Martin's case in the context of civil rights or police practices, as he did in the case of Henry Louis "Skip" Gates Jr. The 2009 Gates case began when police arrested the African American Harvard University professor after a worried neighbor saw him entering *his own home*. Obama's comments questioning the actions of the police in that case met enormous challenges in the mainstream. Three years later, in the more serious case of Trayvon Martin, Obama framed his comments in the context of personal discourse. The problem he seems to be arguing is that one categorical life experience, like race, can be masked by or defined by others. Therefore, someone who could be his son—who presumably would know the forms of expression, forms of interaction, and forms of meaning making regarded as acceptable by the mainstream—could still have his life experiences circumscribed by the current definition of black "race." Until we can transform the meaning of "blackness" into something comparable to whiteness in the mainstream—or until we can eliminate the significance of "whiteness," as Haney-Lopez (1996) contends—racial hierarchies are here to stay.

# Notes

## CHAPTER 1

1. Despite the scientific discrediting of racial narratives and reasoning based on genetics, some people—even some highly educated ones—continue to operate using these illogical assumptions. For a full treatment of how Americans ignore the science of race to create baseless racial reasoning, see K. E. Fields and B. J. Fields 2012.

2. An intersectional analysis is central to this study, to help elucidate the unique position of low-income black and Latino males before and after the jogger incident. Intersectional analysis investigates the privilege and oppression experienced by people in the unique social locations created from intersecting structures of race, class, and gender. Intersectional analysis was developed by black feminists and other feminists of color; it arose from the theoretical and political need to render the black female subject visible and to interrogate the areas where scholars and society had remained silent about the life experiences of black women and other women of color. Development of this area of study is a response to theories of racial and gender oppression that proved to be inadequate because they could not imagine the position of the black woman as someone who experiences both racial and gender subordination simultaneously. It is also a response to marginalization. Intersectional analysis allows one to reveal the underlying categorical boundaries constructed through systems of oppression that must be negotiated as people use their intersecting identities—of race, class, and gender—to navigate these boundaries. My examination of the Central Park jogger case incorporates the work of scholars who use intersectional analysis (Bardaglio 1994; P. H. Collins 1986; Crenshaw 1991; A. Davis 1981; Ferguson 2000; J. D. Hall 1983; King 1988; Romero 2011; V. Smith 1998; White 1999; Wilkins 2008). These intersectional studies point to the existence of abstract social realities that pertain to the various ways that multiple intersecting forms of oppression—based on factors such as race, class, and gender—create multiple positionalities for members of these large-group categories.

3. I view the mainstream as an ideological and spatial construct that allows dominant forces in a society to maintain hegemony. As it operates, the mainstream is ontologically transitory. See Ferguson 2000.

4. I use the term "race" interchangeably with the terms "racial category" or "racial classification."

5. Here I am using Bonilla-Silva's (2006: chap. 2) frames to interpret information within the ideology of color-blind racism.

6. A comparison of the teens in the Central Park case to the Scottsboro boys began from the earliest days of the incident.

7. This type of reaction from some black women to the attack on the jogger points to why it is important to view as unique the social locations created through intersecting structures of race, class, and gender oppression and domination. Distinct social locations arise from a *multiplicative* effect of race, class, and gender domination as opposed to an additive effect. Deborah King (1988: 49–51) noted:

> The relative significance of race, sex, or class in determining the conditions of black women's lives is neither fixed nor absolute but, rather, is dependent on the socio-historical context and the social phenomenon under consideration. These interactions also produce what to some appears a seemingly confounding set of social roles and political attitudes among black women. . . . Yet, it is black women's well-documented facility to encompass seemingly contradictory role expectations of worker, homemaker, and mother that has contributed to the confusion in understanding black womanhood. . . . These competing demands (each requiring its own set of resistances to multiple forms of oppression) are a primary influence on the black woman's definition of her womanhood, and her relationships to the people around her. To reduce this complex of negotiations to an addition problem (racism + sexism = black women's experience) is to define the issues, and indeed black womanhood itself, within the structural terms developed by Europeans and especially white males to privilege their race and their sex unilaterally. Sojourner's declaration, "ain't I a woman?" directly refutes this sort of conceptualization of womanhood as one dimensional rather than dialectical.

8. Content analysis has both quantitative and qualitative components, and researchers use this methodology in various ways. The approach used in this study is one that equates content and meaning and describes content as the thing that emerges from the text's relationship to "a particular context" (Krippendorff 2004: 19–20).

9. As with all scientific methods, any type of content analysis used must be replicable and must exhibit reliability and validity. "For a content analysis to be replicable, the analysts must explicate the context that guides their inferences" (Krippendorff 2004: 24). I explain the design and procedures of the content analysis in the text. Here I am concerned about content validity. I am coding articles for words and terms and using the words and terms as indicators for concepts in the society as well as components of the news stories. The indicators about society are representations of culture, social structure, and institutions. For example, I measure words and terms that are indicators for categorical life experiences such as race, class, and gender. I include additional categorical experiences that are relevant to this particular story, such as age, the jogger's status as a victim, and violence.

10. There is much debate about whether or not the media create or reflect reality. This work does not engage in that debate.

11. "Smaller story topics" are anecdotes, clauses, or phrases that serve as representations of subjects, actions, or events that are incorporated into a main or larger story (i.e., overall argument or plot). For example, the jogger's family background is a smaller story topic. The *Daily News* published at least one free-standing article about the jogger's family that established the family as affluent. But in other published articles in the coverage, the affluence of the jogger's family appeared as a smaller story topic that was relied upon to construct the "facts" (build the argument) in the news article. I employ Gaye Tuchman's

definition of the term "facts," which she describes as "pertinent information gathered by professionally validated methods specifying the relationship between what is known and how it is known" (1978: 82). The gathering of information using field-specific techniques, sources, and manners of presentation allows news stories to create what Tuchman calls "a web of facticity" (1978: 82). The smaller story topics become part of the "web of facticity" in news stories.

12. These "desks" represent divisions (geographical, topical, and administrative) within news organizations. Depending on the size of the paper and the resources available to it, desks vary from a one-person operation to a department-sized operation that produces its own section of the newspaper. Most papers typically have a large city or metro desk. Other types of desks include national, international, business, entertainment, features, and photography. The national desk is responsible for stories coming out of Washington, D.C., and for stories with a national impact. Stories coming out of bureaus around the world move through the international desk. Individual desks do not carry the same weight in all news organization. The importance of each desk carries depends on the nature of the organization. At the *New York Daily News,* the city desk is the most important news-gathering desk. At the *New York Times,* the national and international desks are the two most prominent news-gathering desks.

13. Hard news is often defined as breaking news (unfolding important events) that is presented using traditional or "objective" facts that respond to the questions who, what, where, when, and why. In newspapers, hard news stories are often written in the inverted pyramid style, with the most important information (facts and sources) near the top of the inverted pyramid and the balance of the information falling in descending order of importance down to the pyramid's tip, at the bottom. Feature stories do not rely as often on the inverted pyramid structure and instead use the human element and colorful or slice-of-life details. Editorials are opinion pieces that incorporate the writer's viewpoint and may use first-person language. News analyses are stories that are presented as analyses of recent news events; they are sometimes labeled as such.

14. An article in the *New York Times* was classified as prominently placed if any of the following applies to it: (1) the article appears in the main section before page fifteen, because this section of the paper is distributed nationally; (2) the article appears in the B section on pages one through three, which is toward the front of that section; or (3) the article is an editorial. In the *Daily News* prominence is based on the placement of ads that break up the presentation of news in the front part of the paper. Because the paper rarely places full-page ads before page seven, the stories placed on pages one through seven are considered to be of the greatest significance relative to the other articles published in that book. As with the *New York Times, Daily News* editorials are also considered prominent.

15. There are other components of prominence that I did not measure, such as length of stories and size of type. For an example of a content analysis that measures length of stories, see Martindale 1986.

16. The attack on the jogger took place late in the evening on April 19, 1989. She was discovered by passersby early in the morning on April 20. The first newspaper stories appeared on April 21.

17. I borrow from Neuman's (2011) discussion of the work of the ethnographer.

18. My early forays into autoethnography began as structured memoir writing. Structured memoir writing is a technique developed by Erika Duncan, the founder of Herstory, a women's memoir-writing group based on Long Island, New York. Duncan developed her technique as a way of helping women, who historically represent a marginalized group, to discover their voices and tell their stories. Central to Duncan's pedagogy

is a construct she calls the "stranger-reader." Duncan teaches writers to structure and weave their stories in a way that allows the stranger-reader, someone who knows nothing about them, to walk in their shoes and experience their moments of realization. It is a method of writing based on empathy. See Duncan 2008.

19. Some of these personal narratives were developed in Herstory memoir-writing workshops.

20. Symbolic production is "the production of symbols as opposed to the production of tangible goods" (Ford 1992: 119).

## CHAPTER 2

1. In this study I use Omi and Winant's (1994: 55) definition of race: "Race is a concept which signifies and symbolizes social conflicts and interests by referring to different types of human bodies." I use the term "race" interchangeably with "racial category."

2. The 2002 reexamination of the case that led to the court vacating the convictions made clear that the jogger likely started her run about 9:00 P.M. See Dwyer and Flynn 2002.

3. In 1989, 3,254 rapes were reported in New York City. This figure comes from the National Crime Victimization Survey, which is part of a study conducted by two statisticians from the Bureau of Justice Statistics in the U.S. Department of Justice. See Patrick A. Langan and Matthew R. Durose, "The Remarkable Drop in Crime in New York City," paper presented at Italy's National Statistical Institute Conference on Crime, Rome, Italy, December 3–5, 2003.

4. Blacks made up 2 percent of the journalists working for mainstream newspapers in the United States in 1968; that number grew to only 5 percent in the early 1990s, according to Voakes (1997).

5. Like the main character in Ralph Ellison's *Invisible Man* ([1947] 1989), the marginalization I experienced in the mainstream given my features—as a dark-complexioned African American woman—made me a somewhat of a cipher, a zero in the context of the mainstream. Forces outside of me often determined the meaning of the features that classified me as black and female. In a mainstream setting such as the hospital, administrators could not imagine that I could be one of the journalists they had to be wary of.

6. This is the last line of Langston Hughes's poem "I, Too" (Hughes 1959: 275).

7. Joseph Conrad's *Heart of Darkness* ([1902] 2008) is instructive in ideas about racial domination. The book's protagonist is Captain Marlow, who is at the helm of a leaky steamboat snaking its way up the Congo. Marlow, infused with the culture of European imperialists, views as subhuman the African working side by side with him, the man helping him to keep the boiler of his spongy vessel operational. Marlow said, "He was there below me, and upon my word, to look at him was as edifying as seeing a dog in a parody of breeches and a feather hat, walking on his hind-legs" (Conrad [1902] 2008: 48). Marlow's fireman is an integral part of the steamboat's operation, but the European system of thought prevents Marlow from seeing the fireman as a person like himself. Marlow is a skeptical sort, however. Given the behavior of Europeans in Africa that he has witnessed, he has not fully bought into the imperialist perspective equating Africans with animals. Upon observing the social dynamics between the imperial powers and the Africans, Marlow allows himself to peek behind the ideological curtain. Another level of awareness about the humanity of the oppressed Africans is slowly seeping into his consciousness. But he doubts that either he or his fellow Europeans are courageous enough to admit it:

"Well, you know, that was the worst of it—this suspicion of their not being inhuman. It would come slowly to one" (Conrad [1902] 2008: 47).

8. "The combination of all these factors—tougher drug laws, mandatory sentencing and additional judges, the advent of 'crack' cocaine, and finally Tactical Narcotics Team sweeps—caused a dramatic increase in commitments of drug felons to state prisons during the 1980's. This is best illustrated by the fact that in 1982, 9.5 percent of the inmates in DOCS [New York State Department of Correctional Services] were under custody on drug charges, while by 1992 that share had grown to almost 35 percent" (Silver and Farrell 1998).

9. Background on the Church of the Heavenly Rest is provided on the church's website: http://www.heavenlyrest.org/.

## CHAPTER 3

1. Joan Didion's (1991) essay contrasts the jogger incident with the largely unnoticed murder of a white woman (less affluent than the jogger) by a city official, noting that the events New Yorkers have been encouraged to be concerned with have been cherry-picked based on criteria other than criminality.

2. It is important to note that Angela Davis (1981), in her essay "The Myth of the Black Rapist" in *Women, Race and Class,* takes Brownmiller (1975) to task for failing to properly interrogate race in her groundbreaking work *Against Our Will.*

3. I view the mainstream as an ideological and spatial construct that allows dominant forces in a society to maintain hegemony. As it operates, the mainstream is ontologically transitory.

4. The content analysis, which incorporates qualitative and quantitative techniques, examined a sample of 251 stories published from April 21, 1989, to December 31, 2003, in two major newspapers, the *New York Times* and the *New York Daily News.* The articles represent a sampling of the stories in which the Central Park jogger incident and its aftermath was the subject of the story and not simply a reference mentioned in an article on another subject. The full data set is a collection of approximately 502 newspaper articles—206 from the *New York Times* and about 296 from the *Daily News.* The *New York Times* articles were selected in two steps. Once a Lexis-Nexis search had produced a list of articles and publication dates, those dates were searched by microfilm and the articles that met the selection criteria were copied, along with the full pages on which they were published. The *Daily News* stories from 1996 to 2003 were collected in the same fashion. However, 1996 represents the first year that the *Daily News* began participating in the Lexis-Nexis database. For the years from 1989 to 1996, the *Daily News* articles were retrieved by going through microfilm for the entire period and copying relevant articles—in which the Central Park Jogger incident and its aftermath was the subject of the story—with the same procedure used to copy the *New York Times* articles. The following features of the content of each story are examined: (1) the placement of the story, (2) the desk that produced the story, (3) the type of story, (4) the date of publication, and (5) the sources used. I also measured the occurrence of words and terms in the stories that are indicators of (1) race, (2) class status, (3) violence, (4) gender, (5) victimhood, and (6) age. I also measured the number of "smaller" story topics used in the coverage. For the examination, the fourteen-year period of the Central Park jogger coverage is divided into four phases: The first phase is the aftermath of the incident, which runs from April 21, 1989 to June 9, 1989. This is the period during which I participated in the reporting. It represents the time when the narrative of the coverage was being constructed. The second stage represents, primarily, the

coverage of the legal case against the defendants. It begins June 10, 1989, and continues through the initial legal resolution of the cases in mid-March 1991. The defendants were divided into three groups, because there were three separate legal cases involving them. The first trial had three defendants, the second trial had two, and there was a plea bargain agreement resolving the case for the sixth person. The third time period runs from the remainder of 1991 through 2001. During this phase, coverage of the incident as the subject of a story almost completely subsided. However, the Central Park jogger incident continued to be used as a reference in stories published on other subjects. The final time period runs from the beginning of 2002 until the end of December 2003. In this period, the district attorney's office received new information that a man claiming to be the lone attacker of the jogger had confessed to the crime. The office then opened up a new investigation that confirmed that the DNA of the new suspect (Matias Reyes) matched DNA from the crime and petitioned the court to vacate the convictions of the initial defendants. This period also incorporates a little bit of the aftermath of the court ruling. The four time phases in which the articles have been grouped form sampling clusters. From each cluster, a sample was randomly selected. To ensure randomness, each article in the data set was given a unique number. Each number was written on a piece of paper, which was folded and placed in a box. From that box, half of the numbers for each cluster were randomly selected. Thus, data were collected from a total of 251 articles ($N = 251$).

5. In response to feminist assertions that women should feel free to go where they want when they want, Joan Didion (1991) countered with an essay in the *New York Review of Books* that challenged some normative expectations, among them that cities were supposed to be safe. In most poor black and Latino communities, they are *not* safe.

6. See Helen Benedict's (1992) study of media coverage of sex crimes. I was interviewed by Benedict about my views on the Central Park jogger case and the amount of input editors were willing to accept from female reporters working on the story.

7. This occurred over time, though some historians see it happening sooner rather than later. I follow the timing of scholars who view the late nineteenth century as the period in which the ideology of white dominance crystallized (B. J. Fields 1990; Fredrickson 1971a, 1971b; Hodes 1997).

8. It eventually became illegal to rape an enslaved black woman in Georgia. "The 1861 Georgia code . . . asserted that rape was 'the carnal knowledge of a female, whether slave or free, forcibly and against her will.' Despite this more inclusive definition, the new code did not punish equally all those convicted of rape" (Bardaglio 1994: 760).

9. The newspapers the Penny Press replaced were called the "blanket sheets." The cost and physical structure of the blanket sheets were indicators of socioeconomic differentiation between the two types of newspapers. The target audience of the blanket sheets appeared to be a group with more financial resources than the intended audience of the Penny Press (Saxton 1984). "Selling for six cents a copy and described as 'blanket sheets' (35 inches by 24, they unfolded to a four-foot width), such papers obviously were intended to be spread out on the library table at home, or across the counting-house desk. Circulation was by subscription and subscriptions cost ten dollars a year, the equivalent of a week's wages for a skilled journeyman" (Saxton 2003: 95).

10. Pasley (2000) does not specifically identify these editors as coming from the Penny Presses, but this new media development overlapped with the Jackson administration. Other sources cite Jackson's relationship with Penny Press editors (see Fellow 2010: 106–107).

11. As the abolition movement became more radical, some Penny Press papers denounced the radicalism of the abolitionists (Roediger 1999: 78). Franklin (1980) defines the period after 1830 as the time of the rise of the militant abolitionists. During this period, newspapers run by militant abolitionists often faced violence (Franklin 1980: 180–185; Mindich 2000). Incidents such as these were reported: "Elijah P. Lovejoy was run out of St. Louis for criticizing the leniency of a judge in the trial of persons accused of burning a Negro alive. Later in Alton, Illinois, he was killed when a mob destroyed for the fourth time the press on which he printed the *Alton Observer*. In Cincinnati a mob destroyed James Birney's press in 1836, and he barely escaped with his life" (Franklin 1980: 185). Much of this type of violence during this period was instigated by early Penny Press editors. Mindich (2000: 19) cites incidents in which the violence was directed both at abolitionist editors as well as indiscriminately at free African Americans who happened to be in the vicinity. Mindich (2000) contextualizes the violence, arguing that much of this period was marred by mob violence that was both partisan in nature and anti-abolitionist. Angela Davis (1981) also notes that before the Civil War, more white abolitionists were lynched than blacks.

12. The case of the Scottsboro boys arose out of a 1931 incident in which nine black male youths traveling as hoboes on a freight train in Alabama got into a fight with young white males on the train. The white males charged the blacks with assault, and two white women also traveling on the train leveled rape charges against the boys. Despite a later recantation of the rape charges by one of the women, the boys were repeatedly convicted in a series of trials and retrials. Most served long prison sentences. Emmett Till was a fourteen-year-old Chicago boy visiting family in Money, Mississippi, in the summer of 1955. He is said to have whistled at a white woman. In retaliation, a group of white men took him from his uncle's home in the early morning hours, brutally beat him, shot him in the head, and threw his body in a river. Till's mother held an open-casket public funeral in Chicago to reveal the cruel treatment her son had experienced. After a public outcry, his killers were tried and acquitted.

13. Captain Marlow is the steamboat captain in Joseph Conrad's *Heart of Darkness* ([1902] 2008) who has trouble looking beyond the European system of thought to see that Africans are human beings (see Chapter 2, note 7). Bigger Thomas is the protagonist in Richard Wright's novel *Native Son* ([1940] 1993). Thomas is a young black man who experiences whiteness as an oppressive force that causes insurmountably negative social conditions and places him in a position in which he inadvertently kills a young white woman. The killing changes him, releasing more violent behavior that leads to him raping and deliberately killing his black girlfriend.

14. Du Bois's ([1903] 2003) term "double-consciousness" can be described as the simultaneous self-awareness blacks have based on their understanding of their own humanity and an awareness of themselves as they are viewed through the eyes of their oppressors.

## CHAPTER 4

1. Though the prominence the media conferred on Wall Street and its denizens was not always positive, the greed-fueled materialistic world of money and investments was nonetheless an iconic one in the culture. That world was the subject of the 1987 Oliver Stone movie *Wall Street,* in which the lead character, Gordon Gekko, declared, "Greed is good." That film, some claimed, marked the beginning of a series of big-screen negative portrayals of business leaders. See also Wilson 2002.

2. The other legs of the economic recovery of the 1980s were the insurance industry and real estate. "N.Y.'s Economy Fell in September," *Crain's New York Business,* November 26, 1990, p. 4.

3. Eighteen of Nelson Mandela's twenty-seven years of imprisonment were spent on Robben Island.

4. The focus on the celebrity angle sometimes reached the absurd, as was the case when the *Daily News* ran an article in one of its early editions that referred to Mandela as one of the world's most famous ex-convicts.

5. A fat box is a small story that appears in a boxed format. The box separates the story from longer stories surrounding it while drawing the readers' eyes.

6. In a critique of the propensity of the mainstream press to rely on a particular group of sources, *New York Times* columnist Russell Baker (1986) wrote an opinion piece titled "The Usual Suspects."

7. The battle to integrate Stuyvesant Town has a long history. Stuyvesant Town, which was originally owned by Metropolitan Life Insurance Company and developed as a New York City–subsidized rental apartment complex for veterans, prohibited blacks veterans from renting any of its units. Tenants concerned about social justice protested this policy with limited success. Stuyvesant Town remains to this day a largely white zone.

8. All information about the Civilian Complaint Review Board comes from the board's website: http://www.nyc.gov/html/ccrb/html/about/history.html.

9. Interracial interaction in school could exist only if one did *not* attend a neighborhood high school, that is, a school that served strictly the students in its immediate geographic vicinity. At the time, New York City operated both neighborhood high schools, which served localized communities, and specialized high schools, which drew students from across the city. Many specialized high schools—some of which still exist today—required students to pass an admissions test and each one had a subject area focus, such as math and science or the arts.

10. C. Wright Mills (1956) provides an analysis of the ascendant ruling elite.

11. See also Bauman 1998. Using different language, Bauman writes about the phenomenon of the consumer economy that allows consumers to regularly adopt and change identities based on what they consume.

12. "No More TLC for Cabbies," *New York Daily News,* November 12, 1999.

13. In a memoir-based account of her time as a reporter at the *Washington Post,* Jill Nelson (1993) makes the case that blacks in mainstream institutions are regularly subjected to litmus tests about their positions on racial concerns.

14. From my previous experience in elite schools and then in jobs in corporate America, the War on Drugs (which began during the Nixon administration and was reasserted by the George H. W. Bush administration in 1989) was a distant, vague phenomenon. In those worlds, the most commonly discussed component of the War on Drugs was Nancy Reagan's "Just Say No" campaign, not the changing policies around incarceration, because the people in those environments were not the targets of the policies. See Alexander 2010.

15. Breaking news, which is a type of hard news, reports a currently unfolding significant or consequential event that occurs, such as an earthquake or the death of someone prominent, or newsworthy information released during a planned press conference. News personnel create a story that typically runs in the following day's paper or is broadcast immediately on television or the Internet. Beat reporting is coverage of an area or subject to which a reporter is assigned. The reporter is responsible for keeping the news organi-

zation and its audience apprised of all major or newsworthy developments. Sometimes breaking news develops on a beat. At other times, the beat reporter uses his or her knowledge of the area or subject, as well as sources, to generate stories that are not breaking news. A feature story is one that relies on colorful and descriptive language to convey its message. It is oftentimes not structured in the same formal way as traditional news stories and is frequently based on news events.

16. The sheer volume of people in Grand Central Terminal at the time of the shooting could also be reason enough to place this story on the front page. But, the significance of the specific location of the event cannot be underestimated.

17. Tompkins Square Park has been the site of a number of violent protests over the years. In 1873, an intense clash broke out when the permit was suddenly rescinded for a planned meeting of immigrant workers in the park. Seven thousand people gathered in the park, and sixteen hundred police, some mounted and using clubs, beat the workers (Johnson 2003: 30–32). In 1967, it was the site of another clash between the police and counterculture groups in the East Village (Johnson 2003: 259).

18. David Dinkins served from 1990 through 1993 as the first and only African American mayor of New York City. Instituting an *all-civilian* Civilian Complaint Review Board was part of his platform. See Johnson 2003.

19. One reason that the issue of capital punishment would have particular resonance for staff in the Governor's Office on Minority Affairs is the well-known overrepresentation of blacks on death row. While blacks in the United States make up about 13 percent of the population, Bureau of Justice statistics indicate that they constituted about 42 percent of inmates awaiting execution at the end of 2011. (See Bureau of Justice Statistics data on capital punishment, available at http://www.bjs.gov/index.cfm?ty=pbdetail&iid=4697.)

20. The death penalty was reinstated in 1995 by Governor George Pataki, a Republican, who defeated Mario Cuomo in 1994.

21. See, generally, chapter 1—"A Tale of Two Cities"—in Austin 2001.

22. Greene and Pranis (2007) make the point that some youth leaders worked with city-run youth programs that offered organized summer recreation and employment as part of New York City's relatively successful policy of using social work-type approaches to keep down gang violence. Greene and Pranis (2007) describe these programs as operating largely in the 1950s and 1960s.

## CHAPTER 5

1. Walter Mosley is a famous contemporary African American novelist. He is best known for his detective stories that feature the character Easy Rawlins.

2. Gaye Tuchman's (1972, 1973) studies of media elaborate on the process media workers go through in turning the phenomena of everyday life into news events.

3. This view was part of the public policy debates over welfare dependency and criminal justice policies in the 1970s and 1980s. Sociologist John J. DiIulio Jr. (1989) argued that welfare dependency should have been considered a given in urban black communities because criminals were largely responsible for the demise of these communities because their predatory behaviors scared off the working class and business and economic opportunities. These debates filtered into the public discourse through the mainstream media during this period.

4. When journalism is taught in college courses, a list of variables is identified as representing news values, or items those in journalism would use to determine the strength

or weakness of a story. Some of the standard news values include conflict, timeliness and proximity, progress, impact, disaster, prominence, human interest, novelty, sex, and animals (see Leiter, Harriss, and Johnson 2000: 30–39). Race is often not articulated as being part of this list. To me, the Outward Bound story had seemingly strong standard news values: It had consequence and conflict, which were reactions to an intensely covered story that involved sex and violence (the primary operational news value here again is conflict). In Chapter 2, I discuss race as something I believe has been operating silently as a news value. This story had that too.

5. In his study of newsmaking, Gans (1979) notes that internally journalists must work to sell their stories to more powerful editors.

6. New York City is made of five boroughs: Manhattan, Queens, the Bronx, Brooklyn, and Staten Island. At the time, the *Daily News* had four suburban sections; Brooklyn and Staten Island were collapsed into one.

7. See circulation figures in a period article about the *Daily News*: Pitt 1990.

8. In mainstream newspapers, the editorial section is both a geographic location in the office separate from the newsroom and a physical location in the newspaper separate from the news reports. Editorials are the province of management, and in the paper they articulate the management/owner's official positions on issues. See Tuchman 1978 and van Dijk 1993b.

9. C. Vernon Mason and Alton Maddox were two black civil rights attorneys who had worked with the family in the Tawana Brawley case. They would have been likely sources due to their history of advocacy for racial justice in New York City. But, at the time, I was concerned with mainstream media attitudes that presumed that blacks lacked objectivity about issues of race. I wanted to limit factors that might prevent the story from running.

10. The text quoted here is taken from the abbreviated story that ran, not from the original story I wrote.

11. Media messages are polysemic: It cannot be assumed that all members of the audience will take the same meaning from media messages. See Hall 2007.

12. The mainstream media were predominantly white. As late as 1997, there were still few journalists of color. A 1997 American Society of Newspaper Editors report (Voakes 1997) found that 11 percent of the journalists working for mainstream daily newspapers were individuals of color (black, Latino, Asian, and Native American).

13. Since the 1970s, those who study media have grounded many of their analyses in a critique of the presumption that media content is developed in a natural or taken-for-granted process. Instead, these studies recognize and acknowledge the institutional goals and agendas that are incorporated in the social practices used by news organizations to create news. Thus, they have focused their attention on news production specifically. Some of the early and most notable examples are British sociologist Stuart Hall and American sociologist Gaye Tuchman. See, for example, S. Hall et al. 1978 and Tuchman 1978.

14. A privileged space is an area or zone in the social world that raises a particular perspective to the level of authority and then treats it as dominant.

15. Sometimes reporters from desks other than the main one spearheading the reporting of a story will contribute to the coverage. However, the subject of their contribution is often indirectly related to the main subject of coverage.

16. I define prominent placement as follows. In the *New York Times*, (1) any article published in the main section before page fifteen is considered prominent because this

section of the paper is distributed nationally; (2) any article in the "B" section on pages one through three, which is toward the front of the section, is considered prominent; and (3) editorials are considered prominent. In the *Daily News*, prominence is based on the placement of ads that break up the presentation of news in the front part of the paper. Because the paper rarely placed full-page ads before page seven, at that time, the stories placed on pages one through seven are considered to be of the greatest significance relative to the other articles published in that book. As with the *New York Times*, editorials are also considered prominent.

17. The first time period runs from the first day of newspaper coverage, April 21, 1989, until the day the jogger was discharged from the hospital in New York City and went to the Connecticut rehabilitation facility, June 9, 1989.

18. Colin Moore and C. Vernon Mason were known in New York for the heavy media coverage they received in the Howard Beach, Bensonhurst, and Tawana Brawley cases. See Chancer 2005: 3–60.

## CHAPTER 6

1. The term "coverage" refers to a collection of news reports about a subject.

2. Van Dijk notes that "the power of the media is not defined only by their broad ideological influence on their audiences. . . . [A]s institutions, broadcast organizations, television networks, and newspapers, they also participate in complex networks of elite organizations or other powerful social actors" (1993b: 243).

3. Hard news stands in contrast to "soft news," such as feature stories or human interest stories that rely more heavily on "colorful" slice-of-life details and are structured or ordered in a less formal format.

4. Linguist and media critic Noam Chomsky refers to institutional memory as a type of context. Chomsky charges that the goal of elite newspapers is to create propaganda. Major U.S. papers like the *New York Times* have the authority to directly and indirectly influence smaller media outlets and thus set any agenda nationally and internationally. Chomsky largely sees the media as a tool for propaganda in which elite media institutions such as the *New York Times*, the *Washington Post*, the *Wall Street Journal*, and the *Los Angeles Times* determine, select, shape, control, and restrict discussion in order to serve the interests of the dominant elite groups. This can be done directly because major papers such as the *Times* and the *Post* have their own wire services, where smaller papers acquire stories for their own pages. The indirect influence comes from the amount of authority these papers wield and the credibility that comes with it. Chomsky identified a list of functions major media carry out in the course of doing business that, he says, represents the elements of a propaganda model used to support the power centers. The major media serve this purpose in many ways: through selection of topics, distribution of concerns, framing of issues, filtering of information, emphasis and tone, and by keeping debate within the bounds of acceptable premises (Herman and Chomsky 1988: 298). Chomsky argues that the propaganda model is hidden in the context, which is the underpinning of news stories. He defines context as the institutional memory necessary for understanding why and how. See interviews with Chomsky in Wintonick, Achbar, and Symansky 1992.

5. This makes the news desk perhaps the most important desk in a news organization.

6. The mainstream media did not construct the confessions as problematic until the district attorney's office reopened its investigation thirteen years after the convictions. At that time, a major report defining the confessions as problematic was published in the

*Village Voice,* an alternative newspaper (Hornung 1990). The city's black newspapers also reported on the problematic nature of the confessions.

7. "Media language" is equivalent to the term "media discourse" used by sociolinguists. (See Chapter 1.) For an example of this homological relationship, consider that of the twenty-six articles classified as having high racial content because they contained between four and eight race indicators, nineteen were prominently placed, fourteen were hard news, and sixteen included photos.

8. This represents singular logic in a discourse or narrative. It stands in contrast to dialogic (Fairclough 1995; see also Barthes 1977).

9. Hall et al. (1978: 57) uses the terms "*primary* and *secondary* definers of social events" to discuss how the media's use of sources allows ideas from dominant groups to prevail. Secondary definers are subordinated in media language/discourse.

10. This article was not part of the sample in the content analysis I conducted.

11. Not everyone who was a suspect during the initial investigations was eventually charged.

12. By this time, I had returned from Albany and had begun transitioning to covering other matters. The *Daily News* was in a state of turmoil; its owner, the *Chicago Tribune,* was battling the many unions of the *News.* A strike would ensue the following year, during part of the coverage of the second jogger trial.

13. The reference to my personal priming is meant in the technical sense of how the framing of stories primes audiences to think in a particular way (see Entman 2007).

14. "A Profile in Courage" [editorial], *New York Daily News,* July 18, 1989, p. 26.

## CHAPTER 7

1. Oftentimes, raising the issue of this narrative in the context of crime is perceived as a defense for the commission of the crime. This rape, like all rapes, was indefensible.

2. The term "mutant" did not occur in any of the articles in my sample, but it was used in a *Daily News* article by African American columnist and former city desk editor Bob Herbert (1990).

3. Joey Fama is the white teen convicted of killing Yusuf Hawkins, the black teen who, along with some friends, went to Bensonhurst, Brooklyn, to buy a used car.

4. I looked for a relationship between articles in the entire sample that were prominently placed and those that contained high numbers of various age indicators. I identified six words and terms that were indicators of age. The articles in the sample included anywhere from zero to five age terms, and articles with three to five age terms were considered to have a high age content. Using a chi-square test, high age content was found to be statistically significantly related to the prominent placement of articles.

5. Bob Herbert's 1990 column did link the phenomena of rising youth violence and racial tensions, but this connection was not frequently made in the mainstream media discourse. However, the mainstream media at the time did draw similarities between the racial attitudes of the white ethnic Bensonhurst and Howard Beach communities with those of the supporters of the suspects in the Central Park jogger case. The implication was that they were all equally racist.

6. Dr. Satcher's 2001 report is discussed in the context of the War on Drugs in Chapter 4.

7. The motion to vacate the charges filed by the office of the Manhattan District Attorney stated that semen was found inside the jogger as well as on a sock recovered from the site of the attack. Those pieces of information appeared in press reports (e.g.,

Alvarez 1990b). Press reports also indicated that semen belonging to the jogger's boyfriend was found on her running pants (e.g., Alvarez 1990b).

8. One interesting distinction between the two cases is that the black press and other alternative presses no longer matter in the ways they did during the Scottsboro and the Emmett Till cases. In Scottsboro, the left press played a significant role in the discourse, and during the Till case, the black press played an important role. In the more contemporary era of the initial jogger coverage, where there is a concentration of ownership of mainstream media, the black and other alternate presses had little impact on the discourse. See Goodman 1995 and Houck and Grindy 2008.

# CHAPTER 8

1. Mentioning the attack on the Central Park jogger and the murder Michael Griffith in the same context suggests that even at the federal level there was an attempt to create moral equivalence between the two incidents and to suggest that both were possibly symbolic of the perils of racial border crossings.

2. Hall et al. (1978) also credit a conservative backlash, starting in the 1960s in Great Britain, as part of the reason for that moral panic around muggings.

3. At the time of Robert Stutman's retirement in 1990, a *New York Times* report (Kerr 1990) stated that he was critical of U.S. drug policies because of the meager spending on drug treatment and education.

4. Although the idea of race as a social construction has been the dominant paradigm, biologically based ideas of race still existed and continue to exist. In science, when new paradigms emerge, followers of the old theories often continue to try to prove the worth of the old paradigm. See Kuhn 1962.

5. The findings from my content analysis point to the ways in which media producers conceptualize the world outside their institutional doors.

6. This does not make class the most important concept in the coverage. In the context of media systems, analyses that rely on frequencies will not indicate the degree or level of importance. In media, importance is determined by prominent placement of stories. Therefore, the frequency of inclusion of indicators for the concept of class does not determine how important class was to the media content makers. Krippendorff (2004: 195) notes that in content analyses "simple frequencies say nothing about relationships between content variables." Additional analysis would be needed to determine the relationships between the concepts and prominent placement in media.

7. Interracial rapes are more frequently covered by the media than rapes in which the perpetrator and victim are from the same racial category.

8. See also note 4 above.

9. See also Krajicek 1999 on the history of DiIulio's concept of the "super-predator." Satcher (2001) argues in his study on youth violence that the notion of a "super-predator" is one of the "myths" about young people and violence.

10. Marvin E. Wolfgang's (1983) birth-cohort studies form the basis of all of this work by John J. DiIulio Jr. and James Q. Wilson.

11. In what was essentially a repudiation of their earlier work, DiIulio and several prominent criminologists who had supported the "super-predator" theory joined a 2012 friend of the court brief supporting the petitioners in two cases heard together in which the U.S. Supreme Court would be ruling on the "constitutionality of sentences of life without parole for juveniles convicted of homicide offenses, including felony homicide"

(p. 2). The brief stated that "Empirical research that has analyzed the increase in violent crime . . . demonstrates that the juvenile superpredator was a myth and the predictions of future youth violence were baseless" (p. 8). See U.S. Supreme Court brief in the cases of petitioners *Kuntrell Jackson v. Ray Hobbs, Director, Arkansas Department of Corrections,* and *Evan Miller v. Alabama,* 10-9647 and 10-9646, amici curiae brief filed by Carl Micarelli, Counsel of Record, January 17, 2012.

12. Ryan and Ziedenberg (2007: 3) directly cite the Central Park jogger case in their report. "Sometimes all it takes is *one case* to change the course of public opinion and national policy. The Central Park Jogger case did just that." Their conclusions are not scientifically drawn, and the organization they produced their study for—Campaign for Youth Justice—is engaged in a national campaign to end youth incarceration in adult facilities across the nation.

13. All but two of the eighteen racial words or terms refer to black and Latino race.

14. Wacquant (2002) argues that mass incarceration operates like slavery as an institution that defines blacks in the United States. He noted that the inmate population in the United States was predominantly white until 1988.

15. See also the U.S. Supreme Court brief cited in note 11 for this chapter.

## CHAPTER 9

1. As discussed in Chapter 8, this is the theory of the "super-predator," which would eventually be debunked. James C. Howell (2009) cites criminologists James Fox, James Q. Wilson, and Alfred Blumstein, as well as political scientist John J. DiIulio Jr., as examples of researchers who promulgated the false idea that a growing crime wave would develop after the 1990s from an emerging group of young "super-predators." Howell (2009: 5) notes that DiIulio drew a direct connection to race in building his ideas.

2. The 2012 friend of the court brief filed in the U.S. Supreme Court (discussed in note 11 for Chapter 8)—in which DiIulio participated—also specifically rejected the concept of "wolfpacks," stating that "another aspect of the juvenile superpredator myth was the belief that antisocial youths prowl in 'wolfpacks' and the superpredator exercises a contagious influence on unsuspecting peers, with the implication that he should be quarantined for life" (p. 20).

3. According to 2010 U.S. Census data, the total U.S. population was 308,745,538 and the total population under eighteen years old was 74,181,467.

4. In the context of rape, these hierarchies support white male patriarchy because they are kept alive by the myth of black male sexual predators in search of white women to rape (A. Davis 1981; Smith 1998). This myth sustains the notion that white women exist in a heightened state of danger and thus continue to need white male protectors. Keeping that myth alive also maintains its counterpart: that is, that black women are promiscuous (A. Davis 1981; Smith 1998). Thus, the myth also privileges white women over black women, because it treats less seriously the rape of a black woman by either a black or a white man. In effect, the myth makes it less plausible that a black woman *could* be raped. Likewise, it is less plausible that a white man could be a rapist.

5. It is clear that all women are susceptible to rape, and the data indicate that rapists come from *all* racial categories. However, in the United States, "cases of interracial rape are constituted simultaneously as crimes of race and of gender" (Smith 1998: 32).

6. "The Central Park Five, Again" [Editorial]. *New York Post,* April 21, 2011.

7. "'Juvenile Delinquency' Does Not Apply" [Editorial]. *New York Daily News,* April 22, 1989, p. 11.

8. Marvin D. Free Jr. and Mitch Ruesink (2012: 29) discuss their finding of increased likelihood of wrongful convictions in interracial rapes in the context of witness error. There were 109 cases of rape in their sample of 343 wrongful convictions. The researchers were able to identify the race of seventy-four of the rape/sexual assault victims: "Over 81 percent were white." While possible police and prosecutorial misconduct and not witness identification is responsible for the wrongful conviction of the kids in the jogger case, it is important to note that there is a greater likelihood of wrongful conviction in *interracial* rapes.

9. The claim Matias Reyes made about the police officer overlooking the blood on his pants was disputed in an NYPD review of the case. The police review, led by attorney Michael Armstrong, was conducted after Manhattan District Attorney Robert Morgenthau moved to have the convictions of the Central Park Five vacated. In the police review, led by attorney Michael Armstrong, Reyes's claim is disputed. The police report can be downloaded from http://news.findlaw.com/cnn/docs/cpjgr/nypd12703jgrrpt.pdf.

10. Since its formation in 1989 under President George H.W. Bush, the Office of National Drug Control Policy, run by the "drug czar," has issued an annual National Drug Control Strategy. As discussed in Chapter 8, the first "drug czar" was William Bennett.

11. The Obama administration's first National Drug Control Strategy (2010) promised to change direction from the previous focus on law enforcement and to "balance . . . prevention, treatment, and law enforcement." Subsequent strategies have built on this plan. The full report for 2010 is available at http://www.whitehouse.gov/sites/default/files/ondcp/policy-and-research/ndcs2010.pdf.

12. "The 2012 National Drug Control Strategy: Building on a Record of Reform," Executive Summary. Available at http://www.whitehouse.gov/sites/default/files/ondcp/2012_national_drug_control_strategy_executive_summary.pdf.

13. "2012 National Drug Control Strategy." See note 12 above.

14. American Civil Liberties Union, "Fair Sentencing Act." Available at https://www.aclu.org/fair-sentencing-act.

15. See note 4 for Chapter 7.

16. In Chapters 7 and 8 I discuss the growing importance of age as a social categorical factor in the drug war.

17. "President Obama's Remarks on Trayvon Martin (Full Transcript)," *Washington Post,* July 19, 2013. Available at http://articles.washingtonpost.com/2013-07-19/politics/40672554_1_trayvon-martin-stand-your-ground-president-obama-s.

18. For example, the NYPD's Street Crime Unit reported 18,000 stops in 1997, as compared to 140 in 1996 (New York State Office of the Attorney General 1999: 65).

# References

Abbott, Andrew. 2007. "Against Narrative: A Preface to Lyrical Sociology." *Sociological Theory* 25:67–99.

Alba, Richard D., and Victor Nee. 2005. *Remaking the American Mainstream: Assimilation and Contemporary Immigration.* Cambridge, MA: Harvard University Press.

Alexander, Michelle. 2010. *The New Jim Crow: Mass Incarceration in the Age of Colorblindness.* New York: New Press.

Allen, Theodore W. 1997. *The Invention of the White Race: The Origin of Racial Oppression in Anglo-America.* New York: Verso.

Alvarez, Lizette. 1990a. "Cop Describes Jogger: Bloody and Thrashing." *New York Daily News,* July 4, p. 5.

———. 1990b. "DNA Prints Fail to ID Jogger's Attackers." *New York Daily News,* July 14, p. 3.

———. 1990c. "Jogger's Trail of Blood Recalled by Detective." *New York Daily News,* July 10, p. 5.

———. 1990d. "Jogger-Trial Images Conflict." *New York Daily News,* August 6, p. 12.

———. 1990e. "No Evidence of Rape, Says Lawyer in Cross-Exam: Jogger Defense Curve." *New York Daily News,* July 7, p. 5.

Alvarez, Lizette, and Timothy Williams. 2012. "Documents Tell Zimmerman's Side in Martin Case." *New York Times,* June 21. Available at www.nytimes.com/2012/06/22/us/documents-tell-zimmermans-side-in-martin-shooting.html?_r=0&pagewanted=print.

Annin, Peter. 1996. "Superpredators Arrive: Should We Cage the New Breed of Vicious Kids?" *Newsweek,* January 22, p. 57.

Arce, Rose Marie. 1989. "Roof Rape Victim a Fighter." *New York Daily News,* June 28, p. 7.

Arce, Rose Marie, and Gene Mustain. 1989. "The Dead-End Kids: Nothing to Lose, so They're Fearless." *New York Daily News,* January 26, p. 7.

Austin, Joe. 2001. *Taking the Train: How Graffiti Art Became an Urban Crisis in New York City.* New York: Columbia University Press.

Bagdikian, Ben Haig. 1983. *Media Monopoly.* Boston: Beacon Press.

———. 1997. *The Media Monopoly.* 5th ed. Boston: Beacon Press.

———. 2004. *The New Media Monopoly.* Boston: Beacon Press.

Baker, Houston A., Jr. 1995. *Black Studies, Rap, and the Academy.* Chicago: University of Chicago Press.

Baker, Russell. 1986. "The Usual Suspects." *New York Times Magazine,* August 17.

Banton, Michael. 2009. "The Idiom of Race: A Critique of Presentation." In *Theories of Race and Racism: A Reader.* Rev. ed. Edited by Les Back and John Solomos. New York: Routledge.

Bardaglio, Peter. 1994. "Rape and the Law in the Old South: 'Calculated to excite indignation in every heart.'" *Journal of Southern History* 60:749–772.

Barol, Bill, Karen Springen, and Jennifer Foote. 1988. "The Eighties Are Over." *Newsweek,* January 4, p. 40.

Barron, James. 1990. "Holdout on Rape Verdict Still Sees Discrepancies." *New York Times,* August 19, p. A33.

Barthes, Roland. 1977. *Image, Music, Text.* Translated by Stephen Heath. New York: Hill and Wang.

Bauman, Zygmunt. 1998. *Work, Consumerism and the New Poor.* Philadelphia: Open University Press.

Bay, Mia. 2009. *To Tell the Truth Freely: The Life of Ida B. Wells.* New York: Farrar, Straus and Giroux.

Becker, Elizabeth. 2001. "As Ex-Theorist on Young 'Superpredators,' Bush Aide Has Regrets." *New York Times,* February 9, p. A19.

Bell, Alan, and Peter Garrett, eds. 1998. *Approaches to Media Discourse.* Oxford: Blackwell Publishers.

Bell, Derrick A. 1992. *Faces at the Bottom of the Well: The Permanence of Racism.* New York: Basic Books.

Benedict, Helen. 1992. *Virgin or Vamp: How the Press Covers Sex Crimes.* London: Oxford University Press.

Bennett, William. 1989. "National Drug Control Strategy." Office of National Drug Control Policy, September 5. Washington, DC: The White House.

Bennett, William J., John J. DiIulio Jr., and John P. Walters. 1996. *Body Count: Moral Poverty . . . And How to Win America's War against Crime and Drugs.* New York: Simon and Schuster.

Berger, James O., and Donald A. Berry. 1988. "Statistical Analysis and the Illusion of Objectivity." *American Scientist* 76 (2): 159–165.

Berger, Leigh. 2001. "Inside Out: Narrative Autoethnography as a Path toward Rapport. *Qualitative Inquiry* 7:504–518.

Berke, Richard L. 1989. "Bennett Asks Tough Drug Fight, Declaring Crack Biggest Problem." *New York Times,* August 1, p. A14. Available at http://www.nytimes.com/1989/08/01/us/bennett-asks-tougher-drug-fight-declaring-crack-biggest-problem.html?scp=1&sq=William+Bennett&st=nyt.

Berkowitz, Harry. 1989. "The Manager Behind the Mogul: Donald Trump Giving His Hand-Picked People a Free Hand." *Washington Post,* September 23, p. E39.

Blumenthal, Ralph. 1988a. "Dozens Are Seized in New U.S. *New York Times,* December 2, p. A14.

———. 1988b. "Questions and Answers in the Brawley Inquiry." *New York Times,* February 24, p. B5.

———. 1989. "F.B.I. Begins Inquiry on Brooklyn Youth's Slaying in Racial Attack." *New York Times,* August 30, p. B4.

Bochner, Arthur P. 1984. "The Functions of Human Communication in Interpersonal Bonding." In *Handbook of Rhetorical and Communication Theory,* edited by Carroll C. Arnold and John W. Bowers, 544–621. Boston: Allyn and Bacon.

Boyle, Maree, and Ken Parry. 2007. "Telling the Whole Story: The Case for Organizational Autoethnography." *Culture and Organization* 13: 185–190.

Bonilla-Silva, Eduardo. 2006. *Racism without Racists: Color-Blind Racism and the Persistence of Racial Inequality in the United States.* 2nd ed. New York: Rowman and Littlefield.

Bourgois, Philippe. 1989. "Just Another Night on Crack Street." *The New York Times Magazine,* November 12, p. 53.

———. 1995. *In Search of Respect: Selling Crack in El Barrio.* New York: Cambridge University Press.

Broussard, Sharon, Larry Celona, Ingrid DeVita, James Duddy, Tony Marcano, Patrice O'Shaughnessy, Claire Serant, and Stuart Marques. 1989. "'Wilding' Teens Held in Rape: 7 Are Called Part of Wolf Pack." *New York Daily News,* April 22, p. 3.

Broussard, Sharon, and Mark Kriegel. 1989. "Worse before Better: Citizens Arrest Crime in their Nabes." *New York Daily News,* January 29, p. 21.

Brownmiller, Susan. 1975. *Against Our Will.* New York: Simon and Schuster.

Bumiller, Kristin. 2008. *In an Abusive State: How Neoliberalism Appropriated the Feminist Movement against Sexual Violence.* Durham, NC: Duke University Press.

Burns, Sarah. 2011. *The Central Park Five: A Chronicle of a City Wilding.* New York: Alfred A. Knopf.

Bush, George H.W. 1989. "Address to the Nation on the National Drug Control Strategy." Public Papers from the George Bush Presidential Library and Museum, September 5. Available at bushlibrary.tamu.edu/research/public_papers.php?id=863&year=&month=.

Butts, Jeffrey A. 2012. "Transfer of Juveniles to Criminal Court Is Not Correlated with Falling Youth Violence." *Research and Evaluation Data Bits,* no. 2012-05. New York: Research and Evaluation Center, John Jay College of Criminal Justice, City University of New York. Available at http://johnjayresearch.org/wp-content/uploads/2012/03/databit2012_05.pdf.

Byfield, Natalie P. 1989a. "Bullets Destroy American Dream." *New York Daily News,* January 25, p. 7.

———. 1989b. "Cops Targeted Youth?" *New York Daily News,* June 24, p. 11.

———. 1989c. "The Jogger's Painful Path: Her State Horrified Docs, & Now They Fear for Her Recovery." *New York Daily News,* May 14, p. 7.

———. 1989d. "Jogger Talks to Prosecutor: Victim Forgets Rape Details." *New York Daily News,* June 7, p. 23.

———. 1996. "The Crisis of Black Youth in New York City." *Race and Reason,* pp. 30–36. New York: Institute for Research in African-American Studies, Columbia University.

———. Forthcoming. "Modern Newspapers and the Formation of White Racial Group Consciousness." In *Dimensions of Racism in Advertising: From Slavery to the 21st Century,* edited by Edward Lama Wonkeryor and Dana Saewitz. New York: Peter Lang Publishers.

Byfield, Natalie, Rose Marie Arce, and Sharon Broussard. 1989. "In Wrong Place at Wrong Time." *New York Daily News,* January 25, p. 7.

Caldwell, Earl. 1990. "Jogger Rape Case Coming Unglued." *New York Daily News,* January 12, p. 30.

Campbell, Richard, Christopher R. Martin, and Bettina Fabos. 2005. *Media & Culture: An Introduction to Mass Communication.* 4th ed. New York: Bedford/St. Martin's.

Cantwell, Alice. 1991a. "Jog Trial Teens Get 5-Yr. Terms." *New York Daily News,* January 10, p. 3.

———. 1991b. "Plea Deal Ends Jogger Case." *New York Daily News,* January 31, p. 7.

Carby, Hazel. 1986. "'On the Threshold of Woman's Era': Lynching, Empire, and Sexuality in Black Feminist Theory." In *"Race," Writing, and Difference,* edited by Henry Louis Gates Jr. Chicago: University of Chicago Press.

Chancer, Lynn S. 2005. *High-Profile Crimes: When Legal Cases Become Social Causes.* Chicago: University of Chicago Press.

Chang, Jeff. 2005. *Can't Stop Won't Stop: A History of the Hip-Hop Generation.* New York: Picador/St. Martin's Press.

Chapman, John. 1961. *Tell It to Sweeney: The Informal History of the* New York Daily News. New York: Doubleday.

*City Sun.* 1989. "It's an Outrage!" [editorial]. *City Sun,* April 26–May 2, p. 1.

Clark, Pat[rick]. 1989. "Will Jury Hear Rape Tales?" *New York Daily News,* July 30, p. 31.

Clark, Patrick, and Ruth Landa. 1989. "Rape Suspects Laugh over Attack." *New York Daily News,* April 23, p. 2.

Clifford, Timothy. 1989. "Video: Youths Argued Whether to Kill Jogger: Central Park Attack Suspects Gave Details to Cops." *Newsday,* September 25, p. 3.

CNN. 2005. "Bennett under Fire for Remarks on Blacks, Crime." *CNN.com,* September 30. Available at http://www.cnn.com/2005/POLITICS/09/30/bennett.comments.

Coates, Ta-Nehisi. 2012. "Fear of a Black President." *The Atlantic.* Available at http://www.theatlantic.com/magazine/archive/2012/09/fear-of-a-black-president/309064/.

Cohen, Stanley. 2002. *Folk Devils and Moral Panics: Thirtieth Anniversary Edition.* 3rd ed. London: Taylor and Francis.

Collins, Gail. 1989. "Gifted Black & Angry" *New York Daily News,* April 26, p. 5.

Collins, Patricia Hill. 1986. "Learning from the Outsider Within: The Sociological Significance of Black Feminist Thought." *Social Problems* 33:S14–S32.

———. 2000. *Black Feminist Thought: Knowledge, Consciousness, and the Politics of Empowerment.* 2nd ed. New York: Routledge.

———. 2005. *Black Sexual Politics: African Americans, Gender, and the New Racism.* New York: Routledge.

Conrad, Joseph. [1902] 2008. *Heart of Darkness.* Reprinted by Forgotten Books. Available at http://books.google.com/books?id=RSJSNNLrdc4C&printsec=frontcover&dq=heart+of+darkness+joseph+conrad#v=onepage&q=&f=false.

*Crain's New York Business.* 1988. "How's Ed Koch Doin'? For Business, Just Fine." May 9, p. 1.

Crenshaw, Kimberle. 1991. "Mapping the Margins: Intersectionality, Identity Politics, and Violence against Women of Color." *Stanford Law Review* 43:1241–1299.

Davis, Angela. 1981. *Women, Race & Class.* New York: Vintage Books.

Davis, David Brion. 1975. *The Problem of Slavery in the Age of Revolution: 1770–1823.* Ithaca, NY: Cornell University Press.

Davis, Kathy. 2008. "Intersectionality as Buzzword: A Sociology of Science Perspective on What Makes a Feminist Theory Successful." *Feminist Theory* 9:67–85.

Didion, Joan. 1991. "New York: Sentimental Journeys." *New York Review of Books,* January 17.

DiIulio, John J., Jr. 1989. "The Underclass: III. The Impact of Inner-City Crime." *Public Interest* 96 (Summer): 28–46.

———. 1995. "Moral Poverty: The Coming of the Super-predators Should Scare Us into Wanting to Get to the Root Causes of Crime a Lot Faster." *Chicago Tribune,* December 15, p. 31.

Dorfman, Lori, and Vincent Schiraldi. 2001. "Off Balance: Youth, Race & Crime in the News." Building Blocks for Youth. Available at http://www.cclp.org/documents/BBY/offbalance.pdf.

Dressner, Julie, and Edwin Martinez. 2012. "The Scars of Stop-and-Frisk." *New York Times,* April 6. Available at http://www.nytimes.com/2012/06/12/opinion/the-scars-of-stop-and-frisk.html?ref=stopandfrisk.

Duara, Prasenjit. 1996. "Historicizing National Identity, or Who Imagines What and When." In *Becoming National: A Reader,* edited by Geoff Eley and Ronald Grigor Suny. New York: Oxford University Press.

Du Bois, W.E.B. [1903] 2003. *The Souls of Black Folk.* New York: Modern Library.

Duncan, Erika. 2008. *Paper Stranger: Shaping Stories in Communities.* Vol. I. Centerreach, NY: Herstory Writers Workshop, Inc.

Durkheim, Emile. [1912] 1995. *The Elementary Forms of Religious Life.* Translated by Karen E. Fields. New York: Free Press.

Dwyer, Jim. 2002. "Convict Says Jogger Attack Was His 2d." *New York Times,* October 5, p. B1.

Dwyer, Jim, and Kevin Flynn. 2002. "New Light on Jogger's Rape Calls Evidence into Question." *New York Times,* December 1, p. A1.

Ehrenreich, Barbara. 1986. "Is the Middle-Class Doomed." *New York Times Magazine,* September 7, p. 44.

Ellis, Carolyn, Tony E. Adams, and Arthur P. Bochner. 2011. "Autoethnography: An Overview." *Forum: Qualitative Social Research* 12 (1). Available at http://www.qualitative-research.net/index.php/fqs/article/view/1589/3096.

Ellison, R. [1947] 1989. *Invisible Man.* New York: Vintage Books.

Entman, Robert. 1992. "Blacks in the News: Television, Modern Racism and Cultural Change." *Journalism Quarterly* 69 (Summer).

———. 2007. "Framing Bias: Media in the Distribution of Power." *Journal of Communication* 57:163–173.

Entman, Robert, and Andrew Rojecki. 2001. *The Black Image in the White Mind.* Chicago: University of Chicago Press.

Ewen, Stuart. 1996. *PR! A Social History of Spin.* New York: Basic Books.

Fairclough, Norman. 1995. *Media Discourse.* New York: Edward Arnold.

———. 1998. "Political Discourse in the Media: An Analytical Framework." In *Approaches to Media Discourse,* edited by Alan Bell and Peter Garrett. Hoboken, NJ: Wiley and Sons.

Feagin, Joe R. 2001. *Racist America: Roots, Current Realities, & Future Reparations.* New York: Routledge.

Fellow, Anthony R. 2010. *American Media History.* Boston: Wadsworth Cengage Learning.

Ferber, Abby. 1998. *White Man Falling: Race, Gender, and White Supremacy.* Lanham, MD: Rowman and Littlefield.

Ferguson, Ann Arnett. 2000. *Bad Boys: Public School in the Making of Black Masculinity.* Ann Arbor: University of Michigan Press.

Fields, Barbara Jeanne. 1990. "Slavery, Race and Ideology in the United States of America." *New Left Review* 181:95–118.

Fields, Karen E. 2002. "Individuality and the Intellectuals: An Imaginary Conversation between W.E.B. Du Bois and Emile Durkheim." *Theory and Society* 31:435–462.

Fields, Karen E., and Barbara J. Fields. 2012. *Racecraft: The Soul of Inequality in American Life.* New York: Verso.

Fishman, Mark. 1978. "Crime Waves as Ideology." *Social Problems* 25:531–543.

Foderaro, Lisa. 1989. "Angered by Attack, Trump Urges Return of the Death Penalty." *New York Times,* May 1, p. B6.

Ford, Richard T. 1992. "Urban Space and the Color Line: The Consequences of Demarcation and Disorientation in the Postmodern Metropolis." *Harvard Blackletter Journal* 9:117–147.

Foucault, Michel. 1972. *The Archeology of Knowledge & The Discourse on Language.* New York: Pantheon Books.

Fowler, Roger. 1991. *Language in the News: Discourse and Ideology in the Press.* London and New York: Routledge.

Franklin, John Hope. 1980. *From Slavery to Freedom: A History of Negro Americans.* New York: Alfred A. Knopf.

Fredrickson, George. 1971a. *The Black Image in the White Mind: Debate on Afro-American Character and Destiny, 1817–1914.* New York: Harper and Row.

———. 1971b. "Toward a Social Interpretation of the Development of American Racism." In *Key Issues in the Afro-American Experience, Vol. 1,* edited by Nathan Huggins, Martin Kilson, and Daniel Fox. New York: Harcourt Brace Jovanovich.

Free, Marvin D., Jr., and Mitch Ruesink. 2012. *Race and Justice: Wrongful Convictions of African American Men.* Boulder, CO: Lynne Rienner Publishers.

Galvin, Jim. 1985. "Rape: A Decade of Reform." *Crime & Delinquency* 31:163–168.

Gans, Herbert J. 1979. *Deciding What's News: A Study of CBS Evening News, NBC Nightly News, Newsweek & Time.* New York: Pantheon Books.

———. 2005. "Race as Class." *Contexts* 4(4): 17–21.

Gearty, Robert. 1989. "Rev. Gigante Defends His Bailout." *New York Daily News,* June 12, p. 7.

Geertz, Clifford. 1973. *The Interpretation of Cultures.* New York: Basic Books.

Gitlin, Todd. 1980. *The Whole World Is Watching: Mass Media in the Making & Unmaking of the New Left.* Berkeley: University of California Press.

Glaberson, William. 1990. "Reporter's Notebook: As Jogger Trial Unfolds, the Fear Hits Home." *New York Times,* July 23, p. B1.

Glenn, Evelyn Nakano. 2009. "Citizenship and Inequality." In *Race and Ethnicity in Society: The Changing Landscape,* edited by Elizabeth Higginbotham and L. Margaret Andersen. Belmont, CA: Wadsworth, Cengage Learning.

Goodman, James. 1995. *Stories of Scottsboro.* New York: Knopf Doubleday.

Green, Amy. 2012. "Zimmerman's Twin Lakes Community Was on Edge Before Trayvon Shooting." *Daily Beast,* March 28. Available at www.thedailybeast.com/articles/2012/03/28/zimmerman-s-twin-lakes-community-was-on-edge-before-trayvon-shooting.print.html.

Greene, Judith, and Kevin Pranis. 2007. *Gang Wars: The Failure of Enforcement Tactics and the Need for Effective Public Safety Strategies.* Justice Policy Institute.

Grogger, Jeff, and Michael Willis. 2000. "The Emergence of Crack Cocaine and the Rise in Urban Crime Rates." *Review of Economics and Statistics* 82:519–529.

Gross, Jane. 1985. "Witness Says Officer Used a Choke Hold on Stewart's Neck." *New York Times,* August 22, p. B5.

Habermas, Jurgen. 1989. *The Structural Transformation of the Public Sphere: An Inquiry into a Category of Bourgeois Society.* Cambridge, MA: MIT Press.

Hall, Jacquelyn Dowd. 1983. "'The Mind That Burns in Each Body': Women, Rape, and Racial Violence." In *Powers of Desire: the Politics of Sexuality,* edited by Ann Snitow, Christine Stansell, and Sharon Thompson. New York: Monthly Review Press.

Hall, Stuart. 2007. "Encoding, Decoding." In *The Cultural Studies Reader,* 3rd ed., edited by Simon During. New York: Routledge.

Hall, Stuart, Chas Critcher, Tony Jefferson, John Clarke, and Brian Roberts. 1978. *Policing the Crisis: Mugging, the State, and Law and Order.* London: MacMillan.

Hancock, LynNell. 2003. "Wolf Pack: The Press and the Central Park Jogger." *Columbia Journalism Review,* January/February 2003. Available at http://www.cjr.org/archives. asp?url=/01/3/hancock.asp.

Haney-Lopez, Ian. 1996. *White by Law: The Legal Construction of Race.* New York: New York University Press.

Harding, Sandra. 1986. *The Science Question in Feminism.* Ithaca, NY: Cornell University Press.

Harlow, Caroline Wolf. 1991. "Female Victims of Violent Crimes." U.S. Department of Justice Office of Justice Programs Bureau of Justice Statistics. Available at https://www.ncjrs.gov/pdffiles1/Digitization/126826NCJRS.pdf.

Harris, Lyle V. 1989. "More Patrols Set for Park." *New York Daily News,* April 29, p. 3.

Hays, Constance L. 1989. "Park Safety: Advice from Runners." *The New York Times,* April 21, p. B3.

Herbert, Bob. 1990. "A Case that Stunned the City: Park Rape Scene Is Still Jarring." *New York Daily News,* June 26, p. 4.

Herman, Edward S., and Noam Chomsky. 1988. *Manufacturing Consent: The Political Economy of the Mass Media.* New York: Pantheon Books.

Hodes, Martha. 1997. *White Women, Black Men: Illicit Sex in the 19th Century South.* New Haven, CT: Yale University Press.

Hornung, Rick. 1990. "The Central Park Rape: The Case against the Prosecution." *Village Voice,* February 20, p. 30.

Houck, Davis, and Matthew Grindy. 2008. *Emmett Till and the Mississippi Press.* Jackson: University of Mississippi Press.

Howell, James C. 2009. *Preventing and Reducing Juvenile Delinquency: A Comprehensive Framework.* Thousand Oaks, CA: Sage Publications.

Hughes, L. 1959. *Selected Poems of Langston Hughes.* New York: Vintage Books.

Ingrassia, Robert. 2002. "Judge Blasts Jogger 5 Reversal." *New York Daily News,* December 21, p. 4.

Isikoff, Michael. 1989. "Drug Buy Set Up for Bush Speech: DEA Lured Seller to Lafayette Park." *Washington Post,* September 22, p. A1.

Johnson, Marilyn. 2003. *Street Justice: A History of Police Violence in New York City.* Boston: Beacon Press.

Jones, Alex. 1989a. "Mayoral Pick Creates Fight within Paper." *New York Times,* September 7, p. B1.

———. 1989b. "New York's Daily News Prepares for a War with Its Union." *New York Times,* September 25. p. D9.

Jonsson, Patrik. 2012. "Geraldo Rivera (Again) Says Trayvon Martin's 'Thug Wear' Got Him Profiled." *The Christian Science Monitor,* May 19. Available at www.csmonitor. com/layout/set/print/USA/Justice/2012/0519/Geraldo-Rivera-again-says-Trayvon-Martin-s-thug-wear-got-him-profiled.

Jordan, Winthrop D. 1968. *White over Black: American Attitudes toward the Negro, 1550–1812.* Durham: University of North Carolina Press.

———. 2000. "First Impressions." In *Theories of Race and Racism: A Reader,* edited by Les Back and John Solomos. New York: Routledge.

Kaufman, Michael T. 1989. "Park Suspects: Children of Discipline." *New York Times,* April 26, p. A1.

Keenan, Kevin. 2005. *Invasion of Privacy: A Reference Handbook.* Santa Barbara, CA: ABC-CLIO.

Kerlikowske, R. Gil. 2010. "National Drug Control Strategy." Office of National Drug Control Policy, Washington DC: The White House.

———. 2012. "National Drug Control Strategy." Office of National Drug Control Policy, January 5, Washington DC: The White House.

Kerr, Peter. 1990. "Retiring Agents Sharply Attack Drug Policies." *New York Times,* March 1, p. B1.

King, Deborah. 1988. "Multiple Jeopardy, Multiple Consciousness: The Context of a Black Feminist Ideology." *Signs* 14:42–72.

Klein, Joe. 1989. "Race: The Issue." *New York Magazine,* May 29. Available at http://nymag.com/news/features/46795.

Koch, Ed. 2012. "Stop-and-Frisk and the Marijuana Misdemeanor Arrests Outrage: Good Luck to the Legal Aid Society Lawsuit." *HuffingtonPost.com,* June 26. Available at http://www.huffingtonpost.com/ed-koch/stopandfrisk-and-the-mari_b_1626941 .html.

Krajicek, David. 1989. "It's Called Spillover: Silk-Stocking Areas Share Run on Crime." *New York Daily News,* January 23, p. 5.

———. 1999. "'Super-Predators': The Making of a Myth." *Youth Today* 8 (April): 4.

Kriegel, Mark. 1989. "Lived a Dream Life." *New York Daily News,* April 21, p. 2.

———. 1997. "Park Rapist Still Insults Our Senses." *New York Daily News.*

Krippendorff, Klaus. 2004. *Content Analysis: An Introduction to Its Methodology.* 2nd ed. Thousand Oaks, CA: Sage Publications.

Kuhn, Thomas. 1962. *Structure of Scientific Revolutions.* Chicago: University of Chicago Press.

Larson, Cedric. 1950. "New York City Police Department Launches New Public Relations Policy." *Journal of Criminal Law and Criminology* 41:364–376.

Leiter, Kelly, Julian Harriss, and Stanley Johnson. 2000. *The Complete Reporter: Fundamentals of News Gathering, Writing, and Editing.* 7th ed. Boston: Allyn and Bacon.

Leland, John and Colin Moynihan. 2012. "Thousands March Silently to Protest Stop-and-Frisk Policies." *New York Times.* June 17. p. A15.

Lizotte, Alan J. 1985. "The Uniqueness of Rape: Reporting Assaultive Violence to the Police." *Crime and Delinquency* 31:169–190.

Luhmann, Niklas. 2000. *The Reality of the Mass Media.* Translated by Kathleen Cross. Stanford, CA: Stanford University Press.

Martindale, Carolyn. 1986. *The White Press in Black America.* Westport, CT: Greenwood Press.

Marzulli, John. (1989). "'Going Wilding' in the Streets." *New York Daily News,* April 22, p. 3.

Mauer, Mark, and Ryan King. 2007. *A 25-Year Quagmire: The War on Drugs and Its Impact on American Society.* Washington, DC: The Sentencing Project.

McAlary, Mike. 1989. "One Big Joke for Teens: A Song that Didn't Make Hearts Sing." *New York Daily News,* April 23, p. 3.

McChesney, Robert. 1999. *Rich Media, Poor Democracy: Communications Politics in Dubious Times.* Urbana: University of Illinois Press.

———. 2008. *The Political Economy of Media: Enduring Issues, Emerging Dilemmas.* New York: Monthly Review Press.

McCoy, Kevin, and Stuart Marques. 1989. "Jogger Case Looks Strong but Likely to Drag." *New York Daily News,* May 1, p. 5.

McFadden, Robert, Ralph Blumenthal, M. A. Farber, E. R. Shipp, Charles Strum, and Craig Wolff. 1990. *Outrage: The Story Behind the Tawana Brawley Hoax.* New York: Bantam Books.

McFadden, Robert, and Susan Saulny. 2002. "A Crime Revisited: The Decision; 13 Years Later, Official Reversal in Jogger Attack." *New York Times,* December 6, p. A1.

McGrath, Peter, and Howard Fineman. 1984. "A New Voting Bloc." *Newsweek,* December 31, p. 30.

McKinley, James, Jr. 1989. "2 More Youths Held in Attacks in Central Park." *New York Times,* April 23, p. 32.

Mills, C. Wright. 1956. *The Power Elite.* New York: Oxford University Press.

Mindich, David T. Z. 2000. "Understanding Frederick Douglass: Toward a New Synthesis Approach to the Birth of Modern American Journalism." *Journalism History* 26 (1): 15.

Mooney, Mark. 1996. "Race Slay Torments Killer: Remorseful Con Breaks His Silence." *New York Daily News,* October 13. Available at http://www.nydailynews.com/archives/news/race-slay-torments-killer-remorseful-breaks-silence-article-1.745378.

Murch, Donna. 2010. *Living for the City.* Raleigh: University of North Carolina Press.

Mustain, Gene. 1989a. "A Picture Imperfect: Need to Rock Cocaine Boat." *New York Daily News,* January 29, p. 20.

———. 1989b. "Trail of Fear & Loathing in City: A Swath of Scars Spreading Wide and Cutting Deep." *New York Daily News,* January 22, p. 5.

Nelson, Jill. 1993. *Volunteer Slavery: Authentic Negro Experience.* Chicago: Noble Press.

Neuman, W. Lawrence. 2011. *Social Research Methods: Qualitative and Quantitative Approaches.* Boston: Allyn and Bacon.

Newkirk, Pamela. 2000. *Within the Veil: Black Journalists, White Media.* New York: New York University Press.

Newsom, Doug, Judy VanSlyke Turk, and Dean Kruckeberg. 2004. *This Is PR: The Realities of Public Relations.* Belmont, CA: Wadsworth/Thomas Learning.

New York Civil Liberties Union. 2012. "Stop-and-Frisk 2011." Available at http://www.nyclu.org/files/publications/NYCLU_2011_Stop-and-Frisk_Report.pdf.

———. 2013. "Stop-and-Frisk 2012." Available at http://www.nyclu.org/files/publications/2012_Report_NYCLU_0.pdf.

New York State Office of the Attorney General. 1999. "The New York Police Department's 'Stop and Frisk' Practices." Available at http://www.ag.ny.gov/sites/default/files/pdfs/bureaus/civil_rights/stp_frsk.pdf.

Omi, Michael, and Howard Winant. 1994. *Racial Formation in the United States from the 1960s to the 1990s.* 2nd ed. New York: Routledge.

Pager, Devah. 2007. *Marked: Race, Crime, and Finding Work in an Era of Mass Incarceration.* Chicago: University of Chicago Press.

Parisi, Peter. 1998. "The New York Times Looks at One Block in Harlem: Narratives of Race in Journalism." *Critical Studies in Mass Communications* 15:236–254.

Pasley, Jeffrey L. 2000. "The Two National Gazettes: Newspapers and the Embodiment of American Political Parties." *Early American Literature* 35:51–86.

Pitt, David E. 1990. "Workers vs. *The Daily News*: The Issues and the Prospects." *New York Times,* November 13.

Purdum, Todd. 1990. "Safety Improvements Are Planned for Central Park." *New York Times,* April 4, p. B3.

Reinarman, Craig, and Harry G. Levine. [1997] 2006. "The Crack Attack: Politics and Media in the Crack Scare." In *Sociology: Exploring the Architecture of Everyday Life Readings,* edited by David M. Newman and Jodi O'Brien, 47–66. Thousand Oaks, CA: Pine Forge Press.

Rhodes, Jane. 1994. "Race, Money, Politics and the Antebellum Black Press." *Journalism History* 20 (3–4): 95.

———. 2007. *Framing the Black Panthers: The Spectacular Rise of a Black Power Icon.* New York: New Press.

Roberts, Sam. 1983. "When Police Are Accused of Brutality." *New York Times,* October 27. Available at http://www.nytimes.com/1983/10/27/nyregion/when-police-are-accused-of-brutality.html.

Rodriguez, Clara E. 2000. *Changing Race: Latinos, the Census, and the History of Ethnicity in the United States.* New York: New York University Press.

Roediger, David. 1999. *The Wages of Whiteness: Race and the Making of the American Working Class.* Rev. ed. London: Verso.

———. 2005. *Working toward Whiteness: How America's Immigrants Became White: The Strange Journey from Ellis Island to the Suburbs.* New York: Basic Books.

Romero, Mary. 2011. *The Maid's Daughter: Living Inside and Outside the American Dream.* New York: New York University Press.

Rosenthal, A. M. 1989. "The Guilty Verdict." *New York Times,* May 5, p. 35.

Ross, Barbara, Alice McQuillan, and Frank Lombardi. 2002. "DA Hit on Jogger DNA Link." *New York Daily News,* September 25, p. 10.

Ryan, Liz, and Jason Ziedenberg. 2007. "The Consequences Aren't Minor: The Impact of Trying Youth as Adults and Strategies for Reform." *Campaign for Youth Justice Report,* March. Washington, DC: Campaign for Youth Justice. Executive Summary available at http://www.campaign4youthjustice.org/Downloads/NationalReportsArticles/JPI014-Consequences_exec.pdf.

Santangelo, Mike. 1989. "Suspects' 2d Visit from O'C." *New York Daily News,* May 22, p. 18.

Satcher, David. 2001. *Surgeon General Report.* Washington, DC: U.S. Department of Health and Human Services. Available at http://www.ncbi.nlm.nih.gov/books/NBK44297/#A12312.

Saxton, Alexander. 1984. "Problems of Class and Race in the Origins of the Mass Circulation Press." *American Quarterly* 36:211–234.

———. 2003. *The Rise and Fall of the White Republic: Class Politics and Mass Culture in Nineteenth-Century America.* New York: Verso.

Schudson, Michael. 1978. *Discovering the News: A Social History of American Newspapers.* New York: Basic Books.

Shohat, Ella, and Robert Stam. 1994. *Unthinking Eurocentrism: Multiculturalism and the Media.* New York: Routledge.

Sigelman, Lee. 1973. "Reporting the News: An Organizational Analysis." *American Journal of Sociology* 79 (1): 132–151.

Silver, Sheldon, and Herman D. Farrell, Jr. 1998. "Trends in the New York State Correctional System." *Perspectives from the New York State Assembly's Committee on Ways and Means.* New York State Assembly Occasional Paper no. 9, March. Available at http://assembly.state.ny.us/Reports/WAM/Perspectives/199803/.

Singleton, Don, and Don Gentile. 1989. "Teen Gang Rapes Jogger: 'She Put Up Terrific Fight.'" *New York Daily News,* April 21, p. 3.

Slater, Don. 1998. "Analysing Cultural Objects: Content Analysis and Semiotics." In *Researching Society and Culture,* edited by Clive Seale, 233–244. London: Sage Publications.

Smith, Valerie. 1998. *Not just Race, Not just Gender: Black Feminist Readings*. New York: Routledge.

Snyder, Howard, and Melissa Sickmund. 1999. "Juvenile Offenders and Victims: 1999 National Report." Washington, DC: Office of Juvenile Justice and Delinquency Prevention, U.S. Department of Justice. Available at https://www.ncjrs.gov/html/ojjdp/nationalreport99/toc.html.

Stoddart, Kenneth. 1991. "Lifestory: A Device for Dispersing Authority in the Introductory Course." *Teaching Sociology* 19:70–73.

Sullivan, Ronald. 1989a. "Bail Denied for 3 Youths in Park Attack." *New York Times*, April 29, p. 30.

———. 1989b. "Critics Fault Selection of Judge in Jogger Case." *New York Times*, August 7, p. B4.

———. 1989c. "Genetic Tests 'Inconclusive' in Jogger Rape." *New York Times*, October 10, p. B1.

———. 1989d. "Prosecution Says It Has Witness in the Park Attack." *New York Times*, May 11, p. B3.

———. 1990a. "Judge Explains His Ruling in the Jogger Case." *New York Times*, March 1, p. B3.

———. 1990b. "Statements Are Allowed in Jogger Case." *New York Times*, February 24, p. 27.

———. 1990c. "Videotapes Are Core of Central Park Jogger Case." *New York Times*, June 11, p. B3.

Sullivan, Timothy. 1992. *Unequal Verdicts: The Central Park Jogger Trials*. New York: American Lawyer Books/Simon & Schuster.

Tuchman, Gaye. 1972. "Objectivity as Strategic Ritual: An Examination of Newsmen's Notions of Objectivity." *American Journal of Sociology* 77:660–679.

———. 1973. "Making News by Doing Work: Routinizing the Unexpected." *American Journal of Sociology* 79:110–131.

———. 1978. *Making News: A Study in the Construction of Reality*. New York: Free Press.

U.S. Census Bureau. 2010. *American Fact Finder*. Available at http://factfinder2.census.gov/faces/nav/jsf/pages/index.xhtml.

U.S. Riot Commission Report. 1968. *Report of the National Advisory Commission on Civil Disorders*. New York: Bantam Book.

van Dijk, Tuen A. 1988. *News as Discourse*. Hillsdale, NJ: Lawrence Erlbaum.

———. 1991. *Racism and the Press*. New York: Routledge.

———. 1993a. "Denying Racism: Elite Discourse and Racism." In *Racism and Migration in Western Europe*, edited by J. Solomos and J. Wrench, 179–193. Oxford: Berg.

———. 1993b. *Elite Discourse and Racism*. Sage Series on Race and Ethnic Relations, Vol. 6. London: Sage Publications.

Vitale, Alex. (2008). *City of Disorder: How the Quality of Life Campaign Transformed New York Politics*. New York: New York University Press.

Voakes, Paul. 1997. "*The Newspaper Journalists of the '90s: Who They Are . . . and What They Think about the Major Issues Facing Their Profession*." Reston, VA: American Society of Newspaper Editors.

Wacquant, Loïc. 2002. "From Slavery to Mass Incarceration: Rethinking the 'Race Question' in the US." *New Left Review* 13 (Jan–Feb): 41–60.

Wall, Sarah. 2006. "An Autoethnography on Learning about Autoethnography." *International Journal of Qualitative Methods* 5 (2): 146–160. Available at http://ejournals.library.ualberta.ca/index.php/IJQM/index.

———. 2008. "Easier Said than Done: Writing an Autoethnography." *International Journal of Qualitative Methods* 7 (1): 38–53. Available at http://ejournals.library.ualberta.ca/index.php/IJQM/article/view/1621/1144.

Weinraub, Bernard. 1989. "President Unveils $1.2 Billion Plan to Battle Crime." *New York Times,* May 16, p. A1.

Welch, Michael, Eric Price, and Nana Yankey. 2002. "Moral Panic over Youth Violence: Wilding and the Manufacture of Menace in the Media." *Youth and Society* 34:3.

———. 2004. "Youth Violence and Race in the Media: The Emergence of 'Wilding' as an Invention of the Press." *Race, Gender and Class* 11:2.

Wells, Ida B. 1892. *Southern Horrors: Lynch Law in All Its Phases.* New York: New York Age.

White, Deborah Gray. 1999. *Ar'n't I a Woman? Female Slaves in the Plantation South.* Revised edition. New York: W. W. Norton.

Wicker, Tom. 1989. "Making Things Worse." *New York Times,* May 2, p. A25.

Wilkins, Amy. 2008. *Wannabes, Goths, and Christians: The Boundaries of Sex, Style, and Status.* Chicago: University of Chicago Press.

Williams, Lena. 1988. "Studies Find More Reading for Information and Less for Fun." *New York Times,* May 2, p. D10.

Wilson, Clint C., and Felix Gutierrez. 1995. *Race, Multiculturalism, and the Media: From Mass to Class Communication.* London: Sage Publications.

Wilson, James Q. 1995. "Crime and Public Policy." In *Crime: Public Policies for Crime Control,* edited by James Q. Wilson and Joan Petersilia, 619–630. San Francisco: Institute for Contemporary Studies Press.

Wilson, Scott Bernard. 2002. "Crash of the Titans: Though We Can Expect CEO's to Get Increasingly Villainous in the Movies, On-Screen Magnates Have Always Changed with the Times." *Boston Globe,* July 21, p. L12.

Wilson, William Julius. 1978. *The Declining Significance of Race: Blacks and Changing American Institutions.* Chicago: University of Chicago Press.

Wintonick, Peter, Mark Achbar, and Adam Symansky. 1992. *Manufacturing Consent: Noam Chomsky and the Media.* Montreal: National Film Board of Canada. [Video-cassettes.]

Wolff, Craig. 1989. "Youths Rape and Beat Central Park Jogger." *New York Times,* April 21, p. B1.

Wolfgang, Marvin E. 1983. "Delinquency in Two Birth Cohorts." *American Behavioral Scientist* 27 (1): 75–86.

Wolfgang, Marvin E., and Franco Ferracuti. 1967. *The Subculture of Violence: Towards an Integrated Theory in Criminology.* London: Tavistock Publications.

Wright, Richard. [1940] 1993. *Native Son.* New York: HarperCollins.

Young, Alford. 2008. "White Ethnographers and the Experiences of African-American Men." In *White Logic, White Methods: Racism and Methodology,* edited by Tukufu Zuberi and Eduardo Bonilla-Silva, 179–200. Lanham, MD: Rowman and Littlefield.

Zoglin, Richard, Sam Allis, and Ratu Kamlani. 1996. "Now for the Bad News: A Teenage Time Bomb." *Time,* January 15, p. 52.

# Index

*Page numbers followed by f and t refer to figures and tables, respectively.*

**NATALIE BYFIELD** is Associate Professor of Sociology at St. John's University in Queens, New York. She has also taught in Journalism and Media Studies. She is a former Staff Writer for the *New York Daily News*.